LAST CHAIN ON BILLIE

ALSO BY CAROL BRADLEY

Saving Gracie:
How One Dog Escaped the Shadowy World
of American Puppy Mills

LAST CHAIN ON BILLIE

How One Extraordinary
Elephant Escaped
the Big Top

CAROL BRADLEY

St. Martin's Press
New York

www.stmartins.com

Designed by Kathryn Parise

Library of Congress Cataloging-in-Publication Data

Bradley, Carol, 1957–
    Last chain on Billie : how one extraordinary elephant escaped the big top / Carol Bradley.
        pages cm
    ISBN 978-1-250-02569-2 (hardcover)
    ISBN 978-1-250-02570-8 (e-book)
    1. Captive elephants—United States—Anecdotes. 2. Elephants—United States—Anecdotes. 3. Circus animals—United States—Anecdotes. 4. Animal welfare—United States. 5. Animal rescue—United States. I. Title.
    SF408.6.E44B73 2014
    639.97'96—dc23

                                                      2014008568

St. Martin's Press books may be purchased for educational, business, or promotional use. For information on bulk purchases, please contact Macmillan Corporate and Premium Sales Department at 1-800-221-7945, extension 5442, or write specialmarkets@macmillan.com.

First Edition: July 2014

10 9 8 7 6 5 4 3 2 1

For Billie,
and for every other elephant
who has spent her life
in chains

CONTENTS

ACKNOWLEDGMENTS

I relied on the help and support of a number of people to tell Billie's story.

At the top of the list is the cofounder of the Elephant Sanctuary, Scott Blais, who graciously opened up his life and his life's work to me. Scott made the convincing argument that, of all the Sanctuary's inhabitants, Billie best conveyed the suffering circus elephants experience. I could not have written this book without his cooperation.

Former Sanctuary CEO Rob Atkinson allowed me into the Sanctuary's very private world, and employees Steve Smith; Kelly Costanzo; Angie Sherrill; Laurie Holman, veterinarian; Susan Mikota; Deb Maloy; Kat Haselau; and volunteer extraordinaire Sandra Estes, were kind enough to share their experiences. Jill Moore and Todd Montgomery provided answers to my many questions and Carol Durham tracked down the best images of Billie. Sanctuary Vice President and Chief Operating Officer Janice Zeitlin was also pivotal in providing access to the Sanctuary and verifying the accuracy of my manuscript. Consultant Gail Laule helped me understand the issues Billie continues to face, years after her rescue.

Tracing Billie's backstory would not have been possible had circus trainers Buckles Woodcock and Wade Burck not blogged about her at length. The Circus World Museum's archives in Baraboo, Wisconsin, offered a treasure trove of information about the circuses Billie traveled with; archivist Peter Shrake was instrumental in helping me find the nuggets I needed. I'm grateful, too, to circus veteran John Milton Herriott and former "elephant girls" Deborah Lockard and Janice Daniels for sharing their insights. Dan Koehl's thorough database of captive elephants, at www.elephant.se/location.php, proved enormously helpful.

Information I sought from the U.S. Department of Agriculture's Animal Care division either no longer exists or arrived so heavily redacted it was almost useless. Thankfully, People for the Ethical Treatment of Animals (PETA) had voluminous copies of federal inspection reports on the Hawthorn Corporation, which owned Billie, along with invaluable photos of baby elephants in training and more. I am deeply indebted to Jenny Woods and Teresa Marshall for dredging up numerous files on my behalf and to legal counsel Delcianna Winders for clarifying details about the lawsuit waged by animal welfare groups against Ringling Bros. and Barnum & Bailey over their treatment of elephants.

The advice, guidance, and enthusiasm of my agent, Jeff Kleinman at Folio Literary Management, for this book provided a beacon of support over the last three and a half years. My editor, Daniela Rapp, brought a keen focus and a passion for this subject equal to my own. She gave me the time and space I needed to pull this story together, for which I am eternally grateful. I am indebted to the entire team at St. Martin's Press, including production editor John Morrone, copyeditor Sabrina Soares Roberts, Lisa Pompilio for the cover design, Associate Director of Publicity Joan Higgins, Associate Marketing Manager Kelsey Lawrence, Digital Marketing Associate Kelsey Lawrence, and editorial assistant Lauren Jablonski. In vetting the manuscript, Michael K. Cantwell asked insightful questions that helped strengthen the book. My good friend in Montana, Pam Lemelin, helped shape my Web site.

The freedom to devote time to this project would not have been possible without the financial and moral support of my husband, Steve L'Heureux. He understands the worry, the stress, and the exhilaration involved in any creative effort. I thank him most of all.

FOREWORD

by Dr. Dame Daphne Sheldrick

I have worked intimately with elephants for fifty years of my life, rearing their orphaned young and rehabilitating them back to a wild life in Kenya's Tsavo National Park when grown, each at their own pace, and in their own time, when they themselves feel sufficiently confident to sever human dependency and return to where they belong. I have successfully reared from early infancy more than 170 orphaned elephant babies, and watched them grow into adulthood and eventually take their rightful place. However, the former orphans have never forgotten the role we played in their life, rewarding us by bringing back their wild-born young, and allowing their erstwhile human family to actually handle the calf as it shelters beneath its mother's belly, even when attended by perfectly wild elephant friends whom our elephants have "told" that not all humans are cruel and evil.

Elephants duplicate us humans in many ways other than in age progression and longevity. Endowed with a genetic memory, they are programmed at birth with information important to survival and which will equip them to implement their natural role on earth. Emotionally, they are identical to ourselves, with the same strong sense of family, and of death, and with friendships that span a lifetime, recognizing specific individuals whom they trust and love despite years of separation because elephants never forget, which happens to be true. With them, you reap what you sow—treat them with gentle reverence, understanding, and love, as would their natural elephant family, and you will be rewarded a hundredfold. Treat them cruelly and unkindly and they will settle the score in the end, at a time of their own choosing. With the authority of a lifetime, I can categorically affirm that elephants challenge the uniqueness of humans because "they are just like us, but only better than us" with many attributes we lack and others we have yet to fully understand. Although large and immensely powerful, they are inherently fearful and gentle by nature, and they can teach humans a great deal about caring, even when they are still infants. Both sexes exhibit empathy for less fortunate individuals; this extends to others beyond their own species, and both sexes adore and protect the young.

Wrenching a young elephant from its family and consigning it to a lifetime of bondage in a far-off land, simply for the entertainment of humans who know no better, is as evil and as wrong as it would be were innocent humans forcibly subjected to the same treatment. The so-called training of circus elephants involves immense cruelty to break the animal's spirit and make it too fearful to disobey. Forcing it to perform unnatural stunts ends up damaging its frame, resulting in arthritic impairment and a lifetime of pain.

Nowadays, Billie must celebrate every day, for she enjoys a more normal life, thanks to caring humans who spoke up for her and her like. Although the dream of returning to her homeland and her family can never be fulfilled, at least she has other elephant friends and caring humans who treat her kindly. Her story will go a long way toward helping others and saving them from a cruel life of bondage and servitude. Her story will educate people around the world about the nature of her iconic species, sparing many other young elephants miserable captivity. Elephants do not belong in circuses—and nor should they—in the twenty-first century, when the power of social media and the Internet has a global reach.

—◆—

Dr. Dame Daphne Sheldrick, DBE, created the David Sheldrick Wildlife Trust in Nairobi, Kenya, and is the author of *Love, Life, and Elephants*.

PROLOGUE

※━◆━※

Scott Blais opened the gate to the barn, stood back and waited for the elephant to lumber into view. Her trunk appeared first, raised slightly and held stiff with uncertainty, then the rest of her—8,450 pounds of wariness and fear. All of the other elephants had been loaded up and trucked away, because all of the other elephants were predictable: Blais knew he could board them on to the semi relatively easily. There was a reason he'd saved Billie for last.

For twenty-three years she had traveled the country, chained in place in the back of a semi as her circus caravanned from one stop to another. But a decade had passed since her last journey. There was no telling how Billie would react to seeing a truck again.

The elephant stared at the rear of the trailer for a moment, her left eye partially concealed beneath a scarred and puffy eyebrow. Ever so gently, she raised her trunk to touch first the gate and then the ramp. So far so good, Blais thought. She's deciding whether she feels safe in this setting, whether she feels comfortable.

He wondered if she would remember being packed in so tightly with other elephants, her legs anchored in place. Whether she would remember the dark interior of the truck, the chill of traveling in winter, and the searing heat in summer months. Yet this truck was bright inside. It carried the scents of her barn mates, the six elephants that, two by two, had disappeared over the last few days. Could she detect that something was going to be different about this journey, this destination?

The man standing nearby had shown nothing but kindness to Billie. There was no sense of urgency, no one yelling or waving a bullhook or poking her to step on board. For the first time in her life, someone was asking her to walk up the ramp.

The elephant studied the inside of the semi as if she were memorizing every detail. She glanced back at Blais, hesitating. "It's okay, Billie," he called to her softly. "You can do it."

CAPTURING ELEPHANTS

What is it about elephants? The immense, seemingly docile animals have mesmerized American audiences for more than two hundred years.

The first elephant in America arrived in New York in 1796. Just two years old, still a baby, he was purchased for $450 and shipped over from India. Crowds could view the unnamed elephant for fifty cents. *The Boston Gazette* was so taken by the animal that it said he defied description.

Then, around 1800, a sailing boat from England sank in a storm at the mouth of Delaware Bay and somehow an elephant on board broke loose and swam ashore. The following morning local residents who came to see what was left of the wrecked ship were startled to see an enormous and unfamiliar animal wandering about on the sand.

Old Bet was the third to arrive, in 1804. She, too, was put on display; her owner sold off shares of her for $1,200 each and moved her from town to town at night to keep curious onlookers from glimpsing her for free. Her career ended when a posse of farmers in Maine turned their rifles on her for trampling through their gardens. Little Bet followed in 1811. She lasted eleven years before she was shot to death by five young boys hell-bent on discovering whether a mere bullet could take down such a large animal.

In 1880, the first elephant was born in the United States in Philadelphia. Journalists swooned at the news. "No more lovable tot can be imagined than this playful caricature of an elephant," *McClure's* magazine reported. The baby was named Columbia and she was "a complete elephant, even to the delicate pink nostrils at the end of the little eight-inch trunk," the magazine gushed. Crowds thronged to view her.

Four years later circus owner P. T. Barnum procured his own elephant: Jumbo, a ten-foot-three African male sold to Barnum for $30,000 by the Royal Zoological Society in England. Britain was incensed at the prospect of losing its beloved pachyderm; even Queen Victoria protested the sale. But Barnum had paid his money and he insisted on going through with the deal. By the time the elephant arrived in New York Harbor on April 9, 1892, Jumbomania was in full force. Americans snatched up Jumbo hats, fans, neckties, and earrings. Thousands lined the parade route to watch as sixteen horses drew the elephant's crate to Madison Square Garden. Within six weeks, Jumbo reportedly earned $336,000 for the circus. An estimated nine million men, women, and children paid money to see him as he traveled about the country over the next three years.

By now, America was smitten by elephants. Every circus had to have one. Circuses were full of bizarre sideshows: Chinese jugglers, "Fejee" mermaids, snake charmers, Indian chiefs high-stepping to drumbeats. But nothing trumped the elephants. The phrase "seeing the elephant" became another way of saying that someone had seen it all. Early elephants didn't even have to perform; they could simply stand immobile, housed in a cage or draped in chains, and draw a crowd.

As a poem from the era went:

Huh! See that little show.
Ain't got no elephants.
Guess I won't go.

ONE

———— ✦ ————

LOSING A FAMILY

Before the ruckus of the circus, before she'd taken the first whiff of sawdust or popcorn or cotton candy or heard the rabble's roar, she was a baby elephant in the lush, jungly wilds of India. On the day she was born she would have landed with a thud, encased in a birth sac her mother would have torn open with her trunk. She would have stood just three feet long and three feet tall and weighed less than 200 pounds—not much bigger than a Great Dane. To introduce her to her new world, her mother would have nudged her along the ground until she let out her first squeal. Minutes later she would be standing, and within a couple of hours she would have figured out how to scoot her tiny body under her mother's, reach up to grab a mammary gland, and suckle her first meal.

We can only surmise this, of course, because no one witnessed Billie's birth. No one was there to record the day she was born or even the year. And yet it's reasonable to assume that in the beginning she was free to live as elephants should, her days spent in the company of her aunts, sisters, and cousins, at liberty to wander and frolic in the sun, and keeping close to her mother. Baby elephants seldom stray more than a hundred yards from their mothers in their first years.

Then, of course, came the capture, and that was just the beginning. The men who snared Billie would have held her for weeks, fenced in, all four legs shackled, and likely beaten into submission. She may have been starved at first, maybe kept awake all day and all night for several days—whatever it took to break her spirit. The isolation, the food deprivation, all of it was intended to let her know that she was embarking on a new life now and, no matter how big she grew to be, she was no longer in control. Not now or ever again.

She surfaced in America in 1966, at the age of four, at Southwick's Zoo in Mendon, Massachusetts, a small enterprise tucked up a slender, meandering road on what used to be a dairy farm. Danny Southwick imported all manner of exotic wildlife, not just for his family's zoo but for other parties, and one of the areas he imported elephants from was the Delhi region of India, so it stands to reason Billie was captured there, too. By the time she arrived in Massachusetts the zoo had 1,300 types of waterfowl, two lion cubs, a grizzly bear, tigers, a leopard, a camel from Arabia, a chimpanzee, some wallabies, and a hamadryas baboon.

Most of the elephants Southwick's imported were two years old and prematurely weaned. Almost all of them were females and almost all arrived at John F. Kennedy International Airport in New York City, one of thirteen U.S. ports that permitted the entry of wild animals. The elephants were caged in wooden framed boxes, their legs tied to the frames for the duration of the fifteen-hour flight from India.

Unlike the bigger, more volatile African elephants, who arrived as wild as they had ever been, Asian elephants came partially tamed: not yet able to perform tricks, but docile enough to be handled. Danny Southwick's sister, Justine Brewer, who now runs Southwick's Zoo, remembers Billie being four to five feet tall and cute and sweet, not one to cause any trouble. Whether she gave rides to children is unknown; Brewer believes she was too young to do so. But she does remember the elephant's name: Popsicle, Popsy for short.

The family hired a trainer, Junior Clarke, to work with her. In his late twenties with dark, slick-backed hair, Clarke worked for the Providence zoo, and for several years before that he'd partnered with Roy Bush to train eight elephants owned by Hunt Bros. Circus, one of dozens of small circuses that traveled the countryside. Several times a week he drove the twenty-four miles to Mendon to teach the young elephant how to perform simple tricks, the kind zoo-goers expected to see zoo elephants do. Otherwise she was left to mill about in her yard.

Had Popsicle been able to remain with her mother, the emotional part of her brain likely would have thrived, experts now know. Growing up surrounded by her family would have infused her with the resilience needed to cope with stress, communicate socially, and show empathy toward fellow elephants. Scientists have since learned that severing the mother-baby attachment too soon can cause the circuits in a vulnerable calf's brain to thin down, especially in the part that processes emotions. The psychological damage caused by putting a baby elephant in a zoo by herself can be incalculable.

What must it have been like to be in a new place, a tiny enclosure so much more constricted than the open jungle she had been used to? Massachusetts winters are snowy and cold. An elephant accustomed to tropical temperatures would have had to spend much of her life there indoors. For a time she had company, an elephant named Anna, but in all probability Popsy spent much of her time at the zoo by herself. A half-century ago, zoos viewed animals as objects of entertainment and amusement. Little thought was given to their need for enrichment or company.

Popsicle might have spent the rest of her life at Southwick's Zoo if Danny Southwick hadn't decided to sell her the year she turned ten. Maybe she was getting too big to enchant patrons.

An elephant grows at the rate of an inch a month until it turns three and doesn't reach its full growth until the age of twenty-five or so, but she was clearly no longer a baby. Her early records no longer exist and Danny Southwick is long deceased, so no one knows why he chose to get rid of her. Only that he did. The zoo advertised her for sale, and a man named John Cuneo Jr. decided to look into buying her. Which meant that Popsicle's life was poised to change in a very big way.

TRACKING THE ELUSIVE BEASTS

By the 1880s, the two biggest circuses in the country, Barnum & Bailey and Adam Forepaugh, had sixty pachyderms between them and that still wasn't enough. The rival circuses engaged in a fierce battle over who could trot out the first *white* elephant, considered sacred in Asian cultures. Adam Forepaugh tried to trump Barnum with the "Light of Asia," a baby elephant that had been painted with fifty coats of plaster of paris (and had broken out in blisters and sores). Barnum countered by claiming to have imported a white elephant from Burma for $100,000. It, too, was a hoax.

Capturing an elephant was the hard part. In the early 1800s, hunters in Borneo and Java often dug pits, covered them with poles and branches and laced them with food to trap elephants, but that was highly risky: an elephant who plunged into a deep pit could easily emerge with bruises and dislocated bones and often died from stress or self-induced starvation.

In Africa, native hunters sometimes used small dogs adorned with small wooden rattles or bells to track down elephants. The hunter would follow the sound of his dog's rattle and set off on a shortcut to waylay the elephant.

Other hunters tracked down mother elephants who had babies by their side and weren't able to escape quickly enough. While some of the hunters distracted the herd by chasing a single animal, others would hop off their horses, sidle up to the nursing elephants and sever the tendon in one of their hind legs. As the mother elephant, bleeding and hobbled, struggled to stand, the hunters would capture the baby and tie its legs. They would kill the mother, skin and eat her, and harvest her tusks.

The work was incredibly dangerous, often deadly, but importers didn't care. "[Natives] don't cost much—only five to six dollars apiece," Paul Ruhe, a hunter with the Reiche Brothers, once told circus owner W. C. Coup. "The sheiks are paid in advance, and do not care whether the poor huntsmen get out of the chase alive or not."

The human toll was worth it to obtain the prize—baby elephants. Hunters transported the young animals to a compound, confined them, and kept them alive with goat's milk.

TWO

+ ⊠ +

DRAWN TO THE BIG TOP

Let's flash back twenty-two years before Billie was sold to Cuneo. It's 1950, and the *Chicago Daily Tribune* has just published a feature on John Cuneo Jr. and his colorful menagerie. Young Mr. Cuneo has enjoyed working with animals ever since he was five years old, the article explains: a friend of the family gave him four angora goats, and before long the precocious lad had taught the animals to haul him about in a cart. As soon as the goats mastered that trick he taught them to balance on a teeter-totter and walk on their hind legs.

From there, Cuneo moved on to bears. Bears, no matter their background or age, were wild and distrusting and tended to be vicious, he told the reporter. To tame them you first fed them by hand, then petted and played with them, and led them around on a sturdy chain until they got used to following you. If a bear was willing to tolerate being led about, it might be open to learning a few tricks through a "rigid system" of punishment and rewards. To demonstrate, Cuneo instructed his black bear Carlo to ride a scooter, sit up, stand on his hind legs, and collapse on the floor, playing dead. Cuneo rewarded him with a lump of sugar.

The photo accompanying the story must have sent teacups

clattering all over the Windy City. The picture showed a slim Cuneo, looking jaunty in a suit and a fedora pushed back off his brow, holding an unidentified object up to the mouth of the bear. The animal was muzzled and standing on what looked to be a tree stump. The real story wasn't that John Cuneo Jr. had taught a few tricks to a bear—it was that a man of Cuneo's standing was doing tricks with any sort of wild animal.

Cuneo was a bona fide member of Chicago's upper crust. For a good century his family's name had been synonymous with the highest echelons of power and influence. His great-grandparents, Giovanni and Caterina Cuneo, had immigrated from Genoa, Italy, in 1857, started up a grocery and a small farm and used their profits to buy property on the side. Their son, Frank, carried on the tradition; he founded a produce company, Garibaldi and Cuneo, and developed commercial real estate on an even larger scale. The bustling business district along Wilson Avenue was one of his projects. Frank Cuneo helped establish and lead Chicago's Italian Chamber of Commerce and he helped organize the World's Columbian Exposition in Chicago in 1893. Along with Mother Cabrini, an Italian nun who became the first American saint, he founded Columbus Hospital in Chicago. He later established the Frank Cuneo Memorial Hospital.

By the time John Cuneo Sr. was born in 1884, the family was one of Chicago's most prominent. John Senior was every bit as ambitious as his forefathers. He dropped out of Yale University to learn the ins and outs of bookmaking and borrowed $10,000 from his father to start his own bindery. In time, his Cuneo Press grew to become the largest printing company in the United States, with plants in Chicago and four other cities. Along with Bibles, encyclopedias, and a series of movie magazines Cuneo had purchased, his press published an American household staple, the Sears, Roebuck and Co. catalog. Another of Cuneo's coups was to persuade publisher William Randolph Hearst to print magazines like *Redbook* and *Cosmopolitan* in Chicago as opposed to the West Coast, saving a small fortune in postage fees.

John Senior was forty-six when he married Julia Shepherd. She, too, came from wealth. The couple was so rich that in 1937, when most Americans were still reeling from the Great Depression and hoarding what little money they had, the Cuneos were spending freely. Their most ostentatious purchase was a mansion in Libertyville, Illinois, previously owned by Samuel Insull, Chicago's foremost businessman in the 1920s. For years, Insull had owned a 132-acre farm in Libertyville, a bucolic stretch of countryside north of Chicago. In 1914, at the age of forty-eight, he hired prominent architect Benjamin Marshall—the same architect who designed the sumptuous Drake and Blackstone hotels—to design a lavish manor befitting his station in life. Insull had seen a house in Italy he liked, and he wanted Marshall to come up with something similar: an estate with a glamorous, Mediterranean feel. Insull hired Danish landscape architect Jens Jensen, who had designed Columbus Park and reshaped Garfield and Humboldt parks in Chicago, to turn the flat landscape around the house into a park-like setting.

Locals called the house the Pink Mansion. Forty-foot-high vaulted ceilings, arches and pillars made of Indiana limestone, and floors built with travertine stone, imported from Rome, decorated the main hall. The main house had eight bedrooms, ten bathrooms decorated in gold leaf, a glass-enclosed ballroom and an expansive sun room; all told, thirty-two thousand square feet. Two dining rooms and two kitchens enabled the chefs to prepare dinner for large crowds.

John Cuneo Jr. was six years old and his sister, Consuela, four, when the Cuneos moved into the Insull estate. The family kept an apartment on North Lake Shore Drive in the city, but from then on they considered the Libertyville mansion home.

The move put them smack in the middle of one of Chicago's

most prestigious suburbs. Wealthy businessmen had transformed the Libertyville area from a monotonous stretch of farmland to a handful of opulent estates—a "Hampton among the cornfields," as one writer described it.

The Cuneos doted on their children. To protect their first-born, they screened off an expansive porch connected to John Junior's second-story bedroom. Five years earlier, the son of aviator Charles Lindbergh had been kidnapped and killed, and the Cuneos were determined to protect their own son from a similar fate.

A photograph of John Cuneo Jr. taken around the time the family moved to Libertyville shows him posing with his father and grandfather, dressed in a white oversized jacket and a pair of pressed shorts, white socks, and white shoes, his gaze aimed upward in a knowing smile. John Junior inherited his father's round face, downturned eyes, and an expression of amusement that suggested he didn't take life too seriously. There was no reason he should: he was the son of a multimillionaire.

John Cuneo Sr. raised champion Hackney ponies and showed them around the United States, collecting a barnful of trophies. And he kept adding acreage to his estate—eventually it encompassed two thousand acres. In 1946 Cuneo started the Hawthorn Mellody Farm. It was an authentic working dairy farm and before long it became Chicago's third-largest supplier of milk. Cuneo's middle managers searched the country for top-producing cows and incorporated innovative new automated milking machines and stainless-steel containers to keep the product sterilized. Cuneo was so proud of his state-of-the-art facility that he added glass windows and invited visitors to come watch the cows being milked.

His efforts paid off: Cuneo's herd set new records in terms of the quantity of milk they produced. He labeled his operation the "Home of Champions" and his attention to detail attracted international attention. Schools bused thousands of children to the farm to tour the barns. Each weekend, hundreds of families drove or took the train to Libertyville to get a taste of farm life. It was the first chance for many of these children to see farm animals up close and get a lesson in how food was produced. The schoolkids loved the farmer's hats they were issued at the start of their tours and even more the H. M. ice cream they were served afterward. In one three-year period alone, more than a quarter of a million children passed through the gates.

Before it became common to use celebrities to plug a product, Hawthorn Mellody's publicist recruited an entire roster of stars to endorse the farm. Actor Dean Martin, singer Peggy Lee, and comedian Jerry Lewis all lent their names to the thriving operation, as did a young actor named Ronald Reagan. Hawthorn Mellody even turned to sports figures such as Nellie Fox, noted second baseman for the Chicago White Sox, to offer an endorsement. In the wake of the dairy farm's success, John Cuneo Sr. decided to expand the operation and add a zoo, a move that profoundly altered the course of his son's life.

The zoo started as a simple affair. Patterned after a children's zoo in the Bronx borough of New York, John Senior envisioned a relatively modest collection of unusual animals kept in a series of small stone sheds and wooden barns surrounded by a chain-link fence. Inside a petting zoo there would be goats and ponies, the kinds of animals children could reach out and touch.

John Cuneo Jr. had something bigger in mind. He had already trained goats and bears, and now he wanted more exotic animals, lots of them. He set about procuring as many extraordinary specimens as he could, so that by the time the zoo opened its doors on June 5, 1951, he had on display two guanacos, which are cousins to the llama; capuchin monkeys and sloths from South America; arctic and red foxes, raccoons, South American jungle rats, beavers, muskrats, zebras, Tibetan yak, silver pheasant, swans, cranes, and woodchucks. From India, Cuneo imported a cheetah, and from Africa a chimpanzee. He had Canadian wildcats, South American emus, and mouflon sheep from Africa.

John Junior housed squirrels, porcupines, a deskunked skunk, and other smaller mammals in a colorfully painted tugboat dubbed Noah's Ark. The ark was one of the most popular exhibits, thanks in part to a crow that sat in a cage at the top of the boat mimicking some of the conversations he overheard.

Four years later, John Junior expanded the zoo, opening up the horse, chicken, and hog barns for viewing. With a showman's instinct for what would draw the crowds, he installed an authentic steam train that carried riders through a mile of cornfields, where life-size cutouts of cowboys and Indians dotted the landscape. At the end of the ride was Frontier Town, a series of old-timey buildings sporting corny signs like the law-office shingle that read DEWEY CHETUM & HOWE. The fake town even had a wooden boardwalk. A Club of Champs featured memorabilia from some of the greatest sports figures of the day, among them boxing gloves once owned by Joe Louis, a football jersey previously worn by Chicago Bears football star Red Grange, and a pair of Jesse Owens's running shoes.

To a modern-day mind-set, the offerings of the Hawthorn Mellody Farm and zoo sound wholesomely quaint. But in their day they amounted to a one-of-a-kind experience. America had carnivals and circuses and amusement parks, but Disneyland was the only theme park in the country and it had just opened.

—❈—

John Cuneo Sr. may have been hoping the zoo would offer his only son a taste of entrepreneurship. John Junior had gone away to school, but thus far he was known mostly for his horsemanship and a few youthful indiscretions. In one incident his car collided with a truck fifteen miles south of Libertyville, leaving Cuneo with a serious cut on the left side of his head and a possible concussion. A few months after the zoo opened, John Junior was arrested for speeding and fined $15. The following February he was stopped again, this time for driving sixty miles an hour in a forty-five-mile-an-hour zone in the nearby suburb of Skokie, Illinois. Speeding is hardly a serious crime, but when John Junior failed to appear in court after the second stop, authorities issued a warrant for his arrest. Cuneo's response was that he had been in Arizona and unable to appear. Whatever his transgressions, he considered himself privileged enough to disregard them.

He wasn't the first prosperous American to indulge an interest in exotic wildlife. Two decades earlier, eccentric Coca-Cola heir Asa Candler Jr. of Atlanta acquired his own menagerie. According to one account, Candler was traveling through Eastern Europe with his sisters when he happened to attend the closing performance of a struggling circus. The animals were for sale and Candler, on a lark, bought the lions, baboons, monkeys, and elephants and had them shipped home. Before long he had his own private zoo, complete with five elephants—named, appropriately for the family business, Delicious, Refreshing, Rosa, Coca, and Cola. Candler delighted in having the elephants perform tricks for visitors and haul friends of his grandchildren around in enormous wagons. Twice a week he opened his doors to the public.

For Candler, exotic animals were an expensive hobby. For John Cuneo Jr., they were becoming a career. His latest attraction was a two-year-old baby elephant who'd been shipped from India to California by importer Louis Goebel and then flown to Chicago. News photographers were on hand the afternoon of March 29, 1951, when the tiny calf disembarked from a United Airlines plane along with a Malayan sun bear cub. Just fifty-one inches high, the elephant was so darling she looked like a large stuffed animal. She stood patiently as the stewardess brushed her hide in an affectionate farewell. Cuneo paid $800 for her and named her Jessie.

Jessie was one of 264 elephants housed in circuses and zoos in the United States in 1952, many of whom had arrived as babies and were in fragile health. Despite the risks, circuses and zoos clamored for them. Schoolchildren donated nickels and dimes to help pay for the new elephants and hometown newspapers rallied to support the cause.

Together with a series of trainers, Cuneo taught his own elephant to give rides to children and perform tricks. When newspapers caught up with the duo again several months later, the elephant was pronounced ready for the limelight. "Jessie loves to dance and prance for an appreciative audience on the Hawthorn Mellody Farm," read the caption for one photo. Another caption said: "Trainer James Reynolds tickles Jessie's ribs and the two-year-old performer laughs." Photos showed the elephant balancing her two left legs on a wooden rail two and a half feet off the ground; standing on her hind legs atop a drum; and standing on her head, her trunk stretched out on the ground to give her balance, her hind legs jutting up and her tail held out stiffly, parallel to the ground. The elephant was decked out in a black top hat that was comically too small for her head. A wide white harness encircled her face and bracelets adorned with bells were wrapped around her wrists. In each of the photos another trainer, Joe Frisco, stood next to Jessie wearing an elaborately decorated jacket, a bullhook by his side.

For thousands of years, handlers have used bullhooks, instruments shaped like fireplace pokers with a sharp, steel-tipped spike and hook, to control and punish elephants. An elephant's skin is an inch thick on her back and hindquarters but razor thin around and inside of her ears, in the folds of her mouth, under her arms, under her chin, around her feet, or in and around her anus. To drive a message home, handlers will poke one of those tender spots, dig in and yank hard on the flesh. An elephant poked or hooked will respond by turning away from the pain. To inflict further punishment, a handler can grip the pointed end of the bullhook and swing the solid end like a baseball bat. Prime targets are an elephant's ankle, wrist, or other thinly padded spots, where, despite an elephant's size, the whack of a bullhook can inflict significant pain.

— ⊷ ⋈ ⊶ —

Cuneo spent most of those early years concentrating on bears. It should have surprised no one that when he married in 1956 at the age of twenty-five, he took as his bride a Miss Eloise Berchtold of Cincinnati, Ohio, who happened to train bears, too.

As a young girl, Eloise had worked at Cincinnati's Children's Zoo. She performed with the King Circus before moving on to the Bailey Bros. and Cristiani Circus, where she handled a lion and worked a sideshow involving snakes. Her career as a wild animal trainer took off in earnest in 1955, the year Cristiani bought Cuneo's Olympic Bear Act, which consisted of fourteen bears, all of them different breeds. Berchtold and Cuneo were said to have met as a result of the transaction.

Even after he sold his Olympic Bears, Cuneo still had two other bear acts, along with a couple of boxing kangaroos. A film of his Paramount Bears, shot around 1957 in Cuneo's training barn, shows his polar bear, Zero. Plucked from the Arctic Sea near Norway, Zero was "the world's only uncaged performing polar bear." His trainers led him through his routines with white muzzles wrapped tightly around his snout. He performed with two brown bears and a Syrian bear bought from a zoo in Israel. One skit had Zero pushing a cart containing two of the other bears. Wearing tutus and cone-shaped hats, the bears danced, somersaulted backwards, rode scooters, and roller-skated. Zero balanced on a ball and, using his hind legs, rolled it up an incline. For the finale, he climbed onto a motorcycle and rode it around

the ring. It took a moment to situate him on the cycle; his trainers had to strap his paws to the handlebars. Once he was settled
in, the motorcycle started with a jolt. Zero's trainer held on to an
eight-foot leash as the bear slowly, awkwardly circled the ring, a
mournful soundtrack of Russian-sounding music playing in the
background. When he wasn't performing Zero sat hunched over,
his body lurched unnaturally to one side.

Working with animals involved unexpected risks. The same
year he married Berchtold, Cuneo suffered burns on his hands,
his legs, and his feet while trying to start a motorcycle he kept for
a trained bear. He accidentally splashed gasoline on his hands and
clothing, then touched the gasoline can to the motorcycle's battery and spark plugs, causing a spark. He had to be hospitalized.

Later that year, a former trainer of Cuneo's, Paul Lemery, was
mauled to death by a 500-pound bear he'd acquired from Cuneo
two years earlier. The bear, Hans, pinned Lemery to the floor
when he stepped into the bear's cage and slashed him with his
paws. An associate used a .35-caliber hunting rifle to shoot the
bear to death.

The late 1950s was a tough time for circuses. The costs of taking a show on the road had risen significantly, and the circus's
most reliable audience—children—had started to lose interest,
caught up instead with television shows like *Bonanza* and *I Love
Lucy*. Fewer young people showed a desire to learn the circus
trade, and shows had to reach out to European and South American performers to find workers willing to endure the long hours,
low pay, and relentless travel. The list of traveling circuses was
starting to dwindle.

But John Cuneo Jr. had no intention of looking back. Raised
in luxury and heir to his father's millions, the twenty-nine-year-
old looked surprisingly at home under the big top. He stepped
into the klieg lights wearing a business suit, as if he were headed
to a board meeting instead of presenting tigers or elephants. He

lamented to a newspaper about how hard it was to hire competent help, but he gave every indication that he was having the time of his life. He looked forward to the day, Cuneo said, "when the next P. T. Barnum comes along to make big elephants and big stars really big again."

Cuneo was colorful, funny, and daring. And he was inventive. There seemed to be no trick he was too afraid to try. To counter the slide in circus audiences, Cuneo introduced a new act featuring a half-dozen white "Royal Inca" llamas. Zero now did his tricks on a platform thirty feet in the air. Cuneo replaced Jessie the elephant with several baby elephants who performed together, and he brought in an enormous male African elephant, Koa.

Cuneo did not own a circus. He hired his acts out to circuses, which absolved him of the logistical burden of presenting an entire show. He put together a Wild Animal Fantasy and sent it out on the road as part of a three-ring circus produced on behalf of the Knights of Columbus. In a single year, the Wild Animal Fantasy performed at the Cincinnati and Omaha Shrine shows, at the St. Louis Police Circus in Missouri, in Texas with the Hubert Castle Circus, in Des Moines, Iowa, and at Harry Batt's amusement park in New Orleans. After that, the show traveled the Barnes fair route. The act featured a leopard and a white German shepherd (Cuneo alternately referred to his white dogs as "wolf dogs," "snow wolves," and "Russian wolfhounds") rolling a barrel, eight dogs posing with a black panther, and a leopard riding on the back of a zebra. His ads described the show as "The Earth's Strangest Assemblage of Performing Animals." Tigers rolled drums and leapt from one tall platform to another. In one instance, a big cat circled the ring perched on a platform on top of a zebra's back. At the end of the act the tigers exited the ring through a series of four flaming hoops.

Unlike his rival showmen, Cuneo lacked any incentive to keep costs down. Traveling through Europe, he sat in on a performance of the Cirque d'Hiver in France and spied across the ring two Americans, Jack Arthur and Al Dobritch, who were scouting locales for the Canadian National Exhibition tour. It turned out the men were also in search of animal acts. Cuneo offered his show and the Canadian reps immediately signed him to play their Toronto dates. From Paris, Cuneo traveled to Scotland, where he purchased five small Shetland ponies to incorporate into his llama act. In Portugal he bought a Lusitano stallion, a breed so rare there were said to be only about two hundred such horses in the world. Experienced horsemen regarded Cuneo's horse as the most beautiful of its kind in America, with a summer coat the color of "a newly minted copper penny" and the blackest mane, tail, and legs a horse lover "would ever see."

In 1960, Cuneo sold his Wild Animal Fantasy to Dorey Miller, owner of the Al G. Kelly & Miller Bros. Circus. Not long afterward one of the leopards became confused as it entered the arena and promptly attacked the trainer for Kelly-Miller, Fred Logan, leaving him with puncture wounds in his left arm and shoulder. Cuneo had to beat the animal to get him to let go of Logan.

Cuneo still had his bears, but now he began collecting horses and ponies for a Horse Fantasy act. He had a new love interest as well. Cuneo had divorced Berchtold and married Pat Jameson, whom he'd hired to replace Paul Lemery. Their betrothal lasted a short time before Cuneo fell for a third trainer, Herta Klauser. Cuneo met Klauser during a performance at the Chicago Great Railroad Fair. Like Berchtold and Jameson, she was a stunning blonde. She came from a family of bear trainers: her father, Walter Klauser, had worked with Circus Krone in Germany, where Herta was born. Walter Klauser was said to have invented the motorcycle-riding bear trick more than thirty years earlier. One of his bears pedaled a bicycle that was thirteen feet high. Another could balance on his hind legs and roll a globe down steps.

Despite bears' reputation for being the most capricious of animal performers—able to turn from compliant to volatile in an instant—the Klausers had trained their three brown bears to put on a dazzling act. Boo Boo was the best known of the bunch—he was once photographed "playing blackjack" at a table at the Circus Circus casino in Reno, Nevada. Boo Boo was averse to wearing costumes, so the ruffle around his neck later became a tie, and sometimes he yanked it off. The bear had a bit of a temper: he once slapped trainer Jimmy Hall so hard that he tore the sleeve of Hall's costume and sent him twirling.

Cuneo and Klauser were married on January 1, 1970, and spent the next several years together in the ring, Klauser sashaying about in a sparkly tiara, kitten heels, and a skintight outfit not much bigger than a bathing suit. Her bears wore their signature tutus; they were no taller than Herta's shoulders, and unless spectators were looking closely, they would never notice the clamps wrapped around the bears' mouths. A photo from that time shows Herta kneeling on one knee at the conclusion of an act, her head turned to kiss one of her bears. Several feet to the rear stands Cuneo, his hairline receding by then, his right arm outstretched and a huge smile on his face.

ROUNDING UP THE ELEPHANTS

In India, local hunters chased elephants for thirty miles or more toward enormous blockaded corrals called *keddahs*. To round up the elephants, hunters hollered, pounded on drums, and beat trees with sticks. At night the "beaters" lit torches to force the elephants onward. The operation was arduous and time-consuming; as many as a thousand workers might labor for two months to drive the elephants into the trap. The beaters had to slog their way through dense underbrush. Workers trailing directly behind the elephants could follow the paths broken by the gigantic animals, but the men on the sides had to wield machete-like knives to cut their own trails, all the while being bitten by swarms of mosquitos. The hunters had to take care to avoid the baby elephants who wandered about, investigating noises. If an elephant spied a man she would trumpet and the whole herd would charge.

Once the elephants reached the fortifications, they were hustled inside the heavily disguised gate, where as many as sixty men would lower a gate weighted with stones, trapping the elephants inside. Elephants who refused to enter the *keddah* were either shot to death or, if they were lucky, set free. A moat surrounded the outside of the compound and inside was a long water trough to keep the animals from dying of thirst.

An account of a hunting expedition in 1892 described the elephants huddled together in confusion inside a *keddah*, trumpeting and shrieking and turning frequently to chase a beater, but ultimately allowing themselves to be pushed toward an even smaller enclosure. The elephants were strong enough to crash through a two-ton gate easily enough, but the sounds of the guns frightened them into place. Thirty-six elephants were captured as a result of that hunt.

Captors deliberately starved the elephants in the *keddah* for three or four days to lessen their strength, which made them less dangerous. The hungrier the elephant, the faster she would learn that good behavior was rewarded with food. (*Keddahs* were said to fall out of favor when one rebellious elephant, allowed to go free, refused to leave her herd behind and was shot to death as a result of her loyalty. The incident called attention to the barbaric way elephants were trapped and led to a permanent ban of *keddahs*, reportedly in 1952.)

Once a captured elephant calmed down, keepers fed her and training began. Tame elephants would flank either side of a wild elephant along with two men, each holding a bullhook pointed at the elephant's trunk while two other men massaged the elephant's back, chanting phrases like "Ho! My son," or "Ho! My mother." The elephant invariably thrust her trunk about in fury, only to have the trunk strike the points of the bullhooks, also called ankuses. In time the tip of the elephant's trunk became so sore that she would curl it up protectively and emotionally shut down.

After about three weeks the elephant learned the drill. Hobbled and surrounded by three trainers pointing their bullhooks at the elephant's head and her ears, the elephant could now walk alone to the river and sink down into the water without being disciplined. But the wounds on her ears, head, and back caused by bullhooks, and the rope burns around her legs, required daily medicine, and months—sometimes years—would pass before the elephant would allow her feet to be handled without trumpeting in rage and distress.

THREE

⊷ ⬥ ⊶

LEARNING THE ROPES

Before Cuneo plunked down money for Popsicle, he contacted trainer Buckles Woodcock and asked him to fly to Massachusetts to check her out. William "Buckles" Woodcock practically descended from circus royalty. Born in 1935, he was the fourth in a line of elephant trainers. His father was the well-known trainer "Colonel" William H. Woodcock Sr. and his mother, Sarah Orton, nicknamed Babe, had roots in the business that stretched back even further. Her grandfather, Hiram, started a circus in Wisconsin in 1854, and her father, R. Z. Orton, worked with elephants on the Orton Bros. Circus based in Lancaster, Missouri. Babe Woodcock was fond of saying that her family was in the circus business "when the Ringling brothers were still wearing wooden shoes."

Everybody knew Buckles. Six foot two and Sean Connery handsome, with penetrating dark eyes and a broad, open face framed by a shock of dark, slicked-back hair, he got his nickname as a toddler from the harness his mother buckled him into to keep him safe around the elephants. His father may have had other plans for him, but in 1951, when Buckles was sixteen, he left home and landed a job as a bull man, the term given to elephant handlers, with Eugene "Arky" Scott, who worked for Ringling Bros. and Barnum & Bailey. Later, Woodcock helped his dad train four little female elephants, three Asians and an African, who had just arrived from overseas. The African, named Colonel after Buckles's dad, "eats everything in sight and tries to whale everyone with the show," the elder Woodcock wrote a friend. Buckles also worked with a Burmese elephant his dad had purchased from the Al G. Kelly-Miller Bros. Circus. Bill Woodcock Sr. named her Anna May and she was so adept at performing that at her peak she was considered the most famous elephant in America. Anna May appeared on *The Ed Sullivan Show*, *The Merv Griffin Show*, *Circus of the Stars*, *You Asked For It!*, *The Hollywood Palace,* and *Pick of the Night*. She also appeared in the 1959 movie *The Big Circus* with Victor Mature.

Bill Woodcock Sr. had a saying: "Anything that eats can be trained." One of his strategies was to incorporate a dog into the act. For years Woodcock had a mixed breed named Charlie who would run into the ring, cueing the elephants to begin their stunts. While Charlie climbed on top of one elephant's flank and took a seat, two other two elephants would balance themselves on bull tubs, two-to-three-foot-high steel tables just big enough to accommodate an elephant's four feet, and lock trunks. Woodcock called this maneuver the handshake and Buckles replicated it many times during his career.

Except for a couple of years in the army, Buckles Woodcock had been around elephants all his life. He even married into the elephant world. His wife was the former Barbara Ray, an aerialist and leopard trainer who, before she met Buckles, was married to another elephant trainer, Rex Williams. Buckles's father once told him that an elephant trainer needed to possess three things: a strong back, a weak mind, and savage disposition. Neither father nor son had a reputation for treating elephants cruelly. But Buckles had a job to do, and that was to get elephants in the ring where they could dazzle an audience. He approached his job with a dry humor. "Practiced all three rings together early in the morning in the arena," he once wrote in his ledger. "Pretty much a disaster. All they could remember was how to shit."

He spent several years touring with the James Bros. Circus and had just finished breaking in five new elephants for Carson & Barnes when he got the call from Cuneo to check out the young elephant at Southwick's. Cuneo knew Woodcock was more than qualified to determine if the elephant Danny Southwick was looking to sell had any potential in the ring.

One school of thought among trainers was that elephants who had spent any time in a zoo were bad candidates for circuses. They'd spent far too many hours standing idly to have to suddenly learn the complexity of tricks expected of a circus elephant. Even if they could master the stunts, a zoo elephant might never grow accustomed to the rigors of the road. In the early days it was understood that Barnum & Bailey, for one, would never purchase an elephant from a zoo. The circus either bought elephants from smaller circuses or dealt with dealers who could deliver Asian elephants straight off the boat.

Woodcock flew up from his home in Florida, gave Popsicle the once-over and reported back to Cuneo that she looked trainable. Dorey Miller, the founder of Carson & Barnes Circus, heard that Woodcock was at Southwick's and asked if they had any more elephants available. As a matter of fact, they did—a young male. The following year Danny Southwick peddled four elephants to the Bronx Zoo for $4,600 apiece, but Cuneo may not have paid anything for Popsicle: as part of the trade, he gave Southwick's a hippopotamus named Bubbles. Cuneo had Billie shipped the 1,340 miles from Southwick's Zoo to Woodcock's place in Ruskin, Florida, several miles inland from the Gulf Coast. Teddy, the elephant purchased by the Kelly-Miller Circus, rode along in the same cattle truck.

The first thing Woodcock did with any problem elephant was to give it a new name, sometimes the name of one of his sisters-in-law, just to tease them a little. (When she found out he had renamed another one of his elephants after her, his sister-in-law Peggy said: "You gotta be kidding!") Woodcock evidently determined Popsicle to be difficult because the first thing he did when she arrived was to name her Billie after his wife's sister. Billie and Peggy Ray, his two sisters-in-law, happened to be named after Billie and Peggy Henderson, who also hailed from a circus family. In the circus world, six degrees of separation was a lot closer to just one and a half.

Woodcock was willing to work with Billie and Teddy, but he also had his own act to polish. He was working with his father's elephant, Anna May. In a few weeks' time he and his wife, Barbara, would truck Anna May to California, where they would hook up with the Stockton-based Miller-Johnson Circus.

But Cuneo persisted. He wanted his newest acquisition to learn something glitzier. At Southwick's Zoo, Junior Clarke had taught Billie to sit up and lie down, and that was about it. She needed to do more than that if she was going to make it in the circus. Cuneo had his lawyer send Woodcock a set of legal papers reiterating that he was to train Billie to perform a "first class" hind leg walk and one-foot stand.

The one-legged stand was considered the hardest trick to teach an elephant because the slightest redistribution of weight could cause her to fall and injure herself. Trainer Hugo Schmitt imported the stunt from Germany when he joined Ringling Bros. after World War II. An elephant first performed it in this country in 1948. Woodcock phoned Cuneo and suggested he hire Mac MacDonald, another seasoned trainer, to teach Billie the one-leg stand. MacDonald and his wife, Peggy, had not only taught one of their famous Besalou Elephants, Opal, to balance her 6,000-pound self on a single leg, they'd taught her to pull off the stunt while Peggy performed a handstand on top of Opal's head. MacDonald was capable of teaching Billie "first class" tricks, Woodcock told Cuneo, whereas he, Woodcock, just eked out a living. But Cuneo was undeterred. He told Woodcock to press on.

The rule of thumb was that it took several weeks of daily training sessions to school an elephant in the basic tasks of lifting its trunk and falling in line behind another elephant. A dog trainer once told Woodcock that a dog that could understand eight words was a genius. The dumbest elephant Woodcock had encountered understood twenty or thirty words.

Woodcock couldn't devote all of his time to Billie. In addition to Anna May he needed to attend to Teddy as well, and in short order he found himself stuck with two more elephants. One night soon after Billie and Teddy were dropped off, Woodcock answered a knock at his door in the middle of a driving rainstorm. Out by the road sat a candy-striped truck containing four elephants. The driver was John Carroll, a well-known trainer who was in charge of Carson & Barnes's herd. Carroll was there to drop a third elephant off for Woodcock to train. Kelly, as Woodcock went on to name him, was a male elephant so tiny he had to be fed with a bottle. Shortly after Kelly arrived, Kelly-Miller owner Dorey Miller called to say he'd decided to put together a new elephant act and needed Woodcock to train a fourth punk, the term used for baby elephants. Woodcock named the newest elephant Tena. She was so young that she, too, had to be bottle-fed.

Tena and Kelly weren't the first baby elephants the Woodcocks had cared for around the clock. In times past they had elephants so young that Buckles would have to pull his truck over by the side of the road so Barbara could heat up some formula. There was no exact science on what to feed a captive baby elephant. The Woodcocks developed their own concoction, complete with their secret formula of herbs and spices. Woodcock once asked trainer Smokey Jones: How long does it take before an elephant begins to eat hay? As long as you continue to make that stuff, she will accommodate you, Jones replied.

Tena was too young to learn much of anything. With Kelly, Woodcock stuck to the basics. But Billie and Teddy were old enough and smart enough to grasp quite a few tricks. Woodcock taught them what he could and then shot several photos of Billie carrying out her stunts and mailed them to Cuneo, telling him that he, Woodcock, had a circus to catch up with. "Come get your elephant," Woodcock said.

But Cuneo was on the road; he wasn't able to pick Billie up. Never one to miss an opportunity, Cuneo phoned Charlie Germaine, the owner of Miller-Johnson, and arranged for Billie to join that circus, too. Woodcock was the last to learn of the arrangement. Adding one more elephant to his act meant extra pay, and he didn't mind that part. It also meant that he and Barbara needed to make room for Billie on their cross-country trip.

A few weeks later, the Woodcocks left Florida with Anna May, Billie, Teddy, Tena, and a collie mix with soulful eyes named Clarence, a stray Barbara had rescued. Like his dad, Buckles Woodcock liked to incorporate dogs into acts involving novice elephants.

Their first stop was in Texas, at the Carson & Barnes lot, where Woodcock turned the two youngest elephants over to trainer Kenny Ikert. The Woodcocks camped out with Carson & Barnes for several days and then hit the road again, this time for Dallas, where fellow circus veteran Gee Gee Engesser lived. At thirty-six, Engesser was known as the Blond Bombshell of the Circus World. Born Georgedda Zellmar Engesser to a Minnesota circus family, she was swinging on aerial ladders and perching on curled elephant trunks by the time she was three. At eighteen she mastered her greatest feat: grasping the reins of sixteen palomino horses hitched in eight sets of pairs, she would straddle the rear two horses and gallop about the ring at breakneck speed. Cole Bros. Circus described its star act as "the suicidal Roman standing driver."

By 1972 Engesser had divorced her first husband, a tightwire artist named Billy Powell, and married elephant trainer Robert "Bucky" Steele. The couple put together a small menagerie comprised of several ponies, big cats, black bears, and a half-dozen elephants, and traveled with a variety of circuses. At home, the baby of the family, an elephant calf also named Gee Gee, roamed about their property freely. While the family ate breakfast in their kitchen the elephant would wander over to the window, thrust her trunk inside, and squeak for treats.

During their stay at Engesser's, the Woodcocks were joined by Smokey Jones. A striking man with a thick crop of brown hair and strongly chiseled features, Jones had a reputation as the toughest, most cantankerous elephant trainer around, and in the circus community he was widely respected. Hired years earlier to calm down Ringling Bros.' rambunctious herd, he claimed to have taken each elephant, one at a time, into the circus's ring barn in Sarasota, Florida, to find out a bit more about their personalities. "They all promised not to fight this year," he told a writer in all seriousness the following spring.

His strategy was straightforward, Jones claimed. The first time around he would ask an elephant nicely to perform a certain trick. If that didn't work, he issued a command. If an elephant still refused, "I do it for them," he said. "You put the hook just against them, let them jab it into their hide if they want to. Next time they'll do what you want without force."

Jones also carried a long bullwhip, which he'd hurl back and crack as the elephants trundled along to keep them in line. "Just flicking on the feet is best; it smarts because the feet is tender," he explained.

Jones was looking to buy an elephant. Woodcock phoned

Chet Juszyk, an animal importer on the West Coast, to ask if he had any extras. He had one baby elephant due in from overseas, Juszyk replied. Jones joined the Woodcocks' entourage, and soon after they arrived in California, Juszyk called to say Jones's elephant had landed at the airport. She was barely more than a month old. Woodcock and Jones created a stall for her in the back of the truck that held Anna May and Billie. Jones named her Tika and put her to work right away.

It was the end of March, and Miller-Johnson's spring-summer tour was set to begin the following week. Woodcock had planned to work Anna May's act, but now that he had Billie he turned the older elephant over to Barbara and his stepson, Ben, for the first act. Smokey Jones and his stepdaughter, Kari, would work Anna May in the second act. Woodcock would put Billie through her paces.

In the course of three months, Billie's life had been upended completely. She'd gone from a small enclosure at Southwick's with little to fill her days to her first road trip in memory and, after that, an arduous training regimen. She'd spent time around three baby elephants as well as a veteran performer, Anna May, and had ridden across the southern United States, through New Orleans, Houston, El Paso, Tucson, and Phoenix.

Traveling, for an elephant, was never easy and in fact could be downright treacherous. A month earlier a Los Angeles court awarded the DeWayne Circus $4,500 for injuries an elephant named Bimbo Jr. sustained on the road. The truck hauling the elephant had been struck by a car, causing Bimbo to suffer whiplash and leaving her unable to perform her circus routine or to water-ski, her signature stunt.

Yet Woodcock, for one, maintained that elephants were better off in the circus than a zoo. In the circus, he said, they were "constantly getting mental stimulation, not like a zoo elephant who stares at the same four walls every day."

The day after Woodcock's entourage arrived in California, Charlie Germaine called a meeting of all the performers to make an announcement: he had sold the circus. Woodcock's first thought was, My God, this after driving all the way from Florida? Germaine assured the troops that for the upcoming season the circus would still travel under the Miller-Johnson name and all contracts would be honored. He then introduced them to the new owner, Clifford Vargas.

Clifford Vargas came from a Portuguese family and grew up on a farm in Indiana. He started out in the phone business but quit to join the circus, working first for Rudy Jacobi's Rudy Bros. Circus and then for Charlie Germaine. When Vargas bought out Germaine he had to take a crash course in running a circus. He learned the trade from the ground up: where Ringling might rehearse a new show for three or four weeks—refining the choreography, the lighting, and the sequence of acts—before setting out, Vargas would throw everything together at the last minute and hope it jelled. He quickly became one of the most flamboyant and inscrutable showmen of his time. He was feared and disliked by some circus veterans—"he only knew the 'F' word," one recalled—but through raw discipline and perseverance he built his circus into one of the most successful in the country, the only circus that was even remotely on par with Ringling Bros. and Barnum & Bailey. Industry officials later credited Vargas with reinvigorating the industry at a time when smaller circuses were struggling to stay alive.

That night, Vargas threw a party at a nearby club to introduce himself to the performers. He and Barbara Woodcock tore up the dance floor. Vargas was wearing a pair of jeans with a diagonal fly, something Barbara Woodcock thought was "the neatest thing she ever saw." Later that evening Vargas came to the Woodcocks' table with a package containing the racy jeans. "Here, you can have them," he said.

The new program marked a quick turnaround for Miller-Johnson. The show had limped home from a tumultuous season, a smaller version of its usual program that was billed as a variety show. Reviews were lackluster. "When the name Miller-Johnson is mentioned it stirs up visions of two cat acts, three rings of animals and a full program of top name circus performers," a critic for *The Circus Report* wrote of the smaller show. "Makes one wonder what the sponsors thought, especially if they had seen the big circus production that Miller-Johnson had presented in the same Alameda County Fair building just a few short months ago."

The elements were no kinder. In the thick of winter, while driving across the barren plains of Wyoming, performers and crew were caught in a blizzard. As winds whipped about at eighty miles an hour and snowdrifts piled ten feet high, employees were forced to seek shelter at the rear of buildings and behind fences, or just stay put in their cars, turning their engines over periodically to try to stay warm. Cuneo's elephants and some of his tigers were part of that show. Trainer Pat Anthony was able to hole the tigers up inside a gas station. The elephants and the rest of the animals were stranded in trucks as the storm thundered around them.

The circus's spring-summer tour was beefed up but capable of performing in auditoriums, ballparks or, if no other facility was available, their own tent. The season would last thirty-six weeks and, as usual, the grand finale would consist of an elephant act.

It was the first time in years that so many circuses had hit the road with big elephant herds. Ringling Bros.' Red Unit had nineteen elephants; its Blue Unit, eighteen. Beatty-Cole traveled with an even dozen. Hoxie Bros. had ten pachyderms while Carson & Barnes had between twelve and fifteen. Miller-Johnson boasted six.

The circus world was abuzz with reports about Ringling Bros.'

new recruits. At their headquarters in Venice, Florida, trainer Hugo Schmitt had veteran female Taku on hand to help train a dozen big elephants that had just crossed the Atlantic from Billy Smart's Circus in England. On top of that, Ringling had seven baby elephants. The babies underwent two training sessions a day, individually at first and then as a group. Taku would set out with one baby chained to her, followed by the entire group of seven working without chains. Ringling appeared to be readying the elephants to take the place of the older elephants once they retired.

Circuses that couldn't afford entire herds did what they could. Hubert Castle had a guaranteed crowd-pleaser with just one elephant: Bunny, a fourteen-week-old infant who entered center ring at intermission and romped about in the sawdust. Miller-Johnson augmented its elephant act: In addition to Anna May and Billie, the circus booked the Cristiani elephants— Carrie, Babe, Shirley, and Emma—advertised as the "fastest moving herd of performing elephants in America." Emma was distinguished by her beautiful and unusual white eyes; circuses often mistakenly described her as an albino. Barbara Woodcock and Anna May were scheduled to perform a solo act in the show's first half. In the second act, the Cristiani elephants would carry out their routine in the center ring while Anna May would perform her stunts on one of the end rings. Woodcock himself would work Billie in ring three.

It was hard to compete with the Cristiani elephants, who wore glitzy headpieces with frothy pink feathers and tassels that dangled festively down their foreheads. But Barbara Woodcock entered the ring dolled up in a leopard outfit that accented her waist-length blazing red hair. Buckles Woodcock often dressed as an Arab, complete with a black headpiece. A photo from that time shows Buckles, then thirty-seven, practicing with Billie before a show. Still not fully grown, Billie is balanced on a tub, her left foreleg raised slightly. Woodcock is wearing black pants, a satin dolman-sleeved tunic, and a neon orange turban that one wag later said looked like a chunk of cheese.

(In later years, Buckles adorned his elephants with bells, gold headpieces, and bracelets. He even painted their toenails gold. "When working in a display with your competition, we knew no shame," he wrote.)

Anna May's outfit wasn't as showy as the Cristiani elephants, but her stunts were unparalleled. The Woodcocks had taught her to stand on her hind legs, perform headstands, dangle humans from her mouth, play the tambourine, and serve as a landing spot for leopards. One of her most popular acts was to balance on a globe with her trunk wrapped around an American flag. She could also tiptoe across a series of wooden pedestals placed in a single line.

The elephant acts were sandwiched between a variety of other performers: Pat Anthony and his cats; the Cassidy Girls, blond jugglers who balanced on balls; Julius von Uhl and his lion act; Klara and Klarissa on the low wire; the Ralphys and their aerial ladder tricks; the Ashtons on the trampoline; the Ferronis musical clowns; and the Farias family of aerialists, featuring eight-year-old Julio. Traveling with the circus was a five-piece band consisting of two trumpets, an organ, a trombone, and drums.

The circus's trucks were painted orange and white to attract attention as the caravan made its way across the country. By the end of May the circus landed in Pontiac, Michigan. From there it headed to Utica and Syracuse, New York, then to Danbury, New Haven, Hartford, Connecticut, and on to Allentown, Pennsylvania. Next up were stops in West Virginia, Virginia, and Florida. The circus usually stayed put a couple of days at a time but sometimes gave just one performance in a town before packing up and moving again.

The spring show drew rave reviews. "It was a fantastic sight to see the people sitting on the ground all the way to the ring curbs," *The Circus Report* opined enthusiastically. "Who says the tenters are done?" The review went on to describe the show as "well-paced," even if it was "a bit long for the average view."

By July, the newsletter was heralding Miller-Johnson as "a real surprise and revelation." Attendance was good despite little to no advertising. The circus had come up with an irresistible lure: an admittance fee of just seven dollars for a whole family. Crowds grew even bigger as the show moved into West Virginia, Virginia, and on to Florida.

After stops in Florida, the circus headed to Tennessee, then back south to Alabama, Louisiana, Texas, and Oklahoma, with Billie and the rest of the livestock traveling in the back of semis all this time. They drove across country to Arizona and on to California. The caravan meandered up to its final destination in Portland, Oregon, on August 19—a total of more than 12,000 miles.

When the season ended, circus officials were weary but jubilant. Rival shows had encountered thundering storms and raging floods along their stops, but by some fortunate turn of fate, Miller-Johnson managed to stay ahead of the foul weather. From start to finish, the circus had even held on to the same acts, which was rare. Best of all, business was lively: the show in Antioch, California, was even continued by a day, thanks to healthy advance sales.

The circus had ten days to travel halfway across the country to Appleton, Wisconsin, for the start of the fall tour. That meant no rest for cast and crew, or the animals, and it meant that any changes in the program needed to be made quickly. Buckles and Barbara Woodcock peeled off at that point, scheduled to head to Venezuela with their elephants later that fall for a winter tour, and Billie was leaving, too. John Cuneo had plans for her.

For five months Billie had divided her time between the back of a truck, a makeshift yard outside the circus arena and, for a few minutes a day, performing. Her new life didn't suit her. Woodcock told a friend that Billie was "a little snappy." There is no way of knowing whether she'd developed any sort of friendship with Anna May, but if she had, she faced another loss. She would never see Anna May or Buckles Woodcock again. Woodcock had inducted Billie into circus life, but from here on out she was in someone else's hands.

FOOLING THE ELEPHANT

The good cop/bad cop strategy of first punishing an elephant and then comforting it—still practiced in Asian countries—dates back thousands of years. In his *Mirabilia Descripta*, written around the year 1330, missionary Jordanus de Severac described the chilling manner by which captured elephants in Cambodia in that era were tamed. Handlers would ensnare an elephant between two gates. Then a man clothed in red, his face covered, would flog the elephant from above, berating it and depriving it of food or water. The punishment would continue for five or six days before a second man, dressed in a different colored costume, his face visible, would suddenly appear and pretend to strike the villainous beater and drive him away. The bare-faced man would go to the elephant and soothe her, even kiss her, and give her food. The ruse might continue for as long as two weeks. Eventually the second man would climb down beside the elephant and tie her to a tame elephant. After another three weeks the captured elephant would be meek enough to be taken out and trained.

Patience was key. An elephant worked too quickly could die from distress. She needed to learn to desire food and grow accustomed to getting it before she could be put to work. Once an elephant reached that stage, her keepers could put her to use dragging and stacking fallen trees with a surprising degree of nimbleness. In what was then called Ceylon, India, trainers were said to punish a trained elephant not with physical abuse but with psychological discipline. They might halt her allotment of sugarcane or prevent her from eating her food until her companions had had their share. The elephant's shame at having been singled out was punishment enough. Treated kindly, the elephants could work equally well with different keepers once they had grown familiar with the new face.

In Malay, trainers moved a captured elephant out of her stall using a cumbersome system that involved alternating sets of stakes and tying her hobbled front and hind legs to them, over and over, as they pulled the elephant forward a step at a time. Natives would prod the elephant from behind with poles; the elephant was so thoroughly tied up that if she tried to run she would topple over on her side. Her trainer led her to a covered stall with a V-shaped opening through which her head was drawn. The poles forming the V were then pulled together, holding the elephant's head in place behind her ears. From the corners of the stall were crossbars that ran the width of the stall, one positioned under the elephant's stomach, another just behind her forelegs and a third in front of her hind legs. The elephant was practically immobile: she could jiggle her legs or move her trunk, but nothing more.

For two weeks, trappers kept the elephant imprisoned, unable to lie down or move. A keeper assigned to the animal would then work to win her over. He'd feed and pet her, scratch her behind her ears, and give her water and treats of fruit and bamboo shoots, but not enough to satiate her. She was kept hungry and weak.

Gradually the elephant settled down and learned to look forward to the keeper's arrival. At that point she would be led out of the stocks, hobbled only at her knees, allowing her more freedom to play. While the keeper, armed with a bullhook, rode atop the elephant's head, eight or ten men held on to each leg rope and another team of men held the rope wrapped around the elephant's trunk. Six to eight more men followed from behind with whips made of rattan, striking the elephant repeatedly. The beating continued as the men holding the trunk rope led the elephant in a zigzag pattern.

If the elephant tried to run, the men controlling the foot ropes tripped her. When she roared with agony, the beating stopped. The bellow meant the elephant's spirit was shattered, that she was ready to surrender. Immediately her handlers petted and fed her. An elephant who refused to bellow was considered incapable of being trained and was often led out and shot to death.

FOUR

✦ ⚏ ✦

ONE-LEGGED STANDS

Billie's time with Buckles Woodcock prepared her well for her next assignment, which was to join John Cuneo's Hawthorn Five act. Cuneo had purchased the act a couple of years earlier from George A. Hamid Sr., the owner of Hamid-Morton.

A native of Broumana, Lebanon, Hamid had joined his uncle's acrobatic act and toured with Buffalo Bill's Wild West Show in France at the age of nine. He came to the United States the following year, where Wild West icon Annie Oakley taught him to read and write and Buffalo Bill schooled him in the ways of traveling shows. In the 1930s, Hamid teamed up with Robert Morton to create the Hamid-Morton Circus.

Cuneo had provided tigers for Hamid-Morton for the previous five years and Hamid found the acts to be first-class productions. He liked the performances Cuneo was getting out of the elephants, too. To sweeten his offer to sell Cuneo the elephants, Hamid threw in the elephant trailer, the ring curb, and a five-year performing contract. Cuneo jumped at the chance.

The Hawthorn Five had begun years earlier with elephants Siam, Delhi, Bombay, Mysore, and Calcutta, all of whom had arrived from Asia in 1949 and undergone training with Louis Reed.

Three years later Mysore and Calcutta were sold to trainer Tony Diano, and to replace them, Hamid-Morton recruited two more baby elephants, Sherma and Joyce, who were said to be sisters. The story goes that Sherma and Joyce were mishandled from the start, worked by a pair of "show broads" who knew next to nothing about training elephants. Both elephants quickly developed a reputation for being difficult.

Sherma had already killed a man by the time Cuneo acquired her. After she trampled to death a second man—one of Cuneo's handlers—Cuneo was literally ready to shoot her. Trainer Bobby Gibbs talked him out of it. He told Cuneo, "God, no, don't shoot her. I'll take her and retrain her and sell her to the Mexicans." Mexican circuses clamored for elephants and had a difficult time getting any. Gibbs took Sherma to the Circus World Museum in Baraboo, Wisconsin, and began training her in English and Spanish. He thought they had a good rapport, but one day he turned his back to her and without warning Sherma yanked him up with her mouth and trunk, flung him to the ground, and stomped on him, almost killing him. Now Gibbs was ready to shoot her dead, but the head of Circus World, Chappy Fox, begged him not to—tourists were watching. Gibbs spent the next two weeks in an iron lung recuperating from damaged internal organs and mashed ribs. His love affair with Sherma was over. He gave her to the Lion Country Safari in Florida where, in the space of a month, she killed another handler. Accounts vary as to whether she was shipped to Mexico or put to death.

Absent Sherma, Cuneo was down to four elephants, and needed a fifth. At eleven years old, Billie was the youngest of the group and by far the least experienced, but Buckles Woodcock had taught her well enough that she could segue seamlessly into the act. For the first few months Cuneo had her perform alongside two baby elephants he also traveled with, Tena and Ronnie. Bill Golden worked Billie, Cuneo worked Tena, and a third trainer worked

Ronnie. By the time Hamid-Morton kicked off its 1973 winter-spring season, Billie had joined the four adult elephants in the newly configured Hawthorn Five.

At forty, Bombay was the calm presence of the group, the leader. Among other things, she could walk on her hind legs while carrying a pony in her mouth. The stunt was a testament to Bombay's reliability: if she bit down too hard on the pony, she could have crushed it to death. Delhi, thirty-six, and Siam, whose age was unknown, brought experience to the ring while Joyce, twenty-four, was considered technically the most skilled.

Culturally, the early 1970s were watershed years for the United States. The last U.S. ground troops were finally coming home from Vietnam. President Richard Nixon was swept up in scandal at the news that he had known in advance of a break-in at the Democratic National Committee's headquarters in Washington, D.C. The ramifications of Watergate would engulf the nation for the next two years, culminating in Nixon's resignation from office in 1974.

Yet America still seemed bathed in innocence. The scourge of AIDS would not surface for another decade. *The Godfather*, a fascinating look at the mafia, was the most popular film of 1972, but moviegoers also flocked to see *Fiddler on the Roof* and *What's Up, Doc?* Singer Michael Jackson was just starting his solo career and Don McLean's ode "American Pie" captivated radio listeners. Gasoline was only fifty-five cents a gallon. The average American earned $11,800 a year, and a typical new house cost just $27,550. While circuses weren't as big of a draw as they'd once been, audiences were still turning out for them.

Hamid-Morton was one of the first circuses to develop a niche, producing shows for Shriners and other groups, in what are known as sponsored shows. Begun in the 1910s, Shrine Circuses quickly became a major source of fundraising for Shrine organizations. Circuses would appear under the auspices of the local Shrine organization, which is one reason Hamid-Morton was not as well known as some circuses. In turn, the local Shrine group handled promotion and sales. By 1972, 132 temples and 173 Shrine clubs sponsored circus performances, attracting more than ten million people a year.

For Billie, the Hamid-Morton circuit was just as grueling as Miller-Johnson's: four days in Wichita, Kansas, were followed by five days in Kansas City, then four days in Oklahoma City, with stops in Ohio after that. From there the circus traveled to Pennsylvania, Virginia, New Jersey, North Carolina, Maryland, Virginia again, and Wisconsin.

The season was barely under way when a tiger attacked Cuneo during a performance in Kansas City. Cuneo was moving equipment just outside the arena when he edged close to one of the tiger cages. The tiger sprang at him through the bars, tearing his left ear and the left side of his face and ripping his neck, chest, and right arm. Cuneo made light of the attack, saying it was "strictly 100 percent" his fault. "I just got too close," he said. "I did something I've told other people not to do for years." He underwent plastic surgery to repair the wounds, according to one report, and rejoined the circus a few days later at its next stop, in Oklahoma City.

Aside from that mishap, the season unfolded smoothly. *The Circus Report* caught up with the circus in Cherry Hill and praised the show as "fast-moving." While John Cuneo recuperated, Herta Cuneo led Billie and the four other members of the Hawthorn Five through their act. The show featured a scene in which a tiger and a lion rode atop an elephant. When the lion kissed the elephant the crowd went wild.

No one will ever know what was going on in Billie's mind during that time, but the hubbub of the circus had to be bewildering, the pace of travel demanding, especially on an elephant's feet. Elephants walk with their weight on their front feet and their toenails, much like the toenails of human beings, grow a quarter-inch to a half-inch a month. In the wild, elephants keep their toenails worn down by digging and grazing. But in captivity they don't have room to roam, so unless handlers file their nails down, the nail tips clatter against hard surfaces, crack or split, and are apt to absorb contaminants, especially when an elephant is chained up for hours on end and forced to stand in her own waste. A typical elephant urinates fifteen gallons of urine and defecates two hundred to three hundred pounds of waste a day. No matter how diligent the bull men are, a circus elephant is likely to develop infected and painful feet.

That November, the Hawthorn Five performed for the annual Shrine show at Dallas-Fort Worth, a rare ten-day engagement. Four elephants from Oscar Cristiani (the same elephants Billie performed alongside with on the Miller-Johnson tour) and six elephants from the Diano herd also appeared. The next month the Hawthorn elephants traveled to San Francisco to appear with the Polack Circus. The crowd waited patiently through the early acts: the Ronritas on the aerial wheel; the Flying Artons; Miss Astra and her sponge dive from high up onto a thick rubber mat; the Karl Winn Troupe riding their aerial motorcycles; and Señor Antonio on the trapeze. Spectators watched as the Six Clowns performed their toothache, bird magic, and other routines. As always, the crowd had come to see the elephants and the Hawthorn Five did not disappoint.

Billie and Joyce were adept performers. A photo from that year shows them performing the extremely difficult one-legged stands on top of bull tubs. Cuneo is standing between them, dressed as a sultan, complete with a midlength Nehru jacket, and grasping an umbrella, his right arm outstretched to showcase the stunt. To Joyce's left stands a young handler named Janice Daniels, whose arms are also outstretched. She's dressed in a teensy bikini connected with a triangle of cloth and an Egyptian headpiece. Joyce's side is turned to the audience while Billie faces the crowd. The elephants are wearing simple red headpieces with a single gold star on their foreheads and bands around their ankles. Their eyes are coated with black rings of Vaseline, their trunks are curled up, and their mouths are open. It looks for all the world as if they are smiling.

Daniels worked for Cuneo from 1972 through 1974 and has nothing but fond memories of her days with the Hawthorn Five. She remembers taking the elephants for long walks at the many fairgrounds where the circus stayed, dressing up to "dance around" the ring for eight minutes—the circus often put on two shows a day—and afterward indulging the elephants with baths and a giant bucket of fruit. In spite of her youth, Billie was quick to learn a routine—"a smart little teenager," Daniels recalled. She praised John and Herta Cuneo and said their main focus was on grooming, feeding, and exercising the animals.

Deborah Lockard remembers Billie differently. Lockard was one of five young women who rode the elephants that year dressed in sparkly gypsy outfits with gold bras and gauzy, flowing veils. Lockard rode Delhi. Carol Golden rode Bombay. Janice Daniels rode Joyce. Daniels's sister Chrissy rode Siam, and Lockard's sister Donna rode Billie. Lockard felt comfortable walking up to Bombay, Delhi, and Siam and giving them hugs, but she didn't feel that way about Billie and Joyce. Billie had a "mean streak," Lockard said. "We stayed clear of her."

Donna was willing to ride Billie because she was fearless, Deborah Lockard recalled. A few years before joining the act, Donna performed at Atlantic City's Steel Pier with a high-diving horse. Together she and Deborah performed an aerial ballet and the Slide for Life, a high-wire act that required them to zip down a slanted wire hanging only by their necks. While traveling with Hamid-Morton, Donna Lockard met Gee Gee Engesser and

Bucky Steele and learned a lot from them about elephants. She felt capable of handling Billie.

When Siam died in 1973, Cuneo brought in an elephant named Tess. Tess was affectionate and hardworking, and before long Cuneo put her at the head of the pack along with Bombay. Tess was the lead elephant for the walking long mount, a stunt that required elephants to form a line and, in unison, rise up on their hind legs and rest their front feet on the back of the elephant next to them. Because of all the extra weight Tess had to bear to pull off that stunt, Cuneo fed her extra grain mixed with molasses. Lockard suspected the other elephants resented the perks given to Tess.

Cuneo could handle Billie, but he'd taken a dislike to her. "Billie was smart, a gifted performer," he said in an interview. "She could pull off stunts other elephants simply couldn't, or wouldn't, do. But she was a tough elephant. Only worked for somebody she respected. And she hated women. When she was just a little elephant she hit a girl right on the nose."

Donna Lockard is deceased. Long retired from circus life, her sister, Deborah, recalled nothing but good times and defended the circus as a magical form of escape. One of the newspaper clips in her scrapbook shows Deborah riding an elephant under the headline: "Hey kids, young and old, the circus has come to town."

"If I was an elephant and could communicate with humans and was given a choice between freedom in India or Africa, where Mother Nature can hurt me when she wants, etc. or going to a zoo or becoming a Circus Performing Pachyderm, I would choose Circus performer," Lockard wrote in response to questions. "Circus elephants are Special. Where else in town can you get to pet one or ride one or not only see one but see one stand on its head, waltz around, and the infamous ONE-FOOT STAND [sic]? Billie did all those tricks. I believe she was proud of herself doing it."

LONG VOYAGE TO AMERICA

Before an elephant could be shipped overseas she had to be led to the nearest port. In Africa, hunters like Charles Reiche drove wildlife 1,500 miles to Cape Town. Lion cubs, antelope, and other small animals traveled in rudimentary cages balanced on oxcarts or suspended on poles between two camels, but elephants and other bigger animals were expected to walk the long journey.

Coaxing an elephant that far required boldness and skill. The elephant was too wild to be ridden and her captors could not force her along. They relied on a combination of annoyances and enticements and ropes attached to her legs to lure her forward. Many elephants failed to survive. Young, weak, and mourning the loss of their mothers, they collapsed and died along the way.

Getting an elephant aboard a ship was equally problematic. In some cases, traders used slings and derricks to hoist elephants on board. Others placed palm leaves alongside the dock, tied the boat as level as possible with the wharf, then positioned the elephant with her back to the water and prodded her to step backward. It was one thing to maneuver an elephant's hind legs on the boat and something else entirely to convince her to heave her front legs off of dry land. Sometimes an entire day would elapse before the screams of the elephant died down and she allowed herself to be launched on to the vessel.

In the early 1700s, the Dutch would wrap a sailing cloth around an elephant's chest and stomach and force her into the sea between two tame elephants. The tame elephants would turn around midway and swim back to shore, leaving the captured elephant no choice but to follow a small boat to the ship, where sailors would hook tackle to the sailcloth and hoist her on board. The Dutch later improved their method by covering a flat-bottomed barge with planks and lining the ship with green branches, so that the elephant never saw water until she was safely on the ship.

On board, elephants were led down into the bowels of the ship, to dark stables where they would remain for a voyage of some 12,000 miles.

The trauma suffered when elephants were wrenched from their homeland, caged and often beaten and starved into submission, was inestimable. The babies suffered most of all. Keepers couldn't feed a baby elephant on hay alone and expect her to thrive. A baby required, if not goat milk, ten cans of evaporated milk poured into a pail of water several times a day.

The animals had to endure weeks of gale force winds and bracing cold waves. When storms struck they were tossed about like heads of lettuce. In 1894 the British freighter *Hankow* headed for New York with ten zebras, fourteen Javanese ponies, three cassowaries (large birds similar to emus), four monkeys, and three elephants—two adult animals and a baby named Toodles. The ship weathered three months at sea, including a raging storm and ice-cold waves. By the time the boat landed at Pier 29, six of the ponies had died, all ten zebras had washed overboard, and both adult elephants had succumbed to pneumonia. Miraculously, Toodles survived. No bigger than a Shetland pony, his cage had been locked down so thoroughly on deck that he was buffeted from the storm.

One circus's passage from New York to London in 1898 turned tense when high waves caused the elephants' cage on deck to pitch backward every time the boat keeled starboard. One elephant reached through the bars and wrapped his trunk around the watchman like a child seizing hold of a mother's sleeve. Another curled his trunk around the bar of his cage and let it hang inside out, whimpering from time to time as pitifully as a young child.

A ship from Calcutta bound for New York lost four elephants to high waves (the lone leopard on board had already clawed his way out of his cage and jumped overboard, in what was dubbed a suicide). On one boat from Singapore, the ceiling below deck was so low that five elephants had to crawl on their knees past passenger cabins to reach the steerage department. When the ship arrived at Madras, there was no dock to offload them, so keepers opened the doors of steerage and backed the elephants overboard. They landed in the water with a huge splash and a roar, and when they surfaced they blew water as if they were whales. Their keepers paddled over to them on rowboats, climbed onto their backs and rode them to shore.

The biggest risks to transporting animals by boat occurred when traders left them in the inexperienced care of the ship's crew. In 1936 a pygmy elephant, one of five from the Belgian Congo en route to Boston, escaped when a tumultuous storm jostled his crate open. A 400-pound hippo housed next to the elephant got out, too, and attacked him. Passengers were awakened at 5:00 A.M. to the sounds of the elephant's roars and the hippo's bellows. Four hours later the captain had a dead elephant on his hands and a hippo that was contained only after his keepers heaved bales of cotton into the hold, squeezing the hippo against a wall. Before the trip ended a second elephant had died and one of the three giraffes on board slipped and broke its neck.

Elephants who died at sea were tossed overboard.

Newspapers chronicled the trips breathlessly, saluting the importers for their derring-do and recounting with amusement any mishaps that happened along the way. RUM JUMBO TOO MUCH FOR LADY ELEPHANT read the headline in a 1948 issue of *The Daily Boston Globe*. The article told how nine elephants landed in East Boston aboard the freighter *Irisbank* from Calcutta, one of them unconscious after having swallowed a quart of rum. The elephant's keeper fed her the rum after determining that she "did not readily adapt herself to the rigors of the North Atlantic crossing," which lasted fifty-six days.

In 1876, on a steamer from Europe, seven baby elephants from

Burma and India got loose, tussled with one another, and frightened passengers before they were captured. "Poor things!" the newspaper account of their journey said. "How puzzled they must have been by the pitching and tossing and tumbling, the noise of the machinery, and the darkness; and now they will be shut up in houses, and have to go to school."

FIVE

THE HAWTHORN FIVE

In 1974, gasoline was scarce: in some parts of the country many service stations were closed and the ones that were operating stayed open just a few hours a day. Circuses with long stops between shows struggled to find fuel.

The year 1976 was even worse for circuses. A listless economy kept many families home, and people who did venture out were more interested in celebrating the nation's bicentennial or visiting one of America's burgeoning amusement parks: places like Six Flags, which featured musical shows and bigger, more spectacular rides than a traveling carnival could offer. Of the sixty-five circuses that played the United States and Canada that year, some lasted only a week or two, others six or eight weeks before folding their tents and shuffling home.

A circus needed three years to build a route, and shows that had previously relied on unlimited calling to publicize their arrival suddenly found themselves being charged seven to nine cents a call. Many dropped the phone calls. They were scraping by on meager budgets as it was. The George Matthews Great London Circus began the season with three rings, but had to cut back to one, and almost blew away when cold rain and blustery winds thundered through during an appearance in Cleveland, Ohio. By late September, the circus had closed its season for good, along with the Great American Circus, Sells & Gray, Hoxie Bros., and several others. Critics were starting to write off 1976 as the industry's most calamitous year since 1938.

A couple of circuses somehow bucked the trend. Circus Vargas saturated its markets with publicity and counted on word of mouth to spread the news that Vargas delivered show-stopping performances. As a result the circus enjoyed its best season yet, playing forty-nine weeks with a full roster of acts, including seventeen elephants.

Hamid-Morton did well, too. Its costumes were brand-new and its motorized aerial rigging system made it easy to raise, lower, and fold its tent away. After watching a performance in Cherry Hill, New Jersey, reviewer Frank Hoopes praised Hamid-Morton as "the best circus for its size anywhere."

It was more than just the efficiency. Hamid-Morton offered quality performances. Bill Golden presented Cuneo's dozen tigers and black-maned Nubian lion in a "lightning-paced" act featuring tiger pyramids, a rollover, and all twelve tigers lying down. Then came Herta Cuneo's white tiger act. The Cuneos' white tigers were genetic mutations, the result of a captive breeding program. The experimentation required to produce them resulted in striking coats, but the tigers were neurotic and had difficulty hearing. Three of them were cross-eyed. Cuneo's star, Bagheera, was completely deaf. Despite Bagheera's disability, Herta Cuneo taught her to perch atop a pedestal, wait until the elephant Joyce lumbered by, and then soar onto Joyce's back. As Joyce circled the ring, Bagheera would jump first through one hoop of fire, then a second, and then a third. Joyce was dressed in an elaborate blue and white costume that draped down to her knees and covered her forehead. At times she carried not one, but two white tigers on her back.

Cuneo's baby elephants were also trotted out to perform front foot stands on revolving pedestals in the center ring, framed by two adult elephants, likely Billie and Joyce; they, too, had learned the front-foot pedestal trick. The Hawthorn Five performed their one-foot stands, leg carry, and mounts with Debbie Lockard. Ray Valentine Jr. performed somersaults on the tightwire and Princess Mafalda balanced on swords.

Many circuses used the summer to regroup between the spring and fall tours. Not Cuneo. He trucked his animals to Marineland and Game Farm in Niagara Falls, Ontario, where they performed as part of a show featuring Cuneo's tigers and bears and Marineland's sea lions, elephant seals, and killer whales. The animals carried out their act six times a day, seven days a week. When they weren't in the ring the elephants were kept chained in place in a building at the rear.

That fall Cuneo hooked up with a different circus, Page-Cavanaugh, which was led by Charlie Germaine, the man who'd previously owned Miller-Johnson. Germaine's latest production was strictly old-school: no lavish numbers, just an old-fashioned quality show performed, in some cases, under a genuine big top, a blue-and-white-striped tent measuring 150-by-300 feet, with an inside ring surrounded by rows of aluminum seats. "We will play under big tops, buildings, grandstands, . . . even old ladies' driveways if needs be," Germaine announced. "I am not presenting a Broadway theatrical . . . but a *circus!*"

The circus debuted on the East Coast and this time the Hawthorn Five elephants had a new performer: "Miss Margaret" Duke. Duke, an aerialist from Texas, arrived with her husband, Wade Burck, whose job was to handle the tigers. Burck replaced the previous tiger trainer, Bill Golden, who left that spring to join Royal Hanneford.

The year 1976 was a milestone for another reason. Up until that point, little attention had been focused on the welfare of the animals in circuses. But that year, Pat Derby, a former animal trainer in Hollywood, published a memoir, *The Lady and Her Tiger*, which spilled the dirty secrets of some of the brutal practices used to coerce wild animals into performing fanciful tricks. Trainers sometimes half-starved animals—one trainer fed his fox a single chicken neck a day—to make them eager to perform for food, Derby divulged. Others went so far as to break the noses and burn the feet of bears. Derby knew of elephants who'd been electroshocked in the most sensitive of places—their ears, mouths, vaginas, and anuses—to bring them under control.

Derby knew what she was talking about. She'd trained animals for the television shows *Daktari, Gentle Ben*, and *Flipper*, and for movies such as *The Love Bug*. She'd divorced her husband, Ted Derby, because he refused to stop using an electric cattle prod as part of his training regimen.

"Animal work tends to attract a high proportion of sadistic psychotics, on the one hand, and sentimental incompetents on the other," she wrote. Her book became a bestseller, yet millions of Americans seemed either incapable of connecting the dots with regard to performing animals, or simply didn't care. They continued to flock to circuses.

Page-Cavanaugh's fall show featured musicians Vynn and Wynn playing the organ and drums for a long roster of acts: Wade Burck with a dozen Hawthorn tigers and one lion; trapeze artist Winnie McKay; clowns Don Bridwell, Dukie Anderson, and Company; the Boskas, a juggling act; Tim Bickmore, who did rola bola and juggling; Los Latinos, Herbie Weber and Maricela Sanchez Hernandez, on the tightwire; Goofus and Harry the clowns; and Chester Cable, who juggled with his feet. Following intermission, Herta Cuneo presented Bagheera the tiger riding atop Joyce. Then came the Four Flying Ramos, Sergio, Mitzi, Raoula, and Ava; more clowns; Herta Cuneo again with the Hawthorn bears; the Great Huberto on the Slide for Life; and clowns performing a wash day routine. The finale was John Cuneo and Miss Margaret with the Hawthorn Five elephants. The elephants' fabulous long mount ended the show.

SEESAWS, GRASS SKIRTS, AND WATER SKIS

Where circus elephants were concerned, no stunt was deemed too outlandish. Trainers taught elephants to teeter-totter on seesaws. They pedaled around the ring on tricycles. They performed with fireworks. They balanced their big round bodies on wooden barrels, exchanging feet constantly to keep from falling. Adam Forepaugh's 1899 show featured an elephant with a boxing glove attached to the end of his trunk who would spar with his trainer, frequently knocking him out of the ring. John Robinson's Circus had a military act involving three elephants that fired cannons, stepped about in formation, and attended to the "wounded" in battle. The crowd favorite was an Asian elephant named Tillie, who was said to be so intelligent that she could call the circus owner, John G. Robinson, "Papa." Tillie was 120 years old when she died, or so the circus alleged. Her funeral in Robinson's hometown of Terrace Park, Ohio, was a public event.

Jenny II, a well-known elephant in the early 1900s, could ride a tricycle, ring a bell, sound a trumpet, play a flute and an organ, turn the leaves of a music book, play a harmonica while dancing, and lay a baby doll in a cradle, give it a bottle, swing the cradle, and then carry it away. She finished her act by carrying her trainer out of the ring on her head.

Elephants used to perform in mud shows and under tents, but never on an indoor stage. That changed in the early 1900s, when Powers' Dancing Elephants appeared onstage at New York's Hippodrome. The presence of the Powers' elephants symbolized just how big of an attraction the Hip had become. Powers' Dancing Elephants had spent forty years playing year-round in fairs, circuses, theaters, and bull-rings, pulling in $1,500 to $2,000 a week apiece, more than the president of the United States. In elaborately choreographed skits, they played baseball, carried out a-shave-and-a-haircut, bowled, fought one another in a reenactment of a war, and danced the hula, the fox-trot, the Charleston, the two-step, and the waltz.

A perennial trick was to put baby elephants in big baby carriages and have adult elephants push them around the ring. "Mamas in the Park" skits were popular standbys. Some of the elephants wore tall, old-fashioned policemen's hats and carried billy clubs in their mouths. Others were dressed as men in morning coats and top hats.

Some tricks did not require physical exertion. Hollywood studio trainer George Emerson taught one elephant to shimmy in a grass skirt by putting a heavy sack of sand on her back and instructing her to "shake it up." The elephant would do anything to get the sack off her back. In the late 1800s, trainer George Lockhart taught his elephant Boney to close her eyes and blink slowly to feign drunkenness.

As late as the 1950s, comedy acts involving elephants were still crowd-pleasers. The Robinson Circus's barbershop skit started out with four elephants entering a ring decked out with a stand, napkins, towels, and an oversized razor hanging by a mirror. The trainer would station the first elephant in front of the mirror and drape a bib over his chest. A second elephant would grab a big brush and cover the first elephant's face with lather. A third elephant would carry away the bucket. Elephant number two would pick up the razor only to decide it was too dull. The elephant would sharpen the razor on a grind-stone while a fourth elephant turned the crank. Elephant number two then returned to shave the first elephant and dry his face with a towel, which had been hanging over elephant number two's ear. To top off the act, a clown would enter the ring and decide that he, too, wanted a shave. As elephant number two lathered him up, the third and fourth elephants proceeded to make off first with the clown's umbrella, then his coat, and finally his pants. The skit ended with the panicked clown fleeing the stage.

Over time, circuses focused less on comic skits and more on showcasing the elephants' physical prowess. The sight of a group of elephants onstage spinning about, balancing themselves on tubs or resting their front legs on one another's backs was a spectacle. The popular hind-leg maneuver was hard enough to perform on a flat surface: Hugo Schmitt took matters one step further by teaching his elephant Kernaudi to walk up a ramp, cross a short platform, and descend another ramp, all while standing on her rear legs.

Old-school trainers mourned the move away from comedy. "We have an art, but it's fast becoming a lost art smothered by spangles and legs," one lamented.

Elephants were taught to teeter-totter on seesaws that rose higher than their heads. Legendary trainer Gunther Gebel-Williams, who worked for Ringling from 1968 to 1990, had an elephant step on one end of a teeter-totter, catapulting Gebel-Williams into a backward somersault. He'd land on top of another elephant's back. The first elephant he taught this to broke a board with her foot several thousand times before she figured out the exact amount of pressure to apply.

One elephant even learned to water-ski. Queenie was six months old when Liz Dane's father bought her from Henry Trefflich's pet store in New York City in 1953. For the next fourteen years Dane worked with her pet elephant and together they performed three or four times a day at a theme park in Florida. A photo from 1958 showed the elephant, then five, chained to a pair of enormous skis. Dane stood next to her, holding a bullhook in one hand and waving gaily with the other as the duo plowed along behind a boat, leaving a spray of water in their wake.

For years, pyramids—which involved one elephant standing on the backs of two others—were the pièce de résistance of elephant tricks. Trainers subsequently added two three-elephant pyramids with occasionally a seventh elephant doing a hind leg walk in between.

Gebel-Williams taught lions, tigers, and leopards to ride on the backs of elephants. Trainer Gene Garner festooned a young elephant with an entire menagerie of animals. With her teeth, the elephant grasped a ring clung to by a chimpanzee dressed like a Mexican bandito. Meanwhile, a zebra balanced on a red seat with a railing, called a howdah, which covered the elephant's back. Lying on top of the zebra was a tiger, and platforms containing one white dog each were balanced on either side of the elephant. A total of six animals perched precariously on one elephant. Whether the stacked-up menagerie actually moved about the ring or simply stayed put is uncertain.

SIX

━◆━❧❦❧━◆━

LIFE ON THE ROAD

By 1977, the circus industry's fortunes had turned completely around. Circuses were thriving once again and elephant acts, as usual, were the big draw. Carson & Barnes's show boasted thirty-two elephants of all sizes. Circus Vargas featured a pair of elephants who would step on teeter-totters, sending acrobats soaring into the air from the other end. John Cuneo's Hawthorn Five elephants were drawing attention too. Not since the 1950s, when Tom Packs's elephants toured the country, had America seen such a polished five-elephant act.

Packs was a veteran entrepreneur in the amusement industry—he owned a circus, rodeos, thrill shows, ice shows, and other outdoor pursuits—when he decided to work up a few animal acts. He ordered a shipment of animals from Siam, among them eight baby elephants. The elephants were a sensation even before they landed on American soil. The State Department learned that a modern-day Noah's Ark was making its way to the United States, and asked the ship's captain if he wouldn't mind stopping at a series of Pacific Islands along the way to exhibit his cargo. The unscheduled stops lengthened the trip, causing the ship to run low on feed. The captain messaged Packs in a panic, telling him the elephants had grown so hungry they were trying to "kick the ship to pieces." But Packs was unable to find a commercial airline willing to fly out to and drop a load of feed.

Finally, the U.S. Navy stepped in. Four days before the ship arrived in San Francisco, the navy sent a plane 1,500 miles out to parachute a bale of hay down for each of the elephants on board. The navy also lowered several crates of worms to feed the twenty crates of birds. The story got huge play in newspapers. Despite the last-minute rations, three of the elephants died. Packs capitalized on the publicity by flying the surviving elephants immediately to New Orleans, where his circus was performing, so he could show them off. The elephants were malnourished and infested with lice and internal parasites and one of them, Mary, shuffled lopsidedly to compensate for one short leg. But audiences couldn't distinguish a sick elephant from a healthy one.

Packs knew next to nothing about elephants, but he'd stumbled across an ancient book from India that laid bare the time-honored secrets for handling and training pachyderms, borrowed a copy, and had extras made. Then he hired elephant veterans Mac and Peggy MacDonald to train the small herd. Mac MacDonald took one look at the scrawny creatures and nearly walked away, but Packs convinced him to take the job.

The act, dubbed the Besalou Elephants, toured the country to great acclaim. Audiences were captivated by the undersized elephants performing stunts. Vintage photos show one of them, Penny, balancing her front legs on two-foot-high posts alongside Peggy MacDonald, who stood on her hands, too. In another shot the elephants fall into a modified long mount, standing on tubs while Peggy balances one leg on the back of one elephant and her other leg on the back of another.

The act suffered a setback in the summer of 1953 when, during a stunt labeled the Merry-Go-Round, one of the elephants, Tommy, slid off a tub and fractured her hind leg. Tommy's new trainer reset the bone, bound a leather sling of sorts around her leg, and left the elephant behind with short-legged Mary in Indiana for the rest of the season. The following year the circus retired Mary altogether; her limp had become too pronounced. She wound up at the Audubon Zoo and Packs brought in a replacement named Shirley.

The elephants eventually outgrew their adorableness and when they did Packs sold them to importer Louis Goebel, who hired them out to appear in several movies. The elephants were sold again in 1960 to the Rudy Bros. Circus, and once more in 1964, this time to a circus in Mexico. One of the five, Alice, died the following spring. The other four were never heard from again.

Now, two decades later, Cuneo was presenting what some considered the finest five-elephant act to follow the Besalou Elephants. Some if not all of Cuneo's elephants could perform successive hind leg walks, two front foot walks, a walking long mount, and more. The younger two, Joyce and Billie, could execute the extremely difficult one-foot stands. Critics singled out Cuneo's elephant act, together with Herta Cuneo's tiger act, for praise. "Superlatives won't do justice to the Hawthorn Circus Corp.," *The Circus Report* enthused.

There's no question that some trainers genuinely loved their elephants and were able to form strong bonds with them. Dorey Miller, the owner of Carson & Barnes Circus, and his wife, Isla, claimed to have doted on their first elephant, Hattie, who had a paralyzed trunk and needed special care. For a time the Millers even slept in the same trailer as Hattie. "We remember them all, by name, as a part of our family," Miller once said of his elephants. "They are the biggest, the kindest, the most understanding and the smartest animals that live on the earth." In 1977, a twenty-five-year-old elephant with an Italian circus was said to have deliberately starved herself to death after her trainer quit his job. The pair had worked together for fifteen years.

But John Cuneo Jr. seemed more captivated by the spectacle of circus life than by the animals who'd had to sacrifice so much on his behalf. He professed a cavalier affection for certain of his elephants. Joyce, despite her growing reputation for surliness, was the sweetest of the five, according to Cuneo. He said Bombay was as gentle as a puppy. "She would follow you all over the place," he said. "You could leave her loose on the circus and she'd be as good and sweet as she could be."

Billie, though, was something else entirely. "Billie was not a nice elephant," Cuneo said. "She wasn't a pleasant elephant. I'm sorry to say that."

"Bombay would play with a dog—tickle 'em and play with 'em. You get one like Billie, first thing she'd try to do is go to first base with a dog."

He took no responsibility for Billie's demeanor, never seemed to consider that the life he had consigned her to might have robbed her of any chance of normalcy. An elephant's personality had nothing to do with the way she was handled, Cuneo maintained. Two elephants could be treated identically, and one would turn out "obnoxious" while the other was as easygoing as could be. All that mattered to Cuneo was that Billie respected him. If she respected him, he could convince her to carry out fancy stunts: walk on her front legs; walk on her hind legs; do one-foot handstands.

"She did everything for me," he said, looking back on those years. "Anybody else, she'd go after 'em. She was difficult."

In 1977, Cuneo's father died at the age of ninety-two and John Junior headed home to deal with family business. The job of presenting the Hawthorn Five elephants suddenly fell to tiger trainer Wade Burck. Burck had worked with elephants, but he'd never performed with them.

Burck was a hotshot, a North Dakota cowboy who'd broken into circus ranks as a complete outsider—neither a member of the foreign families that had so permeated the circus culture nor a third- or fourth-generation artist, as many circus performers were. He'd loved animals since he was a boy. He'd trained horses on family ranches back home and each year, when the whooping cranes landed in the salt flats near his hometown of Hillsboro, he rode out on his horse to watch them. He left home after high school and wound up as an apprentice keeper at a zoo in Naples, Florida. A trainer who presented John Cuneo's white tiger act for Clyde Bros. Shrine Circus, Lou Regan, later hired Burck as an apprentice trainer—a "shit shoveler." It was the least glamorous job in the circus. For thirty-five dollars a week he raked up elephant dung, surrounded by transients who drank constantly and performers who had no time for a kid so obviously wet behind the ears.

Slowly Burck climbed his way up to training animals. Five years later he was working for Cuneo and traveling with Hamid-Morton on the Shrine Circus circuit from February to June. Summers were spent with the Cuneo menagerie at Marineland in Ontario. After September, Cuneo's menagerie would play the big Texas Shrine dates, which consisted of five big cities in two weeks, and then go to California—the elephants spent their winters at the Great Western Livestock Exposition in Los Angeles. A couple of months later the schedule would start over again, with Cuneo advertising the availability of his Hawthorn Five act for dates in between.

Burck tried to emulate his idol, Gunther Gebel-Williams. He dyed his hair blond and wore scanty costumes: latticework abbreviated tops over low-slung pants. He appreciated the fact that Cuneo had two costumes custom-made for him by Nudie's, a company known for its eye-catching circus attire.

Burck's arrival must have eased Billie's life, at least somewhat. For once, she and the other elephants were under the care of someone who seemed to feel a degree of empathy toward them, the same as Burck did for his tigers. In the ring, he made lots of contact with his tigers—hugging and riding them—which helped build his reputation as a daredevil. To Burck, it made sense to befriend the animals.

"In the old days, when there were plenty of tigers in the world, you'd just beat the animal until it either did what you wanted or attacked you," he once wrote. "If it attacked, you'd shoot it and get another. Well, now you can't replace them, so you better find another way of dealing with them."

Burck looked out for the elephants, too, when he could. One of their regular stops was the old armory in Hartford, Connecticut. Like most armories, it was miserably cold and dank and the elephants were kept in the worst part, a tiny garage in the basement. To get to the performance floor they had to go outside, circle the building, and walk up a ramp that spiraled around the building's perimeter.

The Hawthorn Five elephants knew the layout. Burck would unhook their chains, head them out the door, and then ride the elevator to the performance floor so he could meet them as they rounded the corner of the ramp. He timed it so the elephants could enter the building without having to spend even a few minutes idling in the cold.

Cuneo last performed with the elephants in 1978. His final appearance was at the Arabia Temple Shrine Circus in Houston, Texas. But he remained very involved with the training. Twice a week Cuneo dropped by to supervise Burck's training sessions. Handwritten on a legal pad was a list of the tricks Cuneo wanted the tigers and elephants to do, including the order he wanted the stunts performed and where he wanted each animal positioned. Frequently Cuneo wrote the playlist before he'd even acquired the animals in question. If Burck expressed doubt about a particular animal's ability to perform a certain act, Cuneo waved him off. Nonsense, such-and-such animal did it ten years ago, so it will not be a problem for this one, he'd say.

Cuneo insisted that an animal follow through with a command even if it resisted doing so. And he was adamant about practicing every last detail of a performance, even down to the applause lines. "Why didn't you take a call after that trick?" Cuneo would often ask. Because, Burck told him, they were in the barn, no one was watching, and Burck was there to train the act, not try to sell it.

A series of photos taken during those years captures the elephants performing some of their tricks. One photo shows them lined up in a row—Joyce at the far left, followed by Bombay, Tess in the center, Delhi and Billie on the far right—sitting on their tubs, their front legs raised and held stiffly out in front of them. Margaret Duke poses on Tess's right front leg.

In a second photo Duke stands on a tub and dances the twist while Joyce on her right and Delhi on her left shake their heads back and forth in a simulated dance. A third photo shows the elephants in a T-mount. Tess is in the center, facing the audience. On each side of her, Bombay and Delhi stand on their hind legs, their front feet propped on Tess's back. Joyce stands on her hind legs with her front feet on Bombay's back while Billie strikes the same pose with Delhi. The trick would be difficult enough if the elephants were standing on the ground; the fact that all five are standing on tubs makes it exponentially harder. Not only does Tess bear the weight of two of the elephants, but Duke is standing on top of her shoulders and Tess is lifting her right front foot.

To see the elephants in still photos is one thing. To watch how quickly they carried out their tricks is quite another. Sometime in 1978, a year after Burck took over the elephant act, a friend shot a home movie of the Hawthorn Five rehearsing their act. The footage is grainy and jerky the way amateur films tend to be, but it captures the rapid-fire pace of the elephants as they enter the ring and, one by one, carry out the tricks taught to them by Buckles Woodcock, John Cuneo, and every other trainer who had participated in their schooling.

They start with the Merry-Go-Round, which involves two elephants standing on tubs with their front feet resting on the backs of two other elephants who are circling the tubs at a rapid pace, requiring the elephants on the tubs to rotate quickly in a small space to keep up. The fifth elephant is propped up on a tub with Margaret Duke, clad in a red spangly swimsuit with a peek-aboo cutout just beneath her breasts, resting on the elephant's back. Duke's leg is pointed skyward in a theatrical pose. The elephants wear their usual headpieces of three red circles adorned with blazing gold stars cascading down their faces and onto their trunks and flashy red bracelets encircling each leg. Burck wears red pants with a white cut-out midriff top, the kind of outfit only a circus performer could get away with.

The film goes on to show two elephants, most likely Bombay and Tess, facing each other, holding in their mouths the ends of a taut rope. Duke sits in the middle of the rope as if it is a swing. She grips the rope tightly with her hands as the elephants raise it high, then stretches out one arm and gives a little flourish of a wave. The next scene shows her dangling from an elephant's mouth, her body arched into a back bend, as the elephant circles the outer edge of the ring, stepping back slightly and lowering herself to let Duke jump off. Then two elephants back into a sitting position and Duke clambers up one elephant's forehead.

In the following stunt, Joyce, Bombay, and Billie rise up into a hind leg walk from the back of the ring with Bombay clenching a trapeze, holding Duke in her mouth. (In some of the actual performances, Duke and Burck's three-year-old son, Adam, sat in the trapeze, his tiny hands grasping the ropes on either side.) Walking abreast, the three elephants take a dozen halting steps in unison, their backs hunched over and their torsos tilted forward, until they reach tubs on either side. Bombay sets Duke down and Billie and Joyce place their front feet on the tubs, tuck their hind legs up and under themselves and hoist themselves up on their left front feet, their right front feet thrust forward. They hold the pose for several seconds before stepping down.

The finale shows the five elephants performing a quick-walking long mount, Billie hurrying to bring up the rear. An ordinary long mount is breathtaking enough, but to see the elephants actually walking on their hind legs is spectacular. From a distance the hulking gray line looks like a gigantic caterpillar.

Years later, a trainer for Ringling Bros. testified in court that Ringling stopped teaching its elephants to do one-legged tub stands and perform hind leg walks because they were hobbling the animals at too young of an age, causing them to develop arthritis and rupturing their uteruses. Decades earlier, presumably before anyone knew the damage such stunts could cause, Billie and the rest of the Hawthorn Five performed those tricks daily. The film captures them pulling off the feats. As the elephants file out of the ring, Burck stands on top of a tub and gestures for the sparse audience that had gathered for the run-through.

More remarkable is the scene filmed at the start of the film. The elephants have been unchained and let out to wander on their own to a nearby lake, believed to be at the fairgrounds in Trenton, New Jersey. Burck, shirtless, beckons to Joyce, and the camera shows her walking purposefully past another elephant toward the water. The camera switches to two elephants already submerged up to their thighs. They lower themselves into the gray-green water, which is deep enough to sink down into. One elephant lies on her side, her head halfway submerged. Another smacks the water over and over with her trunk. A third elephant immerses herself entirely. She resurfaces, sucks water up her trunk, brings her trunk to her mouth to drink and repeats this over and over again. The elephants agitate continuously under water, seemingly oblivious to the grooms standing nearby on the bank. Joyce and a fourth elephant watch for a moment before sidling down the bank to join their companions. The first elephant rises up with a bunch of grass wrapped around her trunk, flings off the grass, and settles back down into the water.

It's unclear which of the elephants is Billie. Then, suddenly, Burck points her out in the commentary he wrote to accompany a video release of the film. She has climbed out of the water and is standing on the bank, gazing at the other elephants. She pauses a few seconds before heading back down the grassy bank into the water, swishing her tail and swinging her trunk back and forth. She dips her trunk in the water again before wading in head first. Halfway in, she turns around and backs in the rest of the way, submerging herself up to her eyes. Underwater she jostles about, curling her trunk and raising it high. She turns sideways, submerging her massive head halfway in the water, halfway out. Now she dunks her head completely.

There must have been a slight breeze that day because tiny waves unfurl across the water. Elephants adore baths, and the outing was a rare chance for these five animals to enjoy one, to exert some control over their movements, to shift about free of any tethering, absent any handlers by their side. It's striking how closely the elephants huddle with one another in the water, as if they're intent on savoring the experience together. The film has no sound, so it's impossible to tell whether any of the elephants chirped or trumpeted with contentment. But even without a soundtrack the elephants seem completely in their element. For those few precious minutes they seem to be having the time of their lives.

When the footage appeared on the Internet many years later, Burck posted it on his blog, "The Circus No Spin Zone," along with his thoughts. "Long before it became a 'feel good' publicity stunt to illustrate how much we 'loved' our animals in the circus, as a standard husbandry practice the animals were allowed to play, swim etc. just because it was good for them," he wrote.

The footage next shows Burck putting the elephants in a hind leg stand. The Hawthorn Five line up according to their flow chart: Bombay first, then Tess, followed by Delhi and Joyce. Billie brings up the rear. At Burck's signal the elephants lift their enormous bodies upright, raise their trunks and curl them into the shape of an S. Delhi seems unable to curl her trunk; it bends down at an unnatural angle. Billie curls her trunk perfectly, but she appears to be straining to attempt the hind leg stand. She lowers herself a few seconds before the other elephants, then attempts a second time to stand up. Once again, she sets her front feet down a moment before the others. Burck seems not to notice. He turns around to face the camera, his face relaxed into a loose grin.

Burck's philosophy about animal training was mixed. He had no problem with the concept of confining wild animals, transporting them about the country, and having them perform for a living. He didn't object to beating a camel with a two-by-four to make it understand how to behave. A stud camel would treat his own herd even more harshly—biting and kicking other camels to push them out of danger's way, Burck reasoned. "You can't apply human emotions to animals," he once wrote. But he also believed that the first step in training a tiger was not to instill fear but to overcome the animal's natural fear.

Years after the film was shot of the Hawthorn Five, Burck questioned the rationale of having elephants perform some of the stunts they were expected to do. "At what point in an elephant's life, with the exception of reaching up [to] browse . . . would it go on its hind legs?" he asked. "Anyone ever recall seeing an elephant go to its head with its back feet straight in the air and hold it for four or five seconds? . . . What possible reason would an elephant have to do a one foot stand 'naturally' in the wild: anyone? Ride a tricycle? . . . Who decides when enough is enough?"

Yet Burck also defended the use of bullhooks and other train-ing devices. Briefly, the elephants are seen walking trunk to tail, Adam trotting along beside Delhi. The young boy is no taller than the big elephant's knee and as he walks, he paws the ground with his father's bright red bullhook. Burck wrote that the scene took place at a time "when we were not ashamed to have and use an elephant hook (because we knew how to use it) and didn't carry it with the hook hidden in our hand (or) tape it up to match our costumes . . . in an effort to make it less visible.

"I do recall telling Adam that day, 'It's not a cane, son. Carry it right.'"

In some of their actual performances, Burck entered the ring standing on Bombay's back, Adam behind him straddling the bulky shoulders of Tess. Duke, pregnant with her second child, walked alongside. Delhi, Joyce, and Billie followed from behind. Burck joked that he put Adam in the act as a means of keeping track of the "little monster."

Years later, in an exchange on Wade Burck's circus blog, cir-cus veteran and elephant trainer John Milton Herriott scolded Burck, saying, "If you allowed your young son to be around Billy [sic] without being right on top of the situation you are nuts." Herriott was right: with very little effort, any one of the elephants could have wielded her trunk and sent Adam reeling. But Burck clearly trusted the elephants and the trust seemed to flow both ways.

One of the Hawthorn Five's tricks required Tess to pose on a tub that was perched atop a six-inch-high stand, elevating her slightly above the other elephants. The stunt involved a fair de-gree of risk. Tess could not slide her front feet onto the tub and then heave her hind feet up, as she would do if just one tub were involved. She had to position her front feet carefully on the higher tub, then segue into a front foot stand just long enough to lift her back feet onto the tub as well. "Took a great amount of precision on the old girl's part," Burck wrote years later. The tub once slid off the stand while Tess was on it and Burck blamed himself; he had been standing in Tess's way and she had held herself back when she hoisted her front feet up to keep from kicking him in the mouth.

If all of the handlers felt the way Burck did toward the elephants, life would have been less grueling for Billie and her comrades. But many of the grooms were rough stock, men who were only too happy for any excuse to vent their anger on an elephant. Joyce and Billie were considered the most difficult of Cuneo's performers, so they probably bore the brunt of the punishment.

"Joyce was on a roll," Burck recounted later. "She would just keep going until you put your 'foot down' and said 'enough is enough.' She would be good for a couple of months then it would start all over again. In a ring a real pleasure to work, told once responded instantly, but on the picket line she and Billie were a couple of characters."

Joyce struck a groom one day, and once the man stopped rolling, he picked himself up, brushed the dirt and grass off his clothes, and walked away, never bothering to collect his final pay. In the winter of 1978, Joyce took matters a step further. John Cuneo had his animals in Chicago for the several-day-long Medinah Circus, an annual Shrine affair. The elephants were too large to squeeze through the Medinah Temple entrance, so the circus omitted their act and kept them tethered in the nearby Chicago Avenue Armory. One night a groom, David "Pops" Farr, an Ontario native who had worked for Hawthorn for about a year, was drinking and joking around for some polo fans who were keeping their horses at the armory. He made the mistake of climbing on to Joyce's knee, taking hold of her trunk and wrapping it around him. Witnesses said he inserted his hand into her mouth and shoved her head.

Joyce was in no mood for hijinks. She plucked Farr off her

knee and threw him into a pillar. Fire department paramedics raced to the scene and worked on Farr, to no avail. He died ninety minutes later at a nearby hospital.

Herta Cuneo defended Joyce and told reporters there was nothing mean about her. "She is very smart, calm, and nothing upsets her," Herta said. "If Pops had gotten slapped first, maybe he would have stopped fiddling with her." John Cuneo managed to point the finger at Farr and defend him at the same time. Cuneo insisted the elephants were exercised daily, and told a reporter that Farr was "quite good with the animals. They liked him." He also admitted he probably should have fired Farr sooner.

Hawthorn elephant handler Mark Dial was more critical. He described Joyce as mean and said she'd knocked him down before, too. Dial told a reporter that the only exercise the elephant got was when she was performing—and, unable to perform in Chicago, she and the rest of the Hawthorn Five were left standing in chains, idle, for days on end. "She must have gotten tired of Pops fiddling with her," Dial said.

One of the horse groomers echoed Dial's comments. She said Farr never exercised the elephants, constantly yelled at them, and had even struck the animals with a shovel. "He was always abusing them and drinking," the woman said. "He thought he was a circus performer or something."

If Farr mistreated Joyce, it's fair to assume he also abused Billie—the other "difficult" elephant. The fact that Joyce was Billie's partner in the ring surely caused the incident to resonate with Billie even more.

In an interview, Cuneo gave a detailed account of how one of the Hawthorn Five elephants killed a man after a performance at the Boston Garden. Unbeknownst to him, Cuneo said, the arena's maintenance crew opened the back door to the facility, leaving the elephants exposed to the street. A man walking by spied the elephants, went over to them, and climbed a chest-high fence surrounding them. One of the elephants struck and killed him. No one witnessed the incident and when police informed Cuneo about it, he found the elephants "munching hay like little angels." He suspected the culprit was either Billie or Joyce, who were chained side by side on the far end of the corral. But Cuneo could not remember the year the alleged incident took place and no account of it could be found.

Joyce met all the criteria of a bad elephant and so did Billie. Trainers had considered Billie difficult ever since she hooked up with Buckles Woodcock. Had she lived half a century earlier, she might have paid for her disagreeable personality with her life. But one thing protected Billie, and that was the federal Endangered Species Act. Passed by Congress in 1973, the law forbade any activity that harmed a species listed as endangered—and Asian elephants had been listed as endangered since 1976. A year earlier the United States implemented the Convention of International Trade of Endangered Species, which listed Asian elephants as endangered in 1975. (In 1990, CITES outlawed the trade of Asian and African elephants entirely.) The listing didn't itself guarantee much protection for circus elephants. But then the U.S. Department of Interior urged a crackdown on importing any animals considered endangered. After that, circuses couldn't afford to execute their "bad" elephants because there were none to replace them. They had to find a way to live with the animals.

Two months after Joyce killed the groom in Chicago, Cuneo's ex-wife Eloise Berchtold was killed by an elephant named Teak while they were performing with the Gatini Circus outside Montreal, Canada. Berchtold, forty-two, apparently slipped and fell off of Teak and the elephant "walked over her," a spokesman for the local police department said. The spokesman said the elephant "thought his mistress was playing possum" and stood by her, nudging her body, and refusing to let anyone else near. A police sharpshooter shot Teak to death with a .457-caliber rifle.

It wasn't the first time an elephant attacked Berchtold. Twelve years earlier in Toledo, Ohio, she was performing with Cuneo's African male, Koa, and had leaped off his leg when, without warning, the elephant trumpeted and rammed her across the stage. Berchtold picked herself up, returned to Koa, fed him a carrot, and tried to climb up him again. Again he attacked, knocking her a second time across the stage. Berchtold later speculated that Koa was going through musth, a hormonally charged period when a male elephant's temporal glands secrete a gooey substance and he becomes sexually active, volatile, and unpredictable. But wisely, Cuneo retired Koa after the incident. He never performed again.

FORCING ANIMALS TO PERFORM

The first American to train wild animals was Isaac Van Amburgh, a New Yorker who was obsessed with demonstrating human dominion, an ability to "lay down" with animals the same way biblical character Daniel had done with lions and lambs. In the 1830s, with great flourish, Van Amburgh would step into a cage with a tiger, a lion, and a leopard. Unbeknownst to his audience, he had already beaten the animals into submission. Eventually he incorporated the beatings into his act. Clad in the flashy attire of a Roman gladiator, he pounded his animals with a crowbar to force them to perform tricks. The climax of his act was to smear blood on his arm and shove it into a lion's mouth, daring the lion to bite down.

Almost all circus animals were trained by force. Trainers would clip the claws of young tigers and spend months whipping them, knocking them about with a club, jerking them around by their collars, and firing blank cartridges a few feet from their heads until they were emotionally spent, resigned to carrying out a whole range of tricks. Horses endured whippings, jabbings with pitchforks, getting punched in the face, and having their lips twisted to make them fall in line.

Largely because of their intelligence and docility, elephants were a favorite with trainers. But because of their immense size and strength they were subjected to the worst treatment of all. None of the tricks an elephant performed in the ring were natural movements. Many of the stunts placed inordinate pressure on an elephant's joints and muscles. The only way to persuade an elephant to practice them repeatedly, day in and day out, was to bully her with the threat of retribution if she failed to comply.

Trainers have long claimed that circus elephants enjoyed performing. Legendary trainer George "Slim" Lewis, for one, admitted they did not. To learn new tricks an elephant had to hone muscles she wouldn't otherwise use, which is why baby elephants who hadn't developed much willpower were easier to teach.

Cheerful Gardner broke and trained more than 150 elephants for vaudeville and circus acts into the mid-1900s. He preferred to start with an untamed elephant, about three years old, right off the boat from Burma or Ceylon. As soon as the elephant arrived at his training grounds in Venice, California, Gardner would teach her to respond to her new name and then to perform the tail-up, to grasp the tail of the elephant in front of her with her trunk.

A performing elephant needed to learn to walk down a congested street, stand an arm's length from spectators, and perform outside of a cage in a ring unfazed, and walking trunk-to-tail was a good start: it gave the animal something to focus on and made her less likely to decide to wander off. Once those basic tricks were learned, Gardner and his crew would work with an elephant an hour or two a day inside a ring that was forty-two feet in diameter, the same size as the ring the elephant would one day perform in. The men shouted at the elephants constantly; otherwise the thunderous music blared on performance day would drown out their voices.

Lying down might seem the easiest trick in the world, but not to an elephant. In the wild, an elephant lowers her massive body slowly, bending and tucking her legs first and settling in with care—a cumbersome series of steps that, left to herself, she would undertake only once or twice a day. In the ring an elephant was expected to lie down a handful of times in a single performance, and do so quickly. Teaching an elephant to lie down on command involved tightening the chain around one front and one hind leg, several inches at a time, until the elephant was supporting her weight solely on her remaining two legs, which was exhausting. As soon as the handler saw the elephant flagging, he would issue the command, "Down! Come on down," repeating it until the elephant finally complied. Trainers knew that an elephant first learning to lie down on command would show signs of fear and defeat before giving in. Her eyes would bulge and she would lose control of her bowels, often more than once. When the elephant finally surrendered and keeled over on her side, she had lost the battle.

SEVEN

＋━＝◆＝━＋

ACTING OUT

The Hawthorn Five elephants traveled in freezing cold and scorching heat. They performed in Butte, Montana, elevation 5,538 feet, in November one year, and in Austin, Texas, on a day when temperatures were in the nineties and there was no air-conditioning. The heat inside the arena must have been unbearable.

Burck worked the Hawthorn Five until 1981, when he left to take Cuneo's white tiger act on the road with Circus Vargas. That Burck would continue to work with tigers was astonishing; the year before, he was badly injured after two of the white tigers got into a brawl. One of them, Frosty, pounced on Burck and sank its jaws into his face. Burck knew better than to fight back; he'd be slashed to pieces if he did. Instead he went limp and let Frosty haul him across the backs of four other tigers to the rear of the cage. One of the female tigers smacked Frosty and he let go of Burck. The trainer rolled back on his feet. Then Frosty came after him a second time, puncturing Burck's right shoulder, breaking his collar and ripping open an artery. Burck was throbbing with so much pain he wanted to die. But the tiger wasn't done. When he came at Burck a third time, the tiger bit Burck on his right shoulder again, yanked him to the rear of the cage and started shaking him. From outside the mesh cage, Burck's brother, Mike, who worked for him, slid a stick through the mesh cage and glided it through Frosty's jaws. Mike thrust the stick upward while Burck pulled down, forcing Frosty's mouth open wide enough for Burck to pull away.

He was a mess. His right arm hung flaccid by his side, his face covered in blood. Still, he managed to pull himself upright and finish the performance. Afterward, he headed to the first-aid room to have his shoulder put in a cast and his broken jaw taped up. Then he went back out into the ring to present the elephants, issuing his commands through the side of his mouth. When he finally made it to the hospital, doctors worked on him for nearly six hours. Burck immediately returned to the circus to start getting the tigers and elephants ready for the next day's shows. He performed at three of them and then drove a tractor-trailer to the next town. The incident made him realize that he needed to accept the animals on their own terms. "They aren't capable of thinking like I do, so I've got to think like they do," he once said.

Burck's new assignment with the tigers meant Billie had to get used to new trainers, men with different attitudes and different methods of handling elephants. Like all leased elephants, Cuneo's animals faced a greater risk of abuse because their owner wasn't around to supervise their handling.

By 1982, Billie's chief handler was a trainer named John Caudill, who had worked for the Hoxie Bros. Circus and went by the stage name of Johnny Walker. At a performance of the Hamid-Morton circus in Harrisburg, Pennsylvania, a reviewer praised Walker and his wife, Laura, who rode atop the elephants, for their "fast-moving, highly skilled presentation of ponderous pachydermics." Laura Walker worked with the elephants even though at Marineland that summer, the first time Johnny Walker turned his back, Billie knocked her down. Bombay, Tess, Billie, Joyce, and Delhi entered the ring bedecked in their signature red harnesses and red ankle bands, and now there was a new touch: their cuticles were painted white, the elephant equivalent of a French manicure. The white nails lent their appearance a whimsical touch.

Photos taken the following year show Joyce and Billie sitting down, all four legs thrust outward, with Laura Walker standing on Joyce's forehead and Johnny Walker standing on Billie's. Another photo shows the Walkers with Joyce, Billie, Bombay, Delhi, and Tess as the elephants perform their T-mount formation: four of the elephants raised up in hind leg stands facing Tess, who is lifting her left front leg. All of the elephants are standing on tubs. Laura Walker is standing on Tess's back the way Burck's wife, Margaret Duke, once had. A third photo shows Laura and Johnny Walker with Joyce and Billie at Marineland.

Walker had a reputation for aggression. In 1988, he went after Cuneo's African elephant Tyke while they were traveling with the Tarzan Zerbini Circus in Canada. Tyke had struck Walker's brother and gouged a hole in his back with her lone tusk, according to law-enforcement documents. To pay her back, Walker beat the elephant with such force that she bent down on three legs, screaming, to avoid being struck; witnesses were horrified. Even afterward, when Walker walked by, the elephant screamed and turned away.

"If you don't stay a step ahead of them, if you don't outsmart them, forget it," Walker told a newspaper reporter in 1978, when he was twenty years old. "A trainer has to be firm, quick, and aggressive. Either you have it or you don't." An accompanying photo showed Walker touching the left shoulder of an elephant, the trainer's hand clasped around a long bullhook. The shot may have been intended to show Walker's affection for the elephant, but the elephant appeared to be recoiling.

Walker eventually left Cuneo's employ to start his own circus, Walker Bros. In years to come, he and his son, John Caudill III, would rack up a long rap sheet of USDA violations stemming from elephant abuse. The circus wound up losing its license to own elephants, but got around the revocation by leasing elephants from other circuses.

◄──────►

The Hawthorn Five were part of Cuneo's menagerie that traveled to Japan to perform with Ringling Bros. and Barnum & Bailey in 1989. The circus had sent its Blue Unit to Japan the year before and won the crowds over with its lineup of "amazing elephants, strange clowns, and beautiful showgirls." Japanese audiences paid $50 apiece to fill the 5,000-seat stands throughout the circus's fifteen-week run.

The second tour was a different story. This time the circus played just two cities: Osaka and Tokyo, where the size of the average audience nosedived from 2,700 people to just 860. Dozens of performers, crew and animals, including Billie and the rest of the Hawthorn Five—all fifteen of Cuneo's elephants, as a matter of fact—along with tigers, leopards, baboons, llamas, lions, zebras, horses, camels, and bears, had traveled more than 7,200 miles one way by ship for the gig. Cuneo was proud of what his elephants had to offer—three of the Hawthorn Five could walk forward and backward on their hind legs, with Bombay carrying a girl on a trapeze in her mouth. "We'll never see the likes of that again because nobody has the animals to do that anymore," Cuneo reminisced in an interview.

But the Japan Educational Corp., the promoter for the event, wasn't impressed. It claimed Ringling Bros. had sent substandard performers and animal trainers for the second tour. Because of the contract dispute, Ringling was forbidden to take the animals out of the country. The performers flew home to the States; Billie and the rest of the animals remained in Japan on a docked ship.

The length of time the animals were detained is unclear. The elephants were kept on deck, boxed in by trailers. Ringling Bros.

appealed to the U.S. State Department, which cabled the U.S. Embassy in Tokyo, instructing it to "take all appropriate action" to get the elephants home. Years later, a man identified only as "Warren" commented on Buckles Woodcock's blog that he had fond memories of staying behind to take care of the animals after most of the cast and crew went back home. "At least on the freighter 747 back home, I got to sit in the cockpit whenever I wanted and the flight crew even let me pilot the plane for a while," he wrote.

As soon as the Hawthorn elephants arrived Stateside, Cuneo advertised their availability for circuses and other performances. Interested parties were asked to contact the Hawthorn Corp. at Cuneo's home in Grayslake, Illinois.

By then Billie was twenty-eight years old. How different her life had become since those early days with her mother, when she was free to wander in the jungle of her homeland, surrounded by her family and the sights and smells of nature. She'd spent two-thirds of her life in the circus, performing six days a week, often two performances a day, her life diminished to the same mind-numbing routine: riding thousands of miles a year in the back of a semi, chained in place. Led out to perform eight minutes at a time in one cacophonous, glaringly lit ring after another. Under the klieg lights and to the sounds of earsplitting music, she performed her stunts before children who were often too preoccupied with the plastic swords, whoopee cushions, and inflatable crayons bought for them on the way in. Adults in the audience had no idea what the elephant had suffered in the name of entertainment.

At least she had a new family of sorts: Tess, Bombay, Delhi, and her closest companion, Joyce. But chained in place, Billie seldom had the chance to interact with other elephants the way she would have done in the wild. She had to get used to a revolving door of trainers and grooms, men who regarded Billie as grumpy and mean and routinely whacked her as they passed, for the hell of it.

Eventually, Billie struck back.

Cuneo had replaced Walker with Roy Wells, a thirty-seven-year-old South Dakota native who'd started working with animals at a small park in Ohio. Years after his time with Cuneo, Ringling Bros. hired him to oversee its elephant herd.

In a videotaped interview taken on the road, Wells downplayed the role of the bullhook. He described it as an "ankus" and said it "really . . . is just relatively harmless—it's just used to cue the elephants.

"Ninety percent of the time the elephants will respond to a verbal command," Wells went on to explain, "but in case they don't or they forget what you're asking them, you just gently touch them, and you remind 'em by touching them on the back of their foot, and as you can see it's really dull. It's kinda like the same thing as reins on a horse, you use this to guide them."

He made working with elephants sound like the most gentle, intuitive job in the world. But from his days with Billie, Wells knew firsthand how untrue that was. Billie attacked Wells at least once and maybe twice at the Elephant Roundup in Wisconsin. It's uncertain which years the incidents took place, but records show that Billie was at the roundup in 1990, along with a dozen other Hawthorn elephants.

The roundup was held each year at the Dells Crossroads Park, a facility owned by Jim and Heidi Grogan, in the heart of the Wisconsin Dells tourist mecca a few miles north of the popular Circus World Museum in Baraboo. The official write-up of the Hawthorn Five's appearance praised the elephants for their sophisticated stunts. In one demonstration, Bombay stepped carefully over two performers and then lay her bulky frame directly on top of Cindy Herriott, Wells's wife, as Herriott stretched out on the ground in the center of the ring. Another skit featured Cuneo's African elephant Tyke, who held a ball in her trunk as she went through the motions of a windup, letting the ball wing toward the audience in an underhanded pitch.

Four of the elephants simulated a bowling match, racing to pick up pins with their trunks and handing them to the performers riding on their shoulders. "This will show their dexterity, their ability to follow human commands and the competitive spirit we all know they have," emcee Harry Muller promised in advance.

Finally, Muller chose a dozen members of the audience to play tug-of-war with one of the elephants.

"Folks," he said, "when you go to a show—a circus—and you see those elephants out there and they are doing these things in that elephant act, you might hear someone around you say 'Look at what they're making them do.' The key word here is 'make.' We cannot 'make' them do anything they don't want to do. What we have done is take natural behavior on their part and put it into a script to a time cue on our part."

A spectator witnessed something unusual at one of the roundups. Roy Wells was in the ring with the Hawthorn elephants and they were acting out—flapping their ears in agitation, tossing dirt shavings, and attempting to step down from their tubs. It was a rare display of rebellion, something audiences seldom see.

Was that the same year Billie finally melted down and decided to prove Muller's claim—that no one could make her do anything she didn't want to do? Billie attacked Wells in what Wade Burck later referred to as a "downed and out." No other details are available, although Wells's father-in-law, John Milton Herriott, said Wells wasn't injured badly.

Part of what might have made trainers distrustful of Billie was her wary silence. Research has shown that unexpected attacks on keepers are frequently committed by the very elephants that seem the most passive and dependable.

Wells continued working with Billie for several years. Among their performances was the forty-eighth annual Moslah Shrine Circus in Fort Worth in 1992, where Wells worked the Hawthorn Five and trainer Gary Thomas worked John Cuneo's other five-elephant act. Audience members could ride the elephants at intermission—whether Billie was included in this is unknown—and have their picture taken on a baby African elephant worked by Janie Coronas.

In the spring of 1993 the Hawthorn Five appeared in Pennsylvania for six days with the Irem Shrine Circus, without incident. "Bombay and her four elephant friends are ready to check out all the noise they hear at the 109th Field Artillery Armory," *The Wilkes-Barre Times Leader* reported. "Led by Tess, the 50-year-old Matriarch and people-lover, they prove elephants can show off too. They walk on their hind legs, climb onto tubs and stand on their heads—not easy tricks when you're nearly 9,000 pounds heavy and more than eight feet tall. But it's a circus, and if you go, suspend your disbelief."

Three months later the elephants were in Milwaukee for the Great Circus Parade, a once-a-year chance for circus performers to strut their stuff in front of their peers. Wisconsin has a rich circus heritage; at one time some sixty-five circuses were head-quartered in the state. The parade was an annual affair, a salute to the early years of the circus, when performers would march through town to give the public a chance to glimpse the acts and judge ahead of time whether the show was worth the price of admission. To flaunt their wares, circuses decorated their wagons lavishly.

The 1993 parade was special because it marked the two-hundredth anniversary of the American circus. Near the end of a long procession featuring Barnum & Bailey's old-timey Miniature Pony Chariot, a pygmy hippopotamus, the Ringling Bros. snake den, and the old woman in the shoe, was the "Magnificent Montage of Mammoth Mastodons": nineteen elephants with five trainers, fourteen handlers, and eight women, all of them attired in extravagant costumes. Hawthorn elephants participated uneventfully in the parade.

But a month later, Billie let loose again. The Hawthorn Five and seven of Cuneo's elephants were first trucked 2,000 miles to the West Coast and then put on a ship for Honolulu, another 2,550 miles, to perform with Circus International's "Stars of the Moscow Circus," produced by Paul V. Kaye. The Hawthorn Five were slated to perform for several days in Honolulu followed by four days in Hilo, on the island of Hawaii, along with the Stankeev Trio, comedy contortionists; aerial ballerina Lubov Pisarenkova and her husband, equilibrist Yuri Krasnov; the musical clowns the Troyan Family; the husband-and-wife high-wire act of Nikolai Nikolski and Bertolina Kazakova; the comedy horse act of Gaylord Maynard and "Chief Bear Paw"; the Bisbee Clown Duo; and the Ray Valentine aerial troupe, featuring a flying trapeze and two aerial cradle pairs.

Details about the incident never surfaced publicly and have since been destroyed by the U.S. Department of Agriculture, which claims to eliminate such documents after six years. All that remains is a bare-bones mention in a memo signed a year and a half later by Morley Cook, then associate deputy administrator for the Western Sector of USDA's Animal and Plant Health Inspection Service's office of regulatory enforcement and animal care. It states only that "Billy [sic] attacked trainer in Hawaii—reputation for being very difficult to handle."

The incident must have taken place in front of someone other than Cuneo's employees because Cuneo was unlikely to have reported it on his own. John Milton Herriott, Wells's father-in-law, said Hawaii was where Billie "showed her true colors with Roy." The return voyage back to the mainland was "nerve-wracking" for Wells, Herriott said, and afterward, once Hawthorn trainers got Billie calmed down in California and trucked back to Illinois, Wells chose to resign rather than continue working with her.

Cuneo boasted that Hawthorn had "some fine trainers" handling his elephants over the years: Joe Frisco, Roy Wells, Johnny

Walker, Gary Thomas. It's unclear whether Wade Burck was referring to any of them years later, when he wrote on his blog: "How many 'animal trainers' do you know that have the ignorant, unqualified, I'll-show-you mentality? I have met a number of them over the years, and they are the only ones I know of that have 'insane' animals occasionally."

BLOCK AND TACKLE AND CHAINS

It took an entire team of handlers to teach an elephant to stand on her head. Trainers often chained an elephant's front legs to heavy-duty stakes, added more chains below the knees of her hind legs, then connected the ends of the chains to a block and tackle attached at the top of the building. Next, either a group of men or a pair of horses would haul on the tackle, lifting the elephant's bulky hind quarters so high in the air that the sheer force of gravity, coupled with the constraining power of the front chains, would pull the elephant into place. The first time an elephant underwent the procedure, she would trumpet with fear and rage, flay the ground with her trunk, struggle against the chains—sometimes breaking them—and yank the stakes out of the ground. But after enduring the exercise four or five times a day for up to seven weeks, the elephant usually gave in. In time a trainer merely had to prod her with a bullhook and say the word and the elephant would dutifully launch herself upside down and hold herself in place, sometimes flattening the length of her trunk along the ground for added stability.

One of the most popular stunts was the long mount. To teach that trick, trainers would first pass one chain around an elephant's throat and another around her trunk to hoist it up. Handlers would pull on the neck chain until the elephant began to choke. To ease the pain in her neck, the elephant would rise up on her hind legs and paw the air, grasping for breath. The minute she did so, trainers would back another elephant in under her, so that her forefeet came to rest on the other elephant's back.

To train an elephant to hop on two legs, Cheerful Gardner would first get her to stand on three feet, then lift one of her hind legs in the air. "Jessie . . . foot. Hold . . . foot," he would call out to a young elephant, using a bullhook to demonstrate. He repeated the command several times. Once the elephant held her leg high, Gardner came around to the front and instructed the elephant to lift the opposite front leg. Next he stood eight feet away and held out an apple. The elephant, enticed by the fruit, would hop in Gardner's direction on two legs. The trainer gradually lengthened the distance the elephant needed to hop until he was half a ring away. The "tightrope" he taught his elephants to balance on was really a six-inch-wide, three-inch-deep wooden pole that stood thirty inches off the floor, buttressed on either side by steel plates and painted to look like a rope.

A more difficult trick he taught his elephants was to climb a set of stairs on their hind legs. According to Gardner, elephants could not lift their left legs as high as their right legs; to accommodate them he made the left half of each stair an inch lower than the right.

To teach an elephant to whirl, one trainer would grab the front end of the animal while another trainer grabbed the hind end, each thrusting his end around until the elephant learned to spin on her own at the sound of the word, "Waltz!" To teach an elephant to walk with her forefeet on top of a rolling tub, one trainer would step in front of the tub and another behind it, wedging crowbars between the tub and the ground to hold the tub in place. To perform on a seesaw, elephants had to be held in place with ropes and muscle, and made to practice the trick repeatedly, all morning and all afternoon for months, if necessary, until they couldn't possibly forget.

Only the most daring of trainers tried to teach their elephants the head-carry, which required the elephant to grip the trainer's head in her mouth and twirl around, spinning the trainer's dangling body along with her. The elephant's grasp had to be light enough to keep from squashing the performer's skull or legs, but solid enough to keep the trainer from hurtling out of the ring. Only the most reliable of elephants could be trusted with such a stunt.

Elephants who were agile enough could be taught to step over their trainer as he lay flat in the middle of the ring. Too much pressure by the elephant and the trainer could wind up with a broken neck or a flattened skull. "Foot-in-face" required a trainer to lie flat on the ground so the elephant could lightly touch her front foot to the tip of his nose. In the boldest stunt of all, a trainer would lie on the ground and order his elephant to straddle him, squatting down on all fours and lowering her weight to within inches of his body.

Despite how much trust a trainer might develop with his elephants, there is no easy way to train them, and in the early days no one pretended there was. In 1954, cereal boxes contained postcards describing the amount of time trainers Mac and Peggy MacDonald worked with baby elephants, their specialty. "Extremely wild and uncontrollable after their capture, these amazing Indo-Chinese elephants were patiently tamed and now show instant obedience to their trainers," the postcard read. "Their ten-minute routine is a high-speed act very unusual in the circus world . . . perfected by eight months of constant training, seven hours a day, in Thousand Oaks, California." There was always a risk. An inexperienced baby elephant could easily tumble onto a trainer. Sometimes the collisions were deliberate. A male elephant once sideswiped Peggy MacDonald and intentionally did a headstand on top of her, tearing her arm and breaking a couple of ribs.

EIGHT

A SANCTUARY TAKES SHAPE

Cuneo claimed his company never had problems with animals, but that was far from the truth. Tyke, his African elephant, was exhibit number one. In 1993 alone she raged out of control three times. During a performance in Altoona, Pennsylvania, she blasted through the main entrance of the Jaffa Mosque and ran loose for an hour, forcing 4,500 schoolchildren to evacuate the area and causing $14,000 in damages. The next day she attacked a tiger trainer. Three months later, at a performance at the North Dakota State Fair in Minot, Tyke went on a rampage, trampling a trainer and frightening the public for nearly half an hour before the circus could rein her in.

Cuneo had ready explanations. In Altoona, he said, Tyke was spooked when she backed up against an insubstantial wall and caused it to cave in. The problem in North Dakota was resolved, Cuneo said, when he fired the handler.

African elephants were known to be more hot-tempered, and for years Tyke's trainers had punished her for her outbursts. Tyke was the elephant Johnny Walker beat so savagely—in front of onlookers—in 1988.

On August 23, 1994, a year after Billie attacked trainer Roy

Wells in Hawaii, Tyke was in Hawaii with the Circus International when she lost control for the last time. During a performance she first went after a groom, William Beckwith, who was said to have spooked Tyke when he walked too closely behind her. When trainer Allen Campbell intervened, the elephant turned on him and trampled him to death. As audience members panicked, Tyke broke out of the circus arena and thundered down a city street. She ran amok for half an hour, covering several blocks—almost killing another man—then chased a circus clown across a parking lot. When circus promoter Steve Hirano tried to confine her, Tyke threw him to the ground, splintering his leg. She crushed a series of cars as she careened down the city blocks. The sheer weight of her body knocked one car fifteen feet.

Police caught up with the elephant and began firing at her. Eighty-seven bullets later, she fell to the ground. Employees of the Honolulu Zoo approached the collapsed elephant and gave her a lethal injection, ending her misery. Her autopsy revealed that she died of massive nerve damage and a hemorrhaged brain. Decades later, videos of Tyke's attack inside the ring and her death are still making the rounds on the Internet.

Campbell, the groom, was known as a disciplinarian who didn't hesitate to work his elephants over. At the time of his death he had both cocaine and alcohol in his blood. But the Cuneos refused to accept any responsibility. Herta Cuneo, who was vacationing with her husband nearby in Honolulu, was indignant. "Everybody seems to be more upset about the elephant being killed than Mr. Campbell," she said. "All they are talking about is the elephant, the elephant. We love the elephant, but I think there should be a little justice in this world."

Animal welfare activists, though, blamed Tyke's rampage on her living conditions, saying that years of being kept in chains, unable to exercise any control over her existence, caused her to go berserk. John Lehnhardt, then assistant curator of mammals at the National Zoo in Washington, knew her reputation well and wondered, when he heard the news of an elephant on the rampage, whether the animal in question was Tyke. Controlling an elephant is not the same as dominating one, Lehnhardt said. A beaten elephant will likely return the abuse. Elephants attack because they intend to, and the clues to their intentions are obvious if anyone bothers to notice. But there's no way to predict when the payback will occur.

At the African Lion Safari in Toronto, Tyke's death haunted a pair of elephant trainers. Carol Buckley and Scott Blais couldn't understand why, given Tyke's history of aggression, John Cuneo hadn't simply taken her off the road. Tyke had expressed her unhappiness over and over again. Once she fled the arena in Honolulu, authorities exacerbated matters by chasing her in circles in a police car, sirens blazing. Blais found the video of her death dreadful to watch.

Even though life with the circus was hellish for all elephants, some were more accepting of it than others. Those who couldn't tolerate it should be given a reprieve, allowed to live their lives away from the cacophony, Blais and Buckley felt. To keep a disgruntled elephant on the road was tantamount to hauling around a ticking time bomb. The trainers discussed the possibility that, if another option had existed for Tyke—a place where Cuneo could have retired her—she might still be alive. It was too late to help Tyke. But a sanctuary might provide a refuge for elephants like her.

⊷ ⊶⬥⊷ ⊶

Buckley discovered elephants in the mid-1970s after meeting Fluffie, a year-and-a-half-old female who was born in what is now known as Myanmar and brought to the United States at the age of six months. A tire store owner in Simi Valley, California, bought the elephant and exhibited her at his business during the day. At night he took Fluffie home in a truck and left her parked in his driveway. Buckley was a first-year student at the Exotic Animal Training and Management Program at Moorpark College in Southern California, and once she became aware of Fluffie's existence she offered to take care of her. She soon convinced the store owner to exhibit the elephant for just a few hours on weekends. The rest of the time Fluffie was in Buckley's care.

By the time the elephant was two, Buckley had saved enough money to buy her. She changed the calf's name to Tarra and for the next twenty years the pair traveled the country, performing. Tarra did her tricks in circuses, zoos, and amusement parks, including Knott's Berry Farm in Buena Park, California, where she performed in a small ring. The elephant with the extraordinarily large eyes and delicate ears appeared on *Little House on the Prairie* and other TV shows and had cameo roles in several movies. Buckley placed ads in circus newsletters proclaiming Tarra as "America's Most Talented Musical Elephant" and promising a fast-moving act with original comedy, "a definite crowd pleaser."

Buckley had found her calling. She was captivated by Tarra's curiosity and her capacity to understand ideas. The elephant was so inquisitive she seemed like a sponge, eager to absorb every new thing she encountered. Keeping life interesting for Tarra was a challenge. Buckley had to constantly think of new things to teach her. "Being away from her for even a day did not interest me," Buckley once wrote.

When Tarra was six, Buckley trained her to roller-skate, a skill Buckley insisted Tarra enjoyed. A resident of the Simi Valley later recalled seeing Tarra skate downhill one day while four men on horseback held her back with ropes. Tarra roller-skated in the Ojai Independence Day Parade. At one point Buckley even put Tarra on ice skates and reported that "she balanced beautifully." With Buckley's blond hair, her shiny satin hot pants, and animal-print halter tops and "Baby Tarra"'s star-spangled outfit,

the two cut a memorable swath on the animal entertainment circuit. They were featured guests at the 1980 Republican Convention in Detroit. Two years later they appeared at the Big Apple
Circus in New York; promotional shots showed Tarra sitting on
a tub, her front legs raised high, Buckley perched on one of them.

In 1984, after a performance in California, a spectator grabbed
Buckley and admonished her, saying, "That's abuse. You're abusing your animal by making it skate like that." Buckley disagreed,
but the woman's anger upset her. She began to reconsider the
message Tarra's performances were sending the public. It was the
wrong message, Buckley eventually decided. She retired Tarra's
skates and encouraged the elephant to paint pictures instead. As a
baby, Tarra had often grasped a stick with her trunk and used it to
scrawl abstract images in the dirt. Now, given an array of brushes
and colors to work with, she painted sections of color onto a canvas or vacuumed up a snoutful of nontoxic paint into her trunk
and splashed it back out onto the page. Tarra finished off her art-
work with a signature of sorts, inscribed with a felt-tip pen. Before long, shows and galleries and zoos across the country were
featuring her watercolors.

To make a living, Buckley spent the next few years working
with a series of zoos: the Bowmanville Zoo in Ontario, Canada;
the Chehaw Wild Animal Park in Albany, Georgia; and the
Racine Zoo in Wisconsin. She developed and managed elephant
programs for Knott's Berry Farm theme park in California and
zoos in Santa Barbara and Santa Clara, California; Kansas City;
Granby, Quebec; and Nashville, Tennessee. All the while she was
searching for a way to offer Tarra the life she deserved, living in
nature with freedom to roam.

Buckley wound up taking Tarra to the African Lion Safari in
Ontario, Canada, to breed her. Started in 1969, the safari was a
reserve for exotic animals that also offered elephant shows. When
the elephants weren't performing they were free to wander the

back side of the park, out of sight from the public. It was there that Buckley met Scott Blais.

A native of Maine, Blais grew up in El Paso, Texas, and Albuquerque, New Mexico, before moving with his parents and older brother to Ontario, first to the town of Campbellford and then to Cambridge. The family had Lhasa apso dogs, goldfish, and a couple of rats. After watching a television program about undersea explorer Jacques Cousteau, Blais developed an interest in marine biology. When the family moved to Cambridge, a town west of Toronto, he got a job, along with his brother, at the African Lion Safari, which was twenty minutes from their house. Blais was thirteen; his assignment was to pick up trash. Walking through the park he became intrigued with the animals, in particular a couple of seals that were swimming about in murky water. The following summer he started helping out periodically with the elephant rides. Blais stood at the top of a platform, took tickets from children and helped them clamber onto the back of one of park's two African elephants.

Eventually the elephant superintendent asked if Blais could help out with the shows and with barn maintenance. The man in charge liked Blais's quiet, soft-spoken manner and thought he would work well around the elephants. He started working more closely with the female elephant, Sophie—giving her instructions and using a bullhook to guide her while children rode her. Sophie was compliant, easy to work with.

Blais saw other elephants come in and out of the barn while he was working at the wildlife park, some of whom were on loan for breeding. Circuses would travel through with their elephants and house them at the park for a couple of weeks. Roy Wells stopped by with John Cuneo's Hawthorn Five multiple times.

Like almost all elephant exhibitors, the safari practiced dominance training. A couple of times Blais peeked inside the barn and saw a group of men with pickaxe handles and pitchforks standing around an elephant named Reba, who was known to be aggressive, but he didn't ask what they were doing. He found out the first day he was assigned to Kitty, another Asian elephant. As they rounded a corner by the loading dock, Kitty sped up her pace and nearly clipped Blais; he had to dart out of the elephant's path. A college student working with Blais, Omar Norton, witnessed the incident and told Blais: We're going to stop this. Blais followed Norton around the ring as he struck and poked Kitty with his bullhook. Blais thought the discipline would end there, but the next day when he set out to clean the yard, the elephant men called him back. The other elephants were outside, all but Kitty. "You have to show her you're boss," the chief trainer told him. "Go tell her to lay down."

Blais did so, and his boss handed him a bullhook. He told Blais: "Now you walk around and hit her because she wanted to hurt you." A half-dozen handlers stood watching as Blais circled Kitty. The elephant knew what was about to happen, Blais was convinced of it. He popped her reluctantly. His boss called him over. "She wanted to *kill* you," he told Blais. "She wanted to absolutely kill you. You have to let her know that you are the boss, that she cannot do that. You have to get mad. You have to get even." If the elephant was allowed to get away with her little stunt, he went on to say, she would go rogue, become dangerous, and have to be euthanized.

This time Blais did as he was told. He poked Kitty with the bullhook's sharp end, then thumped her with the handle as hard as he could. He worked her over for thirty minutes and when he was done, both Blais and Kitty seemed defeated. It had to be that way—Blais understood that and Kitty seemed to understand it, too. The other keepers congratulated Blais on a job well done. His boss warned: "Don't let anyone from the public see you do this." From that point forward Kitty obeyed Blais's every request. In spite of what he had done to her, he adored her, as much as he could adore an elephant who cowered in his presence.

The beatings appeared to work. The elephants seemed resigned to their punishment—as if they were acknowledging to themselves, *This is going to hurt like hell.* Afterward, when a keeper told the elephant to jump, the elephant didn't hesitate. The animals' good behavior might taper off a bit with time, but for the most part they fell in line. Blais's calm demeanor made him a natural around the elephants and he loved working around them. His favorite was a mischievous Asian named Wimpie, who relieved her boredom by playfully thwarting the keepers' commands. Tell her to lie down and she'd do a headstand. Tell her to cross her legs and she'd bow. Her handlers beat her for her contrariness, but they were light beatings, not the kind reserved for her aggressively rebellious comrades.

The male elephants posed a bigger challenge. One morning in November 1989, Tusko, the biggest of the males, started roughing up the most submissive of the bunch, an elephant named Rex. Blais and another worker were outside, cleaning up the yard, when their colleague, Norton, came running toward Tusko, yelling at him to stop. Tusko ignored him. Norton turned to go back into the barn to grab his bullhook, intending to separate the elephants and lead Tusko into a separate corral. Before he could do so, the 10,000-pound elephant knocked Norton down from the side and crushed him with his head. The elephant boss came racing from the main barn, but it was too late. Tusko stood there, his mouth wrapped around Norton's head. Norton's chest was smashed flat.

Blais was just seventeen when he witnessed the killing. The theme park sent a grief counselor to his house, but inside the elephant barn there was little talk of what had happened or whether the keepers should rethink their harsh treatment of the elephants. It was simply understood that they happened to be in a dangerous line of work. As Norton told a reporter the summer before,

"If a horse or camel gets mad at you, they'll go after you right away. But an elephant will wait—wait for the best time to nail you."

Blais continued to work with the elephants. He helped train Mugwamp, a twenty-something-year-old Asian who'd never learned any tricks, and now found herself roped up with block and tackle, taking a crash course. Blais also got to know Calvin, a baby imported from the Calgary Zoo. The trainers handled Calvin roughly and that didn't feel right to Blais. But even though Calvin bellowed in protest at his forcible treatment, he was learning his tricks.

Blais also got to help raise Colonel, a male elephant born to Wimpie and an elephant named Buke. Blais even got to take turns with the other handlers sleeping in Colonel's stall. He loved spending time with a creature so innocent.

Then Buckley arrived with Tarra, hoping to breed her. She offered a different philosophy of how to work with these immense beasts. All Blais had ever been told was: If an elephant doesn't do what you say, beat 'em. *Make* 'em do what you say. Buckley had a better understanding of why elephants behaved the way they did—how to coax them with treats and praise to get them to do what you wanted.

Rascha was a good example. An Asian elephant, she recoiled at the nonstop activity around her and behaved apprehensively around the other elephants. When bath time came she was often too nervous to lie down. Instead of forcing Rascha to lie down, and punishing her if she didn't, Buckley would simply ask her to do so. She'd say, "Can you lay down, Rascha?" When Rascha did, Buckley praised her effusively. "Good girl. Thank you." Struck by how much easier it was to work with Rascha this way, Blais began to emulate Buckley. The next time he bathed Rascha he complimented her, reassured her that she was okay, asked her nicely to lie down, then thanked her for doing so. The elephant responded by wrapping her trunk around his ankles and squeaking happy noises. She seemed to appreciate his kind words.

To Blais, this was revelatory. Maybe you didn't have to beat an elephant into behaving after all. Buckley's kinder approach resonated deeply with him and the two trainers spent many hours discussing the right way to work with elephants. They shared frustration over the fact that even though people credited elephants with having some of the most noble of human traits, they treated the animals more harshly than the vilest of humans.

Before long, despite their nineteen-year age difference, Blais and Buckley fell in love. In the aftermath of Tyke's violent death, they began to discuss the need to free elephants from captivity, of starting a facility where elephants could just be elephants.

Buckley's initial idea was to open a restaurant on top of a hill where patrons could look out over a valley and see elephants roaming freely. Vacationing in Costa Rica with friends, she and Blais brainstormed the possibility of creating a sanctuary in that country's lush, subtropical terrain. They could lease an elephant from veteran trainer Bucky Steele to give Tarra some company, offer safari hikes to tourists for a couple of hours of the day, and let the elephants wander freely after that. But when they returned to the States they discovered that Tarra was pregnant, which complicated matters. If they did take Tarra to Costa Rica, they needed some assurance that they could bring her and her calf back to the States if necessary.

Buckley flew back to Costa Rica to iron out details, but government officials there refused to cooperate. They asked her: How can we issue a permit for an elephant that doesn't even exist? Buckley's lawyer warned against taking Tarra out of the United States. Don't be a fool, he said. Costa Rica is not going to let a baby elephant leave the country, because what country doesn't want a baby elephant?

Buckley and Blais were back to square one. They'd planned to stop at trainer Bucky Steele's place in East Texas to pick up a companion for Tarra. Blais dropped out of college and, taking Tarra with them, they headed to Texas to figure out their next step.

Steele was an old-school, tough-as-nails trainer who understood that you didn't have to brutalize an elephant to dominate it. Blais liked him instantly. Yet Steele's own elephants were hardly thriving. One of them was Colonel, the baby born to Wimpie and Buke at the African Lion Safari. Wimpie and Colonel had been traveling with Carson & Barnes Circus, but they were kept apart from each other, which must have been agonizing. Years later, when the circus came through Tennessee, Blais caught a glimpse of mother and son, and the impish, happy-go-lucky youngster Wimpie had once been now seemed a completely different animal. Wimpie had given birth to a second baby since Blais had seen her last, and the calf remained at the safari park. Twice Wimpie had been separated from her babies, and the experience had left her so emotionally withdrawn she seemed closed off to the world. Even her face looked different. Buke, Colonel's father, was in worse shape. He ended up at Steele's ranch in Texas, confined to a modified railroad car when he was in musth, his feet gone to rot. He had to be euthanized at thirty-three.

Buckley and Blais began contacting zoos in search of a home for Tarra, at least for a couple of years, until she delivered her baby. The Fossil Rim Ranch outside of Dallas expressed interest in exhibiting Tarra for a couple of hours and giving her free time the rest of the day. But the zoo backed out after hearing rumors that Tarra was a runner, that given half a chance she would bolt the grounds. In truth, Tarra had a bit of a history of aggression, but she didn't run, Blais said.

Blais and Buckley hooked up with the Nashville Zoo, which was open to the possibility of developing thirty-five acres of adjacent river valley property and letting Tarra and her calf roam there. The idea was that spectators could stand on a rock bluff and look down at the animals. The couple transported Tarra to the zoo and began offering elephant rides and demonstrations on elephant eating practices. Buckley took questions from zoo-goers. It wasn't utopia, but it was a big improvement from life on the road, performing night after night in a ring.

Tarra's pregnancy ended badly. Her labor lasted for several days, and when the baby began to emerge it was apparent that something wasn't right. In the tradition of elephants born in captivity, Buckley and Blais carefully pulled the calf off to the side and tried to resuscitate her. Only later did they realize that her rear half was poorly developed; had she lived, she likely would never have been able to stand. The zoo's veterinarian spent forty-five minutes working with the couple to bring the newborn calf back to life before deciding it was futile. Buckley brought Tarra over to smell the rectum and mouth of the still-warm corpse. Tarra petted her baby gently with her hind foot for a few minutes and then left the room.

Buckley and Blais later learned that Tarra had contracted a virus, which had passed through her into the fetus. And now that the baby was gone, they began to rethink the notion of breeding Tarra. What were they doing trying to introduce a new elephant into the very kind of captivity they were trying to help Tarra escape?

Something else gave them pause. They noticed that when Tarra was in her pen, cooped up and on display, visitors to the zoo wanted to know just two things: Could they ride her, and did she do tricks? If Tarra's back was turned to them, kids would ask if Buckley could turn the elephant around so they could see her face. Some children threw rocks at her, just as Blais had seen kids do at other zoos.

People weren't learning much about elephants in this artificial setting. The public was left to assume that all elephants were good for was performing stunts and snacking on peanuts and hay. What are we really teaching people? Buckley and Blais asked themselves. Isn't there a better way to educate people about what elephants are really about?

They noticed that whenever they brought Tarra out of her exhibit and let her wander about freely in the open part of the zoo, spectators were much more respectful. Instead of watching her for thirty seconds, maybe a minute, before moving on, visitors would stand, mesmerized, for fifteen to twenty minutes—sometimes as long as three hours—just to watch Tarra eat grass.

After Tarra lost her calf, negotiations with the Nashville Zoo broke down. But by now Buckley and Blais knew where they wanted to be. They liked the fertile, semitropical climate of Middle Tennessee. They began to look for property, and just outside the town of Hohenwald, ninety miles southwest of Nashville, they found what they were looking for: 110 acres of rolling meadows and forests backed up to a timber farm. The couple snapped it up. Buckley had some trust money from her father, a thousand dollars or so a month, and what they lacked in money they had in faith. If they needed to take outside jobs to subsidize the operation, they would.

They originally planned to operate a sanctuary big enough for four elephants, with a barn to provide shelter in cold weather and plenty of room to ramble. Would-be supporters asked them: If we give you money, how do we know you can sustain it all the way? You don't, was the reply, but we believe we'll get support. We just don't know how, exactly.

A month after the Elephant Sanctuary opened in March 1995, Buckley staged one final public performance for Tarra, a walkathon to raise money. Buckley strolled the elephant slowly down Hohenwald's main street as a crowd of startled onlookers gathered to watch. Local banker Sandra Estes was driving her mother to a doctor's appointment when she saw the spectators and, curious, pulled into the parking lot of the elementary school to see what was up. She spied Tarra tied to a tree and resting in the shade, her wide, expressive eyes taking in the scene before her. The sight of the elephant was breathtaking: she was the most beautiful thing Estes had ever seen. She vowed to get involved. Estes went on to become the Sanctuary's most devoted volunteer, showing up daily for years to chop vegetables, muck stalls—whatever was needed to help keep the place running.

The private, nonprofit Sanctuary instantly made history. It was the only natural habitat in the United States designated specifically for old, sick, and needy elephants. The elephants lucky enough to wind up there would never again have to perform or entertain the public to earn their living. They wouldn't even have to see the public anymore. They could just live out their days the way elephants should.

COERCION, NOT KINDNESS

George Arstingstall, the first American to breed elephants in captivity, maintained that elephants were the easiest animals in the world to train: they were capable of deductive reasoning, he said—of understanding the rationale behind a particular stunt. But they needed to learn who was in charge. An elephant who failed to respond immediately to the sound of her name or carry out a stunt with the degree of precision Arstingstall expected would be punished severely.

"Don't imagine that you can train an elephant with kindness," Arstingstall once said. "I ruled them all through fear, and not affection.... If I see a keeper becoming kind to an elephant I discharge him and hire another ... the elephant hook has to be in constant use."

Unless they happen to get a glimpse behind the scenes, circus audiences never see a bullhook used to its full capacity. Before a crowd, trainers use a bullhook sparingly; the elephants in the ring do as they are told without seeming to require a heavy hand, or any physical contact at all. By that point the lessons are seared into their memories. Buddhists have a saying: "A first-class horse moves at even the shadow of the whip." With circus elephants, it is the shadow of the bullhook that is always there. Years of training have taught them that misstepping in the ring—or worse, deliberately failing to perform—will guarantee a beating afterward. To reinforce that understanding, trainers have been known to strike their elephants a few gratuitous blows before a performance. Well-trained elephants are often covered with scars from being led by bullhooks. A bullhook is an ever-present reminder that an elephant needs to be thinking about what the trainer wants her to do, and that if she steps out of line there will be repercussions.

NINE

* ❈ *

TROUBLE FOR CUNEO

Tyke's demise triggered an avalanche of lawsuits—ninety-three of them were filed over the next nine years between John Cuneo, the city of Honolulu, the state of Hawaii, and Circus International. The amounts of the settlements were never disclosed. USDA fined the Hawthorn Corporation $12,500 over the incident (although the company never acknowledged any wrongdoing). For a man as wealthy as Cuneo, the fine amounted to pocket change. Worse for him was that he now found himself in the crosshairs of USDA. The federal government was finally starting to understand just how dangerous a circus elephant on the rampage could be.

In a memo dated January 20, 1995, Ron DeHaven, supervisor of the western region of Animal Care under USDA, recommended that every business licensed to have elephants maintain tranquilizer guns strong enough to immobilize a raging elephant and have an emergency euthanasia plan in place. He also recommended that elephant handlers be required to have at least two years of full-time hands-on experience and training before they were put in charge of an elephant; that at least two trained handlers be on hand any time an elephant is being publicly exhibited or giving rides to the public; and that all instances of aggressive behavior by an elephant toward a handler, or a member of the public; or any instances of runaway elephants be reported to USDA.

For the first time, DeHaven also suggested that USDA maintain a list of potentially dangerous elephants and discourage exhibitors from allowing even potential contact between the elephants and the public. (Curiously, the memo stopped short of advocating that dangerous elephants be taken off the road outright.) To bolster his point, DeHaven included a list of eight elephants he felt warranted inclusion on the list. Five of the elephants belonged to John Cuneo. One was Tyke, no longer a danger since she'd been shot to death the year before. Also listed were Tony, a male rumored to have injured several grooms, and Hattie, whom Cuneo had purchased from the Los Angeles Zoo in 1990. She was also said to have injured several handlers. A fourth Cuneo elephant was Misty, who in 1983 broke off her chains at Lion Country Safari in Irvine, California, and crushed the skull of game warden Lee Keaton, killing him. Weeks before that she'd injured a handler.

The fifth Cuneo elephant was Billie. About her, DeHaven's memo repeated what an earlier cryptic USDA document had said about her: "Attacked trainer in Hawaii in 1993. Reputation for being very difficult to handle."

A sixth elephant on the list, Sue, belonged to Circus Vargas at the time of the memo, but was sold to Cuneo later that year. For reasons not given, the list made no mention of Joyce and Frieda, Hawthorn elephants known for their tempers.

In 1994, in Salt Lake City with the Jordan World Circus, Sue was giving rides to children when she wrapped her trunk around her trainer, Rex Williams, hoisted him into the air, flung him to the ground, and stepped on him. He came away with four broken ribs, a broken arm, and internal injuries. When another trainer tried to intervene, Sue kicked her and broke her finger. It took a third trainer to get Sue under control so the children could dismount safely.

Two years later, at the Central Wyoming Fairgrounds, Sue was giving several children a ride when she knocked down and repeatedly kicked one of her trainers. One of the children fell off of Sue during the attack. An assistant elephant trainer said Sue was spooked by a horse, but an eyewitness said the elephant charged the trainer, sent her tumbling, kicked her after the woman curled up into a ball and, when the woman got to her feet, knocked her down again.

Frieda's track record was lethal. In 1983, while she was traveling with Clyde Beatty–Cole Bros. Circus in Atlantic City, New Jersey, Frieda grabbed and threw a man after he wandered into the elephant area and tried to blow into her trunk. The man survived, but he suffered multiple trauma and several broken bones.

Two years later, in New London, Connecticut, Frieda crushed the chest of a woman who entered the elephant pen in a parking lot at the mall, killing her. Circus President John Pugh claimed the woman, forty-seven-year-old Joan Scovell, had been murdered and her body dumped in Frieda's pen. In truth, the incident happened at four o'clock in the morning, after Scovell and her fiancé drove to the area where Frieda and eight other elephants were chained to stakes. Scovell's fiancé admitted the couple had been drinking. He said Scovell ignored his warnings, walked over to the elephants, and tried to climb on top of Frieda. Police said her body was mutilated, as if she'd been trampled repeatedly.

In 1993, Frieda was reported to have killed another man, Christopher Ponte, twenty-two, of Fishkill, New York. In July 1995, Frieda exchanged blows with another Hawthorn elephant, Debbie, after they bumped into each other in a parking lot at the Forest Park bandshell in Queens, New York. The elephants ran out of the tent and crashed into a parked car. Twelve people were injured trying to get out of their way.

Frieda and Debbie got into a second scrape when they ambled away from the lineup outside the North Hanover Mall in Hanover, Pennsylvania, and crashed through a plate-glass window at a Sears automotive center, causing more than $20,000 in damages.

Despite the elephants' dangerous reputations, Cuneo kept them on the road, at least for a time, and permitted trainers to use at least one of them, Misty, to give rides to children. A year and a half after she was labeled as volatile, Misty was traveling with the Jordan World Circus and carrying a child on her back when she suddenly knocked her trainer down and kicked him over and over again. Four days later inspectors found an untreated injury near Misty's left eye.

But by 1996, Tony, Frieda, and Billie were retired for good. Trainer Wade Burck later said that once Billie left the Hawthorn Five, the act was never the same again. By now, Cuneo had his own winter facility in Richmond, Illinois, north of Chicago, twenty-eight miles from his childhood home and just twenty miles from the town of Grayslake, where he and Herta now lived, and that is where he housed the elephants.

The Hawthorn barn was surrounded by pine trees, a ten-foot fence, and an electronically locked gate. Inside the barn was a labyrinth of corrals and hallways and open stalls—a hundred feet long and not a single window. On one end of the concrete and metal building was the picket line where most of the elephants were kept on chains when they weren't traveling. Down a corridor were a storage area, a practice ring, and a small enclosure that housed Billie and Frieda. Their pen was roughly twenty feet by twenty feet, barely big enough to turn around in.

For twenty years Billie had traveled the country with Bombay, Tess, Delhi, and Joyce. Now, suddenly, she had been taken away from them and shut up in a barn. Handlers attached to her left front ankle an eight-foot-long chain. When anyone needed to get into the pen or work with her in any way, they would get Billie to lift up her foot or maneuver it close to the door, then grab the end of her chain and tie her up.

Outside was a small enclosure where Billie and Frieda could mingle, but Illinois' humid winters were too cold and snowy for elephants designed for Asian climates. The elephants languished for months on end in their isolation ward.

Cuneo's problems weren't over. They were just beginning.

Few people noticed that, two years earlier, a Hawthorn elephant named Dumbo had died of tuberculosis. Or that USDA had suspended Hawthorn's license for three weeks after Cuneo tried to ship a baby elephant named Nicholas who tested positive for tuberculosis to Puerto Rico for a performance. (A chest X-ray certified by the University of Wisconsin later revealed that Nicholas did not have an active case of TB.) Cuneo complained that his inability to exhibit Nicholas cost him $25,000.

But in 1996, when two of Cuneo's elephants died of TB within a couple of weeks of one another, the alarm bells rang. Joyce, Billie's longtime companion, was traveling with Circus Vargas when she died soon after she was anesthetized in preparation for a dental procedure. Activists had pointed out how skinny she was—one called her a "bag of bones." Cuneo admitted that Joyce had lost a thousand pounds, but said he thought she was low on iron.

Three days after Joyce's death, a visibly emaciated Hattie collapsed in a trailer and died on her way back to Illinois. She and Joyce were just twenty-six years old. Autopsies found their lungs rife with infection and more than 80 percent clogged. The elephants had continued to perform until they literally couldn't take it anymore.

Joyce was the second of Billie's Hawthorn Five companions to die. Bombay had passed away the year before.

The federal government charged Cuneo with eight violations of the federal Animal Welfare Act, fined him $60,000, suspended his license for forty-five days—and then watered down the penalty. Half of the fine was set aside for research on tuberculosis in elephants and the other half was spent testing and treating Cuneo's elephants—treatments Cuneo should have had to pay for separately. The government subtracted from his license suspension the twenty-one days already imposed because of Nicholas.

The deaths of Hattie and Joyce greatly concerned elephant experts because they marked the first case of zoonotic tuberculosis found in elephants in America since the late 1800s. Tuberculosis is an infectious disease that can spread by way of saliva, sneezes, or coughs, and it can be latent in captive elephants before it finally surfaces. The strain of TB plaguing the Hawthorn elephants—mycobacterium tuberculosis—was considered transmittable to humans. Although casual contact wasn't likely to transmit the disease, carrying children around on the elephants' backs was an obvious health risk. Just two years earlier, an elephant photographed while giving a ride to a small child at a performance of the Garden Bros. Circus in Canada's SkyDome in Toronto was identified as Joyce.

New Mexico officials demanded that Hawthorn take its elephants out of the state or face having the animals quarantined. Florida officials obtained a court injunction stopping Walker Bros. Circus from entering the state with Hawthorn elephants Liz and Lota, who tested positive for tuberculosis.

DeHaven noted that there were enormous epidemiological considerations at stake "since Cuneo buys, sells, trades, and moves elephants like a livestock market." Hawthorn had leased elephants to a dozen facilities—the Utica, New York, zoo; Catskill Game Farm; the Pittsburgh Zoo, Walker Bros. Circus, Alain Zerbini Circus, Tarzan Zerbini Circus, George Carden Circus, Carson & Barnes Circus, the Heritage Zoo, and Riddle's Elephant Farm in Arkansas—where the elephants they mingled with now risked exposure to TB, too. The humid, unventilated, crowded semis the elephants traveled in could be incubators for the disease.

In the summer of 1996 Cuneo's problems deepened: four Hawthorn employees tested positive for TB. The following January, USDA inspectors forbade Cuneo from sending any of his eighteen elephants on the road while they were being treated for TB and banned him from trying to breed his elephant herd. Fourteen of his elephants had a high risk of contracting tuberculosis.

Cuneo blamed the animal welfare group PETA, People for the Ethical Treatment of Animals, for his scrape. "PETA has infiltrated the USDA totally," he told a reporter. "Many people [in the USDA's inspection unit] are also working for PETA.

"People at circuses aren't stupid," Cuneo added. "They see that our animals are clean, fat and happy, and they don't object." He made the comments at his barn where, behind him, stood nine of the elephants, each one chained to the concrete floor of the barn by one front foot and the opposite back foot. As Cuneo spoke the elephants rocked to and fro, eating handfuls of hay, corn, and celery their handlers had set out for the cameras' sake.

If inspectors were hoping the sanctions would serve as a wake-up call to Cuneo, they were disappointed. Two years later they cited him for failing to carry out the tuberculosis protocol and having inadequate plans for veterinary care. He had yet to produce a plan for handling future elephant escapes the USDA had requested. Inspectors found his elephants suffering from problem feet and skin and deprived of exercise. One elephant had blood on her face and earflap.

Several of Cuneo's elephants still traveled the country performing in circuses and giving rides to children. Some of them appeared to have languished in a semi for an extended period, according to one write-up, with no access to water. When the inspector ordered a Hawthorn handler to offer water to the animals, two elephants drank nonstop for eight minutes.

Animal welfare activists turned their focus to an elephant named Lota. In 1990 the Milwaukee Zoo had sold Lota to Cuneo for one dollar after she repeatedly lashed out at one of the zoo's other elephants. The sale was made with the understanding that Cuneo would not send Lota out on the road to perform but would instead keep her at his facility to provide companionship to the Hawthorn herd. The decision stirred an outcry in Milwaukee, especially after footage showed handlers beating the forty-year-old elephant to get her to climb onto a trailer and Lota falling and urinating blood as she struggled to climb aboard, leaving the only home she'd known for thirty-four years. The elephant suffered cuts on her right temple and the bottom of her right rear foot when the chain on her left front leg suddenly broke, causing her to fall. At one point she tried to turn and back out of the truck, but the top half of her body keeled to the ground and she landed on her trunk. Zookeepers were unable to move her, so the truck driver pulled forward, causing the rest of Lota to plunge to the ground. Her handlers managed to get her back on her feet and into a hallway, where they let her stand for fifteen minutes. They took her out to board her again and this time she slipped twice. It took an hour and a half to load Lota onto the truck.

Cuneo broke his promise to keep Lota off the road. Instead, he trained her to perform in the ring and leased her out to Walker Bros. Circus. In the fall of 1997, Lota was diagnosed with the human strain of tuberculosis. Two years later she developed a large open wound on her right hip. She grew so thin that her eyes looked sunken in. Still, Lota continued to perform with Walker Bros., traveling in cold, damp trucks and kept in chains almost around the clock. Circus owner Johnny Walker—the same trainer who had worked with the Hawthorn Five—admitted Lota had a hard time adjusting to the demands of the traveling life. In 2001 she returned to Hawthorn's facility in Illinois emaciated and limping, with a big lump on her left hip, a fluid-filled abscess that extended as far as her midthigh and looked ready to burst.

After Lota contracted tuberculosis, the Milwaukee Zoo realized its mistake and tried to get her back. She was traveling with a circus oft-cited for mistreating elephants. Walker Bros. was performing on behalf of Chicago's Medinah Shrine Temple in 2001 when a woman who was chaperoning a group of schoolkids wrote *The Chicago Sun-Times* to protest a scene the group stumbled onto at the rear of the arena.

"The trainer began verbally abusing and hitting" one of the animals, the woman wrote. "We watched in horror as he swung a stick with all his force and struck the elephant in the back of the leg. This must have hurt because the elephant let out a scream that could be heard throughout the UIC Pavilion. The kids were frightened and asked me why the man was hurting the elephant." The complaint subsequently filed against the circus identified the trainer in question as Johnny Walker.

In Harlan County, Kentucky, another member of the public complained to USDA that the Hawthorn elephants traveling with Walker Bros. had "numerous red and raw spots on their ears from being speared with the hooklike device the trainer uses."

"The traveling quarters for the animals were at best cramped and inadequate," the man wrote. "At no time did I see any water dish or clean food to be provided for any of the . . . elephants."

USDA cited Hawthorn for failing to provide veterinary care to the three elephants. Two of them were Billie's former companions, Delhi and Tess. The third was an elephant named Liz. Born in 1957, Liz had been taken from her family in the wild and sent to America, where she spent her early years at Benson's Wild Animal Farm in New Hampshire along with an elephant named Queenie. In 1987 Liz and Queenie were sold to the Hawthorn

Corporation and leased out to circuses for the next nineteen years.

Walker Bros. kept the Hawthorn elephants inside an orange plastic mesh tent that was mashed down in two places. Parents and children were walking right up to the elephants and petting them and no attendant was in sight. Conditions were hazardous not only for the public, but for the elephants. In Littleville, Alabama, inspectors noted that handlers left a water hose running, spilling water over an electrical cord that was within reach to anyone and everyone, including the animals. USDA inspectors cited Hawthorn for failing to address the health and safety of its elephants traveling with Walker Bros.

Delhi, especially, was suffering: the cuticles on both of her front feet were severely overgrown and she had an open wound on one nail that was draining and bleeding. The area above the nail was swollen and warm to the touch. The elephant limped in pain as she performed her tricks inside the arena, struggling to keep the weight off her injured foot. Meanwhile, Tess's left eye was teary, causing her to squint. Her trainer explained that he had run out of the antibiotic ointment he had been putting in her eye. And once again the elephants were found loose and unattended on the circus grounds, available to any member of the public who felt like approaching them.

For the next three years federal inspectors cited Walker Bros. repeatedly for lacking any written schedule of veterinary care or any records to indicate the Hawthorn elephants leased to the circus were receiving proper care. In 1995 inspectors discovered that Lota had "deep fissures" on her feet serious enough to warrant immediate attention. That fall inspectors noticed puncture wounds on the elephants, two or three behind their left ears and at least one under their chins. One of the wounds on Liz was filled with pus, a sign of infection.

"These charges are very serious," Ron DeHaven wrote in one

report. "Not only are animal lives in danger, but human lives as well."

Hawthorn faced problems elsewhere. Outside an arena in Charlotte, North Carolina, two of Cuneo's elephants, Debbie and Judy, were traveling with a circus when they bumped into one another, started fighting, and escaped the lineup, crashing into the Word of Life Church, where they nearly flattened two church members and sent children fleeing for safety. The elephants smashed through a glass window, crumpled walls and door frames, and knocked a car fifteen feet. The damage came to $75,000 and the elephants themselves were cut and bruised.

This was Debbie's third meltdown. There was the incident in Hanover, Pennsylvania, where she chased Frieda into the plate-glass window of a Sears Auto Store. And two months after that Debbie ran away from a circus tent in Queens, New York, demolishing a string of parked cars and causing injuries to a dozen bystanders who fled the scene.

By January 2002 USDA notified Cuneo that he could no longer exhibit Debbie and Judy publicly.

In May 2002, USDA cited Hawthorn for failure to provide adequate veterinary care for his elephants, especially Billie's former Hawthorn Five ringmate, Delhi. Now fifty-six, her front legs were so "stocked up" they were double their normal size and puffed up to her chest. She was unable to bend the elbows on her front legs and had difficulty bearing weight on them. She could barely walk. A veterinary consultant hired by the government found major tissue damage on Delhi's front feet and abscesses dotting her hips, the area between her eyes, her ear, her head, her front elbows, and her tail. A sore on the side of her head had ruptured and was draining. Her front feet had chemical burns as well. Her handlers were supposed to soak her feet with a mixture consisting of nine parts water and one part formaldehyde. Instead, trainer John Caudill III—Johnny Walker's son—soaked

Delhi's feet in undiluted formaldehyde, which was extremely toxic. Cuneo defended Caudill—"I don't believe he had a malicious intent in the world," he said. "He just thought if two ounces are good, twenty-two ounces would be better." Cuneo fired Caudill, but the damage was done.

USDA brought in a consulting veterinarian, Dr. James Oosterhuis, to check Delhi out. In the past, Oosterhuis had defended highly questionable treatments of elephants. But Delhi's precarious condition concerned him. He prescribed a laundry list of treatments to save her. Handlers needed to exercise her thirty minutes twice a day, as briskly as possible, and soak her feet twice daily for half an hour each time in warm water mixed with Epsom salts or Betadine. They were to examine and scrub her calluses once a day, apply 3 percent iodine to them twice a day, and trim away the dead skin at least once a week. Handlers needed to help Delhi learn to drink water from a hose and eat mash, sweet feed, from a tub so that oral medicines could be mixed into the mash. They also needed to treat the wounds on her skin and weigh her regularly. The elephant badly needed to be exercised, Oosterhuis said, but she was barely getting any: a short walk through the barn to the exercise ring, once around the ring and back to the barn. She should be weighed monthly, the consultant said, and under no circumstance should she go back on the road until she had gained 500 pounds and was back up to at least 7,400 pounds.

Inspectors found Cuneo's African elephants with hard, cracked skin on their backs, ears and heads, and overgrown nails and cuticles. His tigers were suffering, too. Handlers were keeping several tigers in cramped transport cages, barely big enough to turn around in, for months at a time. Others were being fed moldy food and housed in a barn so poorly ventilated it reeked of urine. Inspectors' eyes stung from the fumes. Some of the tigers were in such ailing health that they died. One of them, twelve-year-old Neve, succumbed while being transported back to the Illinois facility. A six-year-old tiger named Java who should have been in prime health had died a few months earlier.

By the fall of 2002, more problems surfaced. In Norfolk, Virginia, a Hawthorn elephant handler traveling with the Sterling & Reid Circus beat an elephant bloody. The handler, David Creech, was convicted on three counts of animal cruelty and fined $600. He escaped a fourth charge, of striking the elephant over the head with a bullhook, only because an eyewitness was uncertain which handler did the striking. Another Hawthorn handler, Jim Zajicek, was charged with obstructing justice.

Even circuses were starting to notice the Hawthorn Corporation's rap sheet. In March 2003 a local Shrine Circus in Edmonton, Canada, announced that it would no longer use animals owned by Hawthorn.

Everywhere Cuneo turned, he was in trouble.

Back in Illinois, the elephants pined away inside the concrete and metal barn. Billie and Frieda now shared their stall with Sue, too, and all three of them, as well as Nicholas, Cuneo's lone male, suffered from nail problems.

Elephants are large terrestrial mammals; they didn't evolve to stand still for long periods on solid surfaces. When they do, they tend to become overweight, and as they move forward, backward and side to side their feet expand and contract, which can lead to cracked nails. Once that happens, a captive elephant's feet can become contaminated with urine and fecal debris, which makes cracked nails fairly risky. Handlers often use a rasp a couple of times a month to hone an elephant's cuticles and keep them short. But Billie, Frieda and Sue were hard to get to, confined as they were in the same small pen. They weren't getting the care they needed.

Billie was considerably overweight, which put her at even greater risk than the others. She needed to be out walking, but that wasn't happening. She was stuck inside, imprisoned, just as she had been for years.

"BAD" ELEPHANTS

In the circus world, a bad elephant is any elephant that fails to get with the program. For every dozen elephants who acclimate, however uncomfortably, to circus life, there are one or two or three who never do adjust, who simmer with rage at their captivity.

For many circus elephants, the constraints of traveling on the road for months on end, kept tethered in place in a boxcar or a semi and denied the ability to roam, forage, and mingle with one another becomes too much. They while away their time rocking back and forth, swaying from side to side or bobbing their heads up and down neurotically; some tug incessantly on their own nipples or gnaw on the ears of the elephant next in line. The most disturbed go berserk, ripping out light fixtures, crushing windows and demolishing their surroundings—and attacking and often killing their handlers and unsuspecting passersby. Since 1990 alone, circus and zoo elephants in America have killed fifteen humans and injured 135.

Circus elephants frequently try to run away. In the early days it wasn't uncommon for an elephant to flee the lineup, dash down a side street and end up in someone's backyard, causing damage. Circuses had a way of beating the rap. They'd send a bull man to inform the homeowner that the fence or trellis or whatever the elephant damaged was actually a violation of the local ordinance, and that the property owner was fortunate the circus did not plan to take them to court as the result of damage suffered by the elephant. If an elephant stumbled into someone's garden, the circus rep would chew the homeowner out for letting the elephant eat "poisonous" vegetables.

Some circuses capitalized on their bad elephants: they deliberately kept a "killer elephant" as part of their herd and publicized elephant attacks as a way to attract crowds. If the elephant wound up with a death sentence, the execution was billed as a special event. Circuses strangled violent elephants, blasted them with cannonballs, drowned and poisoned them and pitchforked them to death. Trainers had one solution for a bad elephant and that was to torture it, for as long as necessary. If the elephant never did surrender, he was punished until he died.

In the 1880s, trainer George Conklin decided to do whatever it took to discipline Chief, an elephant with a quick mind who, as he grew older, "went mad" and tried to kill several of his handlers. Using block and tackle, Conklin's men chained Chief down by all four legs. He "fought like the devil," Conklin recalled later, but finally his men had the animal stretched out to the point that he was immobile, except for his flailing trunk. The men formed a circle and moved in, thrashing him with stakes, sledges, axes, pitchforks, pokers, and hot irons. Chief never did capitulate. Eleven hours later, he was dead.

Conklin instantly regretted the fatal beating and later discovered that he could subdue an elephant by chaining it down and having alternating groups of a dozen men beat it with clubs, for hours at a time, off and on for several days—stopping short of killing it. "He couldn't stand any more clubbing on that sore hide of his," Conklin told a newspaper reporter about one of his victims. "Now there is not a more obedient elephant in the whole herd."

Animal owner W. P. Hall had a reputation for handling so-called bad elephants. He kept his elephants in "Hall's Cellar," the dark, clammy basement of his barn in Lancaster, Missouri. But even Hall couldn't contain an elephant named Virginia, who had the unfortunate habit of stampeding during performances. The Sells-Floto Circus had washed its hands of her and Hall leased her out to Atterbury Brothers when she freaked out and rushed an audience in Crookston, Minnesota, charging through the bleachers and killing a nine-year-old girl. The circus changed her name to Burma and sold her to another circus. No one knows what happened to her after that.

Tipoo-Sahib, Tip for short, quickly established his reputation as a killer elephant. Within a year after the Adam Forepaugh Circus brought him to America in 1882, Tip reportedly slayed one bull man and seriously injured two others. Two years later he allegedly killed another pair of workers and three men and a boy after that. Forepaugh sent him to New York's Central Park Zoo. Tip had barely settled in when he nearly killed two keepers there. Though later accounts say he killed a total of just two people, the city ordered him shot to death. A taxidermist stuffed his body and put him on display.

In 1903, Thomas Edison offered a one-of-a-kind punishment for Topsy, a former circus elephant who had wound up at the Luna Park Zoo in Coney Island, New York. At twenty-eight, Topsy had killed a man who'd tried to feed her a lit cigar, and Edison's solution was to electrocute her to death—an experiment that could also demonstrate the dangers of alternating current, a different form of electricity than the direct-current method Edison invented. Edison had already electrocuted several stray dogs and cats, even horses and cows, but nothing this big. The zoo erected a gallows and charged admission to 1,500 spectators to watch the event. Topsy refused to climb onto the structure that had been built for her, so her executioners went to her. They strapped wooden sandals with copper electrodes to her feet and ran a wire to Edison's electric light facility, fed her cyanide, and then gave the go-ahead to shoot 6,600 volts of electricity through her body. She died instantly. Later that year Edison released a short movie of the killing, *Electrocuting an Elephant*, which showed Topsy's smoking body topple to the ground. The footage is available on YouTube.

Elephants were the most heralded of performers, but when calamity befell them, circus owners often shrugged it off. In 1911, the Yankee Robinson Circus had finished performing in Cumberland, Wisconsin, when handlers led their elephants to a lake to get a drink. Before long the lead elephant, Tom Tom, who was completely blind, stepped off the slab fill and got his front feet stuck in mud. The dammed-up area began filling with water and the martingale chaining Tom Tom's tusks to his feet made it impossible for him to lift his trunk out of harm's way. By the time anyone noticed, it was too late: the top of Tom Tom's back was the only visible part of him left. Circus employees made light of his death. They said the elephant had become so recalcitrant that little could be done with him. "His drowning was probably a relief to all concerned, Tom Tom included," the local paper said.

TEN

✦

SPACE AND SILENCE

The Elephant Sanctuary's mission was to provide three things elephants needed most: an escape from human dominance, plenty of room and air, and the company of other elephants.

Buckley and Blais had long since retired their bullhooks. The elephants under their care would never again experience the fear and pain brought about by a bullhook or a hot shot; a cell phone–sized device that delivers high-voltage, low-current shocks of electricity. Only if the Sanctuary needed to carry out some sort of medical or grooming procedure would the elephants be asked to perform a behavior, and instead of goading them, caregivers would reward them with treats, gentle touches, and lots of praise.

The Sanctuary couldn't offer total freedom, but to the elephants who'd spent decades in confinement, it might seem like it. Elephants are migratory animals who, given the chance, will wander as many as thirty miles a day, exploring creeks and ponds, foraging for branches and leaves, and simply enjoying the surroundings of nature. Hohenwald's weather was just right for that. It was remarkably similar to the climate in Asia, where the elephants had begun their lives: Middle Tennessee's temperatures ranged from 30 degrees Fahrenheit in the coldest part of the winter to 110 degrees in July. Downpours were frequent, and the rolling terrain, year-round vegetation, and long growing seasons offered the very environment elephants needed to thrive. Maples and sweet gum trees dotted the Sanctuary property, interspersed with hardwood and pines, which cooled the hot summer temperatures by about ten degrees.

That first year the Sanctuary consisted of a small barn, forty acres of fenced property, and Tarra. Buckley took care of the business end of the operation. She managed the finances, handled public relations, and served as the public face of the Sanctuary. The media gravitated to the idea of a single woman who'd finally landed a decent home for her elephant. Behind the scenes, Blais did everything else: he bush-hogged the land, installed fencing and kept the barn in working order. The work was never-ending. Blais never felt caught up. He'd go months without leaving the Sanctuary grounds. Even when he did venture out it would be a quick trip, to the hardware store and back, and then his work would begin again.

The Sanctuary was not the kind of place where carloads of visitors could drive up and gape at the inhabitants. Its gates were closed to the public. The occasional newspaper article or TV segment helped publicize the operation, which generated contributions, but to reach supporters on a regular basis the Sanctuary needed a Web site. In 1995, that seemed a Herculean challenge. Buckley and Blais were living in the middle of nowhere, and to even attempt to get on the Internet they needed a dial-up connection through their landline, which meant calling Nashville and paying long-distance charges. Their phone carrier offered free long-distance service on Fridays, so every Friday after 6:00 P.M., when most of his chores were done for the day, Blais sat down in front of the computer and tried to patch together a Web site. He was out of his element. The result was so rudimentary it looked like a page out of a kindergarten coloring book.

Yet just when he and Buckley needed something, the gods had a way of providing it. Almost immediately after the Sanctuary opened, an early supporter, country music singer Shari Sweet, recruited her mother, communications expert Ruth Sweet, to help publicize its existence. Now someone else, a Web-savvy Nashvillian named Carolyn Stalcup, stepped forward and offered to help design the Web site. Both women were lifesavers.

Expenses, though, began to mount. The Sanctuary needed fencing, and even if they installed it in phases it was going to require money. Through a fundraising effort via the Nashville Humane Association, the Sanctuary took in small donations each day, checks for $5 or $10 or $20 or, every now and then, a couple of hundred dollars. But it wasn't enough, and Blais had decided to look for part-time work when he filled in for Buckley one day and drove to town to pick up the mail. He sat in his car opening the envelopes—one of which, to his amazement, contained a check for $10,000. *Ten thousand dollars*. It seemed like a million. Blais broke into sobs, stunned by the generosity of the donor, whose identity he has long since forgotten. That contribution was just the kick-start the Sanctuary needed.

Relief also came by way of a supporter with a connection with the Tennessee Valley Authority, a federally owned corporation that provides electricity, flood control, and economic development to that region of the country. The supporter—another forgotten name—arrived one afternoon with an entourage of TVA brass to show them firsthand the challenges the Sanctuary was up against. They found Blais digging holes with fence posts, a back-breaking and time-consuming task. "Oh, boy, can we help you," one TVA official said. A couple of weeks later the agency sent a tractor, an auger, a welding machine, a bushhog, and a bulldozer and, later, some transmission cables for Blais to use.

He and Buckley eventually learned that if they really needed something, they should go ahead and buy it but then leave it in the box for a couple of days. Because inevitably someone would donate the exact same item several days later. And this way they could take the original back and get a refund.

What the Sanctuary needed were elephants—nothing short of an entire herd to re-create the complex social arrangement elephants were accustomed to in the wild. At the barest minimum that meant five elephants, but ideally there would be twice that many. A herd of ten or eleven would enable the elephants to become socially and psychologically sound, to look out for one another and grieve collectively when any elephant passed on.

Buckley and Blais reached out to zoos that might have outgrown their elephant exhibits and couldn't afford to expand. And they contacted circuses, offering to take off their hands any elephant that had grown too old or ill to perform. But the Sanctuary's unwillingness to breed its resident elephants irritated the Association of Zoos and Aquariums, which had a vested interest in replenishing the captive elephants that were dying out.

The AZA argued that unless the public had a chance to see elephants up close, they would never develop an appreciation of them and, in turn, support efforts to preserve elephant habitats overseas. Blais and Buckley saw things differently. If you keep subjecting elephants to small enclosures and stupid tricks, they felt, people will never develop a true appreciation for these magnificent animals. They saw no point in producing more elephants for the unnatural environments they were trying to rescue elephants from.

The circus community looked upon the Sanctuary with contempt. To them, it seemed wasteful to let an elephant meander about open land when it could be pirouetting around a tub, entertaining an audience. Even would-be supporters of the Sanctuary were skeptical of its mission. At an Elephant Managers Association conference a couple of years after the Sanctuary's opening, an attendee commented that the Sanctuary was a great idea, but could never succeed. "Well, it's happening," Blais replied, but old-school elephant managers didn't believe him.

Early the following year, the Sanctuary got its second elephant. Born in Sri Lanka in 1966, Barbara had worked for a logging company in Asia, moving trees, before she was sent to Florida to be trained for circus work. She performed for circuses for a dozen years. When she was fourteen she was sent to a breeding facility, but she never became pregnant; instead she acquired a wasting disease. A circus owner in Florida asked Buckley to take Barbara off his hands.

She arrived at the Sanctuary 2,000 pounds underweight, so ill that she wasn't expected to live long. Blais and Buckley took turns sleeping in the barn overnight to make certain Barbara was okay. She was so thin and weak that sometimes she couldn't stand up on her own; she needed a push. But the open land beckoned, and Barbara waited early at the gate each morning, eager to be let out to wander.

That same year, Jenny arrived. Captured in 1973 in Sumatra when she was a year old, she had spent years performing for Carson & Barnes Circus. When she was nineteen, the circus sent her to Cuneo's Hawthorn Corporation to be bred. The bull elephant she was paired with injured Jenny's leg severely and the injury reportedly went untreated. Every day for ten months she was put back into the stall with the bull. She failed to get pregnant and returned to Carson & Barnes with a leg injury that prevented her from performing.

The circus wanted nothing more to do with Jenny, and discarded her at a shelter outside of Las Vegas. A new owner adopted her but did nothing to medicate her injury, which had since escalated into foot rot. When the ABC-TV show *20/20* aired footage of Jenny as part of a segment on captive elephants, millions of viewers saw the disturbing footage of an underweight elephant, chained, exposed to freezing temperatures, and unable to escape her own feces. The outcry shamed her owner into donating Jenny to the Sanctuary.

Caring for and feeding each elephant cost anywhere from $1,000 to $1,500 a month. But raising money was easy compared to finding the right caregivers. Employees needed to have a certain temperament, an ability to step back and read the elephants' demeanor and refrain from injecting their own biases into a scenario.

Along with paid staff, animal lovers by the dozens came forward to help. College students and other volunteers donated a week or two of their time to mow briars and broomsage, haul away barbed wire, and pull down old chain-link fences. The volunteers bunked in cabins at a nearby state park. The hard work was worth doing for the chance to catch glimpses of the elephants, learn their backstories and hear the latest on how well they were now thriving.

In 1998, *Time* magazine included Buckley and Blais in its list of Heroes for the Planet. But some Hohenwald residents weren't so enamored of the Sanctuary. In his infrequent forays into town, Blais detected a "What the hell are they doing?" attitude, a feeling that all that time and effort spent on the elephants could be better spent helping needy children. Other residents resented the intense privacy surrounding the Sanctuary. "They're in our community. They should let us in their doors," was the feeling. Blais fully expected the locals to complain when word got out that Barbara had roamed off the property and wound up in a neighbor's backyard, next to his clothesline. To Blais's surprise, several residents commented that they wished Barbara had come to their house. Blais knew the Sanctuary had reached a milestone when an elderly customer walked in to Sandra Estes's bank and told her, "Honey, I hear we're getting more elephants." Not *they*, but *we*.

The Sanctuary's second phase began a couple of years later with the addition of 110 more acres and a six-stall, 6,000-square-foot heated elephant barn. Contractors built a 200-acre corral surrounded by steel pipe and cable fencing. Dirt roads packed down from years of timber trucks crisscrossed the property, just waiting for the elephants. The addition opened in December 1999.

By then, the Sanctuary had taken in a fourth elephant, fifty-year-old Shirley. Shirley had traveled with several circuses in her early days and had the souvenirs to show for it: she'd been burned in a fire aboard a ship in Nova Scotia, on her way to America, and she'd broken her right hind leg after another elephant attacked her during her days with Lewis Bros. Circus. Her leg was poorly set and she walked with a severe limp. Unable to perform, she wound up at a zoo in Louisiana when she was twenty-eight.

After more than two decades of isolation, the zoo decided to retire Shirley to the Sanctuary. National Geographic filmed the elephant's arrival in Hohenwald: her exit from the semi that had delivered her, her introductory shower and the watermelon treats caregivers gave her afterward. Buckley and Blais brought Tarra into the barn to meet Shirley, the first elephant she'd seen in more than twenty years. The two elephants wrapped their trunks together and Tarra reached out to carefully feel each of Shirley's old injuries. The documentary crew were done for the day, so they put away their equipment and headed off to dinner with the staff.

Buckley and Blais were the only ones to witness what happened next. Jenny, who had been outside all this time, entered the barn, spied Shirley, and immediately tried to get close to her. Blais opened up the stall next to Shirley's, but that wasn't good enough for Jenny. She banged on the gate and practically climbed over the stall to join Shirley. Now that she could see the younger elephant up close, Shirley responded with equal enthusiasm. She bent the steel slats stepping on the fence, trying to get close to Jenny.

Elephants have remarkable memories. They can reach back through time to recall the distinctive characteristics of family and friends; a typical elephant can recognize the trumpets and chirps of a hundred other elephants, and can distinguish the scent of her mother's urine, even after being separated for many years.

Shirley and Jenny had a profound connection to each other. That much was clear.

Blais slid open the door and watched as the two elephants embraced each other joyously. It turned out that nearly a quarter of a century earlier, they had traveled together with the same circus. Trainers had housed Shirley with the younger elephants while she recuperated from her broken leg, and for those few weeks together, while Jenny was just an infant, Shirley had nurtured the baby elephant as if she were her own.

National Geographic told the story of their reunion in its 2000 documentary, *The Urban Elephant*. The film earned an Emmy and generated much-needed acclaim for the Sanctuary's work.

Bunny, forty-seven, was the fifth elephant to arrive. She'd been captured in the wild and spent most of her life as the lone elephant at the Mesker Park Zoo in Evansville, Indiana. Zoo officials made the decision to retire her so she could enjoy the long-needed company of other elephants and rest her feet from too many years of standing on concrete. Bunny trumpeted ceaselessly once she set foot on Sanctuary soil in the fall of 1999, and she took to the vast, open landscape so enthusiastically that at times it was hard to locate her.

Sissy came in 2000. Born in Asia in 1962, she was sent to America when she was two and spent thirty-six years living at a handful of zoos in Texas. The seminal incident in her life occurred when she was twenty-nine and floodwaters rolled into her zoo exhibit. Sissy survived the flood, but for twenty-four hours she was submerged up to her trunk. In 1998, after one of her keepers was killed inside her pen, Sissy was relocated to the El

Paso Zoo, where her keepers, aware of her reputation, inducted her by beating her savagely. A videotape of the beating was leaked to the media and the public was so incensed that zoo officials decided to retire Sissy.

That same year, Winkie arrived. Shipped to America from Burma in 1966, she'd spent almost her entire life at the Henry Vilas Zoo in Madison, Wisconsin, where she struck out at new handlers being trained to dominate her. USDA ordered the zoo to either expand its elephant exhibit or find new homes for its elephants. The zoo asked the Sanctuary to take Winkie, and the Sanctuary did so gladly.

Buckley and Blais were no longer romantically involved, but their devotion to the Sanctuary was as intense as ever. In October 2001 the Sanctuary purchased another 700 acres of land, known to locals as the Highland Lake Land for the 25-acre spring-fed lake that offered the ideal relaxation spot for an elephant. And two years later the Sanctuary welcomed an eighth elephant, Tina. Thirty-three and plagued with foot problems, she'd spent many years alone at the Greater Vancouver Zoo in Canada, without any other elephants to keep her company. Her journey to the Sanctuary covered three thousand miles. She lasted less than a year before she suddenly experienced coordination problems and a loss of appetite and died.

Losing Tina was sad news, but otherwise the Sanctuary was thriving. It added another 1,800 acres, property that most recently had served as a timber farm. And it opened its doors to three African elephants. Zula and Tange had been orphaned in a mass killing of their families and, since 1978, had resided together at the Chehaw Wild Animal Park in Albany, Georgia. The third African, Flora, was also orphaned in a cull. She'd spent eighteen years traveling with a circus that bore her name before her owner, David Balding, decided she deserved a better life.

In 2004 alone, sanctuary membership catapulted to 34,000

donors and contributions reached $4.5 million. Nearly a dozen elephants had experienced the closest thing they would find to freedom again. There was room for plenty more.

~~~~~~

CONQUERING AN ELEPHANT

Elephant-handling is hazardous work—the federal government once labeled it the most dangerous job in America. Countless grooms and trainers have been trampled or stomped to death by the very beasts they were determined to tame. An incensed elephant can kill a man in five seconds. The risks inherent in the job have never been matched by the pay. Even in the 1950s, Ringling Bros. paid its bull men just $16.67 a week with food and a bunk in a train car thrown in.

Pat Derby, the ex-Hollywood trainer who founded the Performing Animal Welfare Sanctuary for captive wildlife in California, wrote that animals always know when a trainer is gripped by fear. "The cruelest trainers, almost without exception, are the ones who are most frightened and most desperate to conceal it; and they make the thing they dread happen, inevitably," she wrote.

An ill-tempered elephant could not merely be tolerated. She had to be beaten; there was no getting around it. And once a beating started, a trainer could not stop halfway. If he gave in too soon because he was worn out or afraid, the thinking went, he would never be able to handle that elephant again.

The severity of the beating usually depended on the elephant's history of aggression. The more belligerent her behavior, the harsher the punishment. Every trainer had his own style, but typically a session started by adding an extra chain to an elephant's legs and tightening it to give the elephant less wiggle room. The trainer would approach the elephant from behind her left side and tell her to lie down. If the elephant refused, the beating would begin. Often a trainer wouldn't wait to see whether the elephant complied; he'd begin striking her anyway, pummeling her between her eye and her ear with a bullhook or an iron tent stake. The elephant might start to lie down when a trainer would reach over the top of the animal and hook her upper ear to jerk her head down further, poking, poking, poking. The trainer would aim for the soft tissue, the inner parts of the ear, behind the ear, underneath the tusks or underneath the chin.

Once the elephant was on the ground the trainer would continue to hit her any number of ways, sometimes with the back end of the bullhook, sometimes with a pickaxe handle, sometimes with a baseball bat. The longer the handle, the greater the amount of force that could go into the blow. Trainers aimed for spots that would inflict the most pain: the elephant's ankles or wrists, where it's easier to come in contact with bone. A favorite spot was the top of the elephant's head; striking there made a loud echoing sound.

Handlers often beat elephants between the eyes, on a bulge at the base of the trunk, on the theory that that spot was thick enough to avoid injury. But beating an elephant between the eyes meant a handler was within reach of the elephant's trunk, and that could get him killed. Instead, seasoned trainers approached an elephant from the left side and the rear and whipped her on the fleshy side of the head between her eye and her ear, using the sharp end of a bullhook to keep the elephant from turning her head.

Handlers like to say there is no way they can injure an animal that big, even if they strike the animal's trunk. They used to allege that an elephant's trunk was all gristle. But elephants feel anything that brushes up against them. In most places an elephant's skin is one-half inch to three-fourths of an inch thick, and so sensitive that that she can feel a fly walking on her back. An elephant's trunk is the most dexterous part and, made up of 40,000 muscles, is also exquisitely vulnerable, so much so that elephants tend to keep their trunk ends securely closed—

even coiling them into their mouths—while they sleep. A striking blow to the nerve ends of the trunk can cause acute pain.

Trainers often rubbed their elephants down with whiskey after a beating. The tissue damage will leave abscesses, bleeding wounds, and skin so damaged it will slough off, sometimes for weeks.

One alternative to a beating is to tighten the chain around an elephant's legs slowly, a few inches at a time, until the elephant is forced to support its weight on the remaining hind and front legs. The elephant will grow fatigued quickly and might lose control of her bowels right before admitting defeat and collapsing on her side. The wise trainer tries to make nice with the elephant afterward by squatting down next to the animal's head, speaking gently to her and even giving her a treat.

In one instance Lewis admitted he went too far. Two of the eight elephants he helped train for the Robbins Bros. Circus were young and apprehensive; one in particular, an elephant named Sadie, simply could not grasp the trick Lewis and his colleague, Bloomer English, were trying to teach her. At one point she tried to escape the ring and the two men decided to discipline her. They began beating her, but minutes later the trainers looked up at one another and stopped. Sadie was lying on her side, heaving with sobs. Tears ran down her face. Lewis had never seen anything like it. He and English crouched beside the elephant, stroked her, and spoke to her comfortingly. They never punished her again. Her emotional meltdown was so rare that veteran bull men later expressed doubts that it really occurred. "But we saw and heard, and neither of us ever will forget it," Lewis wrote.

ELEVEN

THE CRACKDOWN BEGINS

Circus owners are no fools. They know that, even though elephants are entitled to protection under the Endangered Species Act, the federal Animal Welfare Act is too weak to provide it. They also know that USDA inspectors lack police authority: They can cite circuses for breaking the law, but they cannot penalize them for their violations. Those decisions are made further up the food chain. Even when charges are filed, elephant exhibitors are usually able to settle them by paying a small fine. The violations seldom go on their records.

In Cuneo's case, the government had given him a lot of slack. He'd managed to keep his license even after his elephants were found riddled with tuberculosis. But the multitude of charges against Cuneo—and the pressure brought about by animal welfare groups—were adding up fast. Finally, on April 9, 2003, the federal government lowered the boom, citing Hawthorn with forty-seven violations of the Animal Welfare Act. The law had long been criticized for setting bare minimum standards for animal care. Now, USDA was saying, Hawthorn wasn't even meeting those. The violations involved a dozen of Cuneo's elephants; trainers were said to have used physical abuse to train, work, and handle the elephants, causing them discomfort and physical harm; failing to provide medical care for an emaciated elephant (Lota) and to an elephant suffering from acute chemical burns and a bacterial infection (Delhi); failing to provide veterinary care to several elephants, including Billie, who suffered from potentially lethal foot problems; and allowing unsafe contact with the public.

Hawthorn wasn't letting its elephants rest long enough between performances, according to the charges. USDA identified not just Cuneo but three trainers under contract with Hawthorn and John N. Caudill Jr., aka Johnny Walker, Billie's former trainer and the owner of Walker Bros. Circus.

Animal welfare groups grabbed the opportunity to call attention to the plight of circus elephants. Debbie Leahy, then-director of PETA's captive and exotic animals division, said the Hawthorn Corporation ought to be put out of business. "We think it's pretty obvious that these animals are in a state of unrelieved suffering. We'd love to see the animals seized," she said.

The Elephant Sanctuary's Carol Buckley echoed her comments, calling Cuneo's business "terrible."

There's no indication John Cuneo lost any sleep over the allegations. He shrugged off the charges and the USDA administrative law judge for USDA who would hear them, calling it a "kangaroo court."

"Where are the marks on them?" Cuneo said of his elephants. "How do you beat an animal without putting a mark on them? It's a bunch of lies."

He told another reporter, "If these animals are so badly cared for, so mistreated, so dirty, nobody would want them. They're the best-looking animals in the country."

By 2003 Cuneo was seventy-two years old. He'd operated his

company for forty-six years. He had nineteen elephants, one lion, and eighty-four tigers, the largest number of registered tigers in the world. He was rich enough to treat his animals well—to the extent that any wild animal can be well-kept in captivity. Yet he had failed to do so. Instead, Cuneo spent his money on himself. One of his purchases was four acres of property for a winter home on Sarasota Bay, Florida, not far from the John and Mabel Ringling Museum, at a cost of $7.1 million.

Cuneo fought the charges all the way.

For a month his employees kept the kind of meticulous records USDA had asked them to maintain. Then, suddenly, that stopped. Federal inspectors discovered the same updates were being copied almost word for word from one day to the next, with only the date changed.

Two months after it levied the boatload of charges, USDA cited Hawthorn again, this time for failing to provide suitable veterinary care to Billie's, Frieda's, and Sue's problem feet. The elephants needed medical treatment every three or four months; nine months had passed since they'd gotten any. Delhi's left front foot was in bad shape again.

A month later, the feds ratcheted up the pressure. Hawthorn had failed to provide appropriate care to its elephant Judy, who'd been exposed to other elephants testing positive for tuberculosis. Delhi wasn't getting the foot care she so badly needed, and wasn't getting weighed every eight weeks to determine if she was gaining much-needed pounds. There was no documentation that any weekly foot trimming had occurred. The only person doing that job was a veterinarian who came to the Hawthorn facility once every four to six weeks. Elephant superintendent Gary Thomas said Delhi was being walked each morning, but inspectors saw no evidence of that. Instead of scrubbing her problem feet and applying iodine to the lesions, handlers were spraying Delhi's feet with some mysterious "healing oil." The frustration of the inspecting veterinarian is evident in the report he subsequently filed with USDA's Animal and Plant Health Inspection Service. "The lack of adherence to these plans may have resulted in the relapse of problems in Delhi's left front foot," Dr. Kenneth Kirstein wrote. "Strict adherence to treatment plans is critical."

Nothing had been done to provide shade to the outdoor corral the elephants were sometimes let out in. Tall, shady trees lined the perimeter of the Hawthorn property and protected the pastures from sunlight early and late in the day, but there was no protection from the sun from 11 A.M. to 3 P.M., when it shone the hottest. Federal regulations required that animals have some way to protect themselves from direct sunlight. Heat and humidity in Illinois could be beastly in the summer. The issue of shade, however, was a moot point for most of the elephants, including Billie, because they were seldom taken outside. They spent long days inside a barn kept so poorly that exposed fiberglass insulation hung down within their reach.

The federal Occupational Safety and Health Administration also weighed in, charging Hawthorn with failing to protect its workers after several of them tested positive for TB. Again, Cuneo came out swinging. He said there was no record of humans getting tuberculosis from elephants and accused authorities of conducting a witch hunt. "We're getting sick of it," Cuneo told a newspaper. "It gets very tiresome. We have very good people."

In late November, Delhi suffered blow-outs on both of her injured feet: the flesh surrounding the infected areas cracked open, producing raw, aching wounds. Despite her distressing state, no diagnostic tests were performed. Delhi's survival was at stake. The following day, November 22, 2003, USDA officials seized the fifty-seven-year-old elephant and transferred her to the Elephant Sanctuary in Tennessee. She was covered with scars, lasting souvenirs of her circus career. Animal welfare activists were stunned: For the first time in history, the U.S. government was rescuing an elephant.

Her first afternoon free at the Sanctuary, Delhi napped beneath the midday sun. But the rest of the Hawthorn herd remained chained up in Illinois. Eight months had elapsed since USDA leveled all those charges against Cuneo's company. Four more months would slip away before Cuneo and the government reached a settlement. Ultimately, Cuneo admitted to nineteen of the forty-seven violations. He agreed to pay a $200,000 fine and turn his remaining elephants over to facilities approved by the USDA.

The settlement was unprecedented. Never before had the federal government ordered the release of so many captive wild animals. And rarely had anyone involved with the circus industry admitted violating the Animal Welfare Act. Doing so meant the violations were now on Cuneo's record. Cuneo reportedly said he went along with the settlement because he didn't want to spend more money going to court. But USDA spokesman Darby Holladay called the agreement "an unprecedented win for Animal Care." Animal welfare advocates who'd spent years protesting the living conditions of circus elephants praised the agreement as a landmark. "Nothing like this has ever happened before," Carol Buckley said. "The animal welfare laws here are weak to begin with, and at no other time has USDA actually enforced their laws like this." She was optimistic about the ramifications of the agreement. "Clearly, these actions will force elephant owners to be more careful about how they treat their animals."

Richard Farinato, director of captive wildlife programs for the Humane Society of the United States, was en route to an animal care conference when he heard about the settlement. "I swear I felt the planet swerve on its axis slightly while in flight," he wrote. "The resolution of this case was truly earth-shaking."

GOING ROGUE

Circuses kept elephants on the road even when they were old and infirm. One of them, Ena, an elephant with the Robbins Bros. Circus, finally reached her breaking point and began using her trunk to demolish everything within reach. To minimize the damage, her handlers kept all four of her legs chained, for such long periods that when it came time to head to the big ring, Ena could barely walk at all. Robbins Bros. sold her to another circus; whether they divulged Ena's temperament seems doubtful. Her new employer assigned her to carry her new trainer about with his head in her mouth. Ena promptly crushed the man's skull.

Even elephants merely trying to escape their captivity sometimes paid with their lives. In 1928, the Sells-Floto Circus was in Lewiston, Idaho, on a scorching hot day—the temperature hovered above 100 degrees—when Mary, a thirsty elephant, broke from her trainers and ran down Main Street, crashing into a storefront window she apparently mistook for a shimmering pool of water. She finally found water in a garage where local residents were washing their cars. Townspeople caught up with her and shot her to death.

An angry elephant is apt to knock a person down first with her trunk. If the animal is really serious, she will pull her victim in and keep pummeling him with her tusks or feet. In worst-case scenarios, an elephant will sit on her target and pulverize him. In her book *Elephants on the Edge*, Gay Bradshaw writes that elephants possess "retaliatory cunning," an ability to deliberately go after someone who has hurt them in the past. An elephant can remember the personal experiences that have left an impression on her, good or bad. Bradshaw credits elephants with a degree of self-knowledge that reflects

an engagement with the outside world, a keen memory of their experiences with people and places, and the patience to wait, plot, and
snatch a passing chance to vindicate past abuse or even forestall it in
the future.

Male elephants are especially dangerous: they're larger than
females and they have long, lethal tusks, something female Asian
elephants lack. Once a year male elephants go into musth, a two-to-
four-month period when the elephant becomes sexually active, capricious, and erratic. By some accounts, underfeeding an elephant
cuts its period of musth to two weeks or less. Circuses typically pulled
an elephant undergoing musth from the lineup. They chained him
headfirst into a corner and sometimes attached a martingale connecting his tusks to his feet. One elephant, Dumbo, wore martingale
chains for twenty years.

Circus owners often mistook the temperament displayed during
musth as a character flaw and tried to beat it out of an elephant—
which often made matters worse. After Black Diamond, a male elephant traveling with the Al G. Barnes Circus, killed three people, his
trainers shackled and chained him and sawed his tusks down. They
clasped an iron bar across his tusks to prevent him from raising his
trunk. But even that couldn't change him.

In Corsicana, Texas, in 1929, Black Diamond found himself in the
hands of H. D. "Curley" Prickett, a man who'd worked with him years
earlier. Prickett had since left the circus and was now employed by a
local landowner, a woman named Eva Speed Donohoo, but when he
heard the circus was coming to town, he asked to escort Black Diamond along the parade route for old times' sake. Donohoo came out
to watch him do so.

Prickett and Black Diamond approached the spot where Donohoo
was waiting and, by some accounts, Donohoo reached out to pet the
elephant. Black Diamond responded by throwing Prickett across a car
and then pounding Donohoo to the ground, dragging her from where
she was standing between two cars and crushing her to death. The

elephant may well have been experiencing musth, but it didn't matter. Townspeople followed the circus when it left Corsicana, demanding justice for Donohoo's death.

The owner of the Barnes circus, John Ringling, sent a message to "Kill Diamond in some humane way." Handlers chained three of Black Diamond's legs to three other elephants and escorted him down city streets as thousands of onlookers jeered. At the circus grounds his handlers chained the elephant to two trees and tried to feed him poisoned peanuts mixed in with nonpoisonous ones. Black Diamond was smart enough to sort through the mix and eat only the nonpoisonous peanuts, so his handlers tried poisoned oranges. He refused them, too. Ultimately a firing squad shot him to death, using more than 170 rounds. Afterward, a butcher peddled ribbons of his hide for a dime each.

Black Diamond's death was a wake-up call to the circus world. John Ringling ordered all of his circus's "dangerous" male elephants destroyed and many other circuses followed suit. The manager of Barnes saved one of its males, Tusko, by selling him to a promoter for $2,800. Barnes had billed Tusko as "The Mighty Monarch of the Jungle, The Largest Elephant the World Has Ever Known, Standing 13 Feet High and Weighing 20,983 pounds or Ten Tons and a Half." In truth, he was ten feet two inches and weighed barely more than seven tons, but he was still the largest elephant in the country. And powerful: In Portland, Ore., he once rammed his way through a solid concrete wall buttressed on one side with a steel plate. His reputation was so daunting that Barnes kept Tusko snubbed down entirely in chains. Martingale chains crisscrossed his tusks, he had cross-hobbles on his four legs and a chain-basket contraption limited his ability to move his head and trunk. Another long chain fastened to his cross-hobbles dragged the ground behind him. If, by some miracle, Tusko was able to run, his handlers could grab hold of the chain and try to tie him to a nearby tree. The chains alone weighed 914 pounds.

Tusko was considered especially dangerous when he was going

through musth. Handlers pummeled pins into the shackles that gripped the chains about his legs. For several years he was kept in a crush cage for three or four months at a time, unable to lie down or even move a single foot. The chains around his legs were so tight they embedded themselves in his flesh to the point that they were invisible. Even then the elephant was considered too volatile to approach.

Black Diamond's legacy left its mark. In the 1930s and 1940s, circuses killed dozens of their male elephants. By 1952, of the 264 captive elephants in America, only half a dozen were mature males.

TWELVE

MIRED IN BUREAUCRACY

Animal lovers celebrated the crackdown on John Cuneo too soon. He wasn't going out of business. For a man of his means, a $200,000 fine was chump change. And in exchange for confiscating Cuneo's elephants, the government let him retain his license to exhibit animals, which mean he got to keep his lion and eighty-seven tigers. Even while he was ordered to give up his elephants, Cuneo applied for permission to send his tigers to Mexico, Canada, Europe, and Asia, and the government granted it on grounds that he had not yet been convicted of anything. Cuneo's company leased animals worldwide to circuses, exhibits, shows, and for commercials. Revoking his exhibitor's license would have jeopardized all those arrangements.

Sixteen of Cuneo's tigers were traveling with a circus in the United States. Another fifteen were headed for a tour in Europe. Seven would begin a fall tour through the South with the George Carden Circus, while a fourth group was tentatively scheduled to travel to China.

Nor was having to give up his elephants that great of a burden. The presence of tuberculosis in the herd had already forced Cuneo to take them off the road. "Cuneo has made a lot of money on the backs of these elephants, and now he's getting rid of them when they're less and less useful to him," Buckley noted. The agreement did nothing to bar him from procuring more elephants once his present herd was sent to new homes.

The settlement specified that Lota would go to the Elephant Sanctuary. Cuneo was supposed to have sent her there six years earlier, but he'd backpedaled, claiming he needed to put her to work to satisfy a contract with a circus after another elephant had to be pulled out. Even though Lota tested positive for tuberculosis, Cuneo sent her back out to perform. At a time when she could have begun medical treatment to help recover from TB, she was traveling in the back of a trailer with four other elephants, struggling to cope with the rigors of the road.

The settlement authorized Cuneo to identify the places he wanted to send the rest of the elephants. The parties needed to meet USDA's approval. Cuneo was supposed to relinquish the elephants by August 15, 2004, which gave him five months.

Animal welfare groups, including the Elephant Sanctuary, watched closely, concerned that because of the presence of tuberculosis, finding homes for the elephants would be difficult. Six cases had been diagnosed in Cuneo's herd in the last eight years, two of the elephants had active cases of TB and the remaining fourteen had been exposed to the disease. Because of the tuberculosis, the elephants were poor candidates for zoos, and the settlement stipulated that the elephants would not be returned to circus life.

"We think they need to remain together as a herd," Buckley told a reporter, "and that's going to be very hard to do."

The general counsel for USDA, Bernadette Juarez, advised Cuneo that the Elephant Sanctuary and PAWS might be the only two facilities that met the requirements of the consent decision. Cuneo objected to sending the elephants there. He wanted them

Four elephants form a pyramid while a young woman stands on the forward-facing elephant's head at the Sells Floto Circus, ca. 1929-1931. *(Courtesy of Circus World Museum, Baraboo, Wisconsin)*

One of the most difficult tricks a circus elephant is expected to learn is to stand on its head, carefully bolstering its weight on its front legs and face, with its trunk stretched out along the ground to help it balance. *(Courtesy of Circus World Museum, Baraboo, Wisconsin)*

A pair of Sells Floto Circus performers wave from atop an elaborately costumed elephant, 1923. Circus elephants often carried a variety of animals, including tigers, dogs, and monkeys on their backs. *(Courtesy of Circus World Museum, Baraboo, Wisconsin)*

A young woman practices perching on the head of an elephant, who in turn is balanced on its hind legs. *(Courtesy of Circus World Museum, Baraboo, Wisconsin)*

An elephant, possibly the renowned Tusko, stands draped in chains outside of a big top, 1928. *(Courtesy of Circus World Museum, Baraboo, Wisconsin)*

One of the Hawthorn elephants, Lota, is anchored so securely in place that she is barely able to move. *(Courtesy of PETA)*

A bullhook—the time-honored tool, and weapon, of elephant trainers. *(Courtesy of PETA)*

Trainers wrap ropes around a baby elephant and grab hold of her trunk to make her stretch out on the ground, the beginning of an arduous training regimen. *(Courtesy of PETA)*

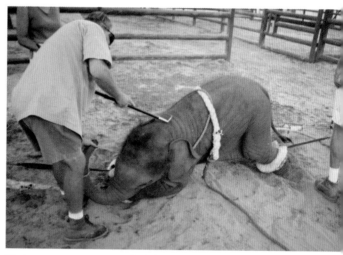

Trainers use bullhooks to force a baby elephant to sit on a tub. According to the late trainer Sammy Haddock, loud music is played to drown out the youngsters' screams. *(Courtesy of PETA)*

Caregivers at the Elephant Sanctuary delight in creating surprise toys for their residents. Billie was especially taken with this colorful giant box. *(© 2011, The Elephant Sanctuary in Tennessee)*

After arriving at the Elephant Sanctuary in 2006, Billie, left, formed a tight friendship with two other elephants, Frieda, center, and Liz. Years later, the three girls remain inseparable. *(© 2008, The Elephant Sanctuary in Tennessee)*

Sanctuary cofounder Scott Blais. He found in Billie an especially sensitive soul whose trust in humans had been all but destroyed. (© *2011, The Elephant Sanctuary in Tennessee*)

Elephants Shirley and Tarra bask in one of the Elephant Sanctuary's open meadows along with Tarra's canine pal, Bella. The Sanctuary's 2,700 acres make it the largest refuge for old, sick, and needy elephants in the United States. (© *2013, The Elephant Sanctuary in Tennessee*)

A breakthrough moment for Billie came when caregivers tossed a large blue ball into the barnyard. She straddled it, kicked it, and ran after it, so caught up in her play that for a few hours her ever-present anxiety seemed to vanish.
(© 2010, The Elephant Sanctuary in Tennessee)

Like all elephants, Billie loves water—dunking in it, splashing her trunk with it, and spraying it with her trunk. Here she opens her mouth wide to catch a hoseful. *(© 2013, The Elephant Sanctuary in Tennessee)*

Finally, on May 3, 2011, Billie achieved a long-anticipated milestone: she finally allowed a Sanctuary caregiver to remove the last chain around her leg. (© 2011, *The Elephant Sanctuary in Tennessee*)

Billie leaves behind a giant Popsicle hanging from a tree and wanders down one of the many paths that beckon on the grounds of the Elephant Sanctuary. (© 2013, *The Elephant Sanctuary in Tennessee*)

to go to circuses, and he argued that any outfit that had a valid USDA license was qualified to take them. He seemed unconcerned that his elephants could very easily expose other elephants, not to mention the general public, to a contagious disease.

Cuneo proposed eight facilities for the remaining elephants (Judy had already been placed). But five of them—Marion Nature Park, Patricia Zerbini Circus, the Animal Park Inc., Riddles Elephant and Wildlife Sanctuary, and African Lion Safari—were unwilling or unable to take the animals. Riddle's operation in Arkansas was not accredited by the Association of Sanctuaries and did not abide by Sanctuary standards. Moreover, Riddle was known to use hot shots on his elephants. George Carden Circus could not meet conditions aimed at reducing the risk of contagion. Besides, USDA would not approve any facility that had elephants on the road and/or might be exposing its own elephants to the Hawthorn herd.

By late May, USDA decided to send three of the younger elephants—Ronnie, Gypsy, and Joy—to the Endangered Ark Foundation in Hugo, Oklahoma, a breeding facility designed to produce more baby elephants for Carson & Barnes Circus. The head of the facility, Barbara Byrd, said her family had lived with elephants for years and would welcome the newcomers. But animal welfare groups were livid. The circus was notorious for abusing its elephants. USDA's own records had documented the problems.

Five years earlier an undercover investigator for PETA had shot footage of Carson & Barnes's animal care director, Tim Frisco, instructing trainers how to work with elephants. The video is shockingly brutal. Frisco shouts profanities and beats an elephant until she shrieks with pain. He can clearly be heard telling the trainers to hurt the elephants. "Tear that foot off!" he yells at the handlers. "Sink it in the foot! Tear it off! Make 'em scream!

"When you hear that screaming then you know you got their attention," he says.

The video shows Frisco singling out an elephant named Becky, shouting "You mother——cker!" at her. The camera shows Becky shrinking back and screaming in response.

"Don't touch 'em. Hurt 'em. Hurt 'em," Frisco tells his subordinates. "When he starts squirming too f——ing much, both f——ing hands—*boom*—right under that chin!" To demonstrate, Frisco swings his bullhook like a baseball bat.

In another scene, Frisco is shown jabbing elephants in the rear end with an electric cattle prod to make them move faster. "I'll kick the sh-t out of you, little prick," he bellows, poking Becky. Becky screams—an agonizing sound of fear coming from so large an animal—and Frisco roars at the trainers, blaming them for making him have to punish the elephants.

Unaware that he is being taped, he admits: "I'm not gonna touch her in front of a thousand people. She's gonna f——ing do what I want and that's just f——ing the way it is."

To avoid going to court, Carson & Barnes agreed to pay $400 in fines in 2002 as a result of the video. The following year the circus was fined $550 when one of its elephant trucks overturned. From 1995 to 2001 the circus was cited as least eight other times for failing to maintain its transport trailers.

USDA had found no evidence of mistreatment at the Elephant Sanctuary. The Hawthorn elephants would have access to their own barn and be kept apart from the other elephants on site so that none of the others would risk catching tuberculosis. Neither the Elephant Sanctuary nor PAWS allowed their elephants to be bred, however, and to Cuneo, that was the sticking point. If his elephants were forbidden to perform, at least they could be put to work reproducing.

USDA vetoed Carson & Barnes and began lining up other potential placements for the Hawthorn elephants. They earmarked six—Lota, Misty, Frieda, Debbie, Tess, and Liz—for the Elephant Sanctuary. Queenie, Lottie, and Minnie would go to PAWS. Joy would be sent to the Nashville Zoo and Judy would go to Chris Hamblen, a private elephant owner in Kountze, Texas. The department was still looking for homes for Ronnie and Gypsy.

That left Sue, Nicholas, and Billie. USDA tentatively designated them to go to the Popcorn Park Zoo in Forked River, New Jersey. Run by the Associated Humane Societies, New Jersey's largest animal sheltering system, Popcorn Park was home to more than two hundred sick, old, abandoned, injured, and abused animals—everything from geese to mountain lions, tigers, camels, wallabies, monkeys, birds, horses, sheep, pigs, goats, and reptiles—on eleven acres. The zoo had taken in one elephant, an African male named Sonny, who died in 1989.

The terms of the agreement called for revoking Cuneo's license if he failed to donate the elephants by August 15. But at the last minute, Cuneo's lawyers filed two motions with USDA's chief administrative law judge seeking to change the deadline and vacate the consent decision and order. Cuneo now said it was important to keep his elephants together and that Scott Riddle, owner of Riddle's breeding farm in Arkansas, was best suited to take them. The Elephant Sanctuary and PAWS lacked the expertise to care for the herd and would neglect his animals, Cuneo argued. He said his employees refused under any circumstances to transport the elephants to either facility "because they so deeply share my concerns."

The administrative law judge sided with Cuneo and stayed the consent decision until he could rule on the two motions. USDA's Animal and Plant Health Inspection Service appealed the ruling to the department's judicial officer. On November 22, 2004, the judicial officer dismissed the appeal and sent the matter back to the administrative law judge.

Meanwhile, at the Hawthorn barn in Illinois, Lota and Misty

were living apart from the other elephants in an uninsulated metal shed, barely protected from the Midwest's extreme temperatures. Their health was too precarious to withstand any more delays. Finally they were getting out. As Sanctuary caregivers loaded them up outside the Hawthorn barn, Lota entered the semi peacefully but Misty, rattled by the yelling going on around her and angered when Cuneo tried to make her spread out on her sternum so he could remove her chains, delivered a parting shot. She reached out and thumped Cuneo with her trunk, knocking him down.

The two elephants arrived in Hohenwald alive but ailing. On top of her tuberculosis, Lota was a thousand pounds underweight and believed to be suffering from a urinary tract infection. Misty appeared much older than her forty years. "You look at Misty, she should be in her prime, but she looks totally used up," Buckley told a reporter. "The good news is Lota is eating ravenously. She loves the food here, so she is eating very well."

The Sanctuary was interested in taking as many of the remaining Hawthorn elephants as they could, Buckley added. "They're going to need care for the remainder of their lives," she said. "I surely hope they don't get absorbed back into the circus industry."

Misty and Lota had made it out, just barely. Tess, one of the Hawthorn Five elephants, was not so lucky. She died on November 1. A necropsy report blamed her demise on cardiopulmonary collapse due to prolonged lateral recumbency—in lay terms, she'd lain down for so long to rest her swollen and throbbing leg that her organs collapsed under her enormous weight. Despite her obvious suffering, Hawthorn's trainers had waited a month before giving her any medication. The government cited Hawthorn for that, too.

Even while the fate of his license was up in the air, Cuneo let conditions slide at his facility in Illinois.

Federal inspectors finally noticed that Hawthorn employees weren't able to work safely around Billie, Sue, Frieda, and Nicholas, the four elephants kept in pens, physically separated from their handlers. "These four are considered dangerous and the male is become increasingly aggressive with the three females," an inspector wrote. "When animals cannot be shifted to the outside because of the weather, it is not possible to separate one elephant from the other three for any routine health care while maintaining employee safety due to space limitations and the lack of a large enough elephant restraint device."

Even if it was possible to separate the elephants, the company had too few workers to do the job: just one full-time caretaker, one groom, and one general helper to care for fourteen elephants. Moreover, the handlers were too inexperienced to handle the elephants safely. And because of what had happened to Billie years earlier, she refused to step into the crush, the restraint device, where routine treatment could have been administered.

Handlers frequently locked elephants in a crush cage. Zoos and circuses use crush cages to administer medical treatment to elephants, and as long as handlers speak to the elephants softly and feed them treats while they're under confinement, most animals don't seem to mind the experience. Billie, though, had every reason to avoid the crush.

It's unclear what she'd done to prompt her punishment—maybe she'd helped herself to another elephant's rations one time too many. But three years after Hawthorn took Billie off the road, an elephant trainer and a bear trainer decided to teach her a lesson. They led her into the crush, latched the doors, and "worked her over"—a euphemism for beating her savagely. Beatings were commonplace for captive elephants. But "working over" an elephant referred to a specific form of punishment. In rapid-fire succession, a handler would order the elephant to perform a series of tricks: sit, stand, lift a foot. An elephant couldn't possibly comply with such swift commands, and for failing to keep up she was flogged mercilessly.

The thrashing came with a message: that Billie must never, ever act on her own. The instant she did so, she would be chastised. Punishments that harsh had a way of dulling an elephant's senses, which gave her handlers even more leverage. Now a handler's very presence, the mere tone of his voice, would remind Billie that she needed to do as she was told.

This time, though, the beating backfired. Billie never got over the incident. Seven years passed and she refused to enter the crush again. Several times the door to the crush swung open and that alone invoked so much rage that she ripped it apart. But there was no way handlers were going to work on her feet otherwise. As a result, she wasn't getting the foot care she needed to keep her feet from getting infected.

In November 2004, one of the protected-contact elephants turned on two of the employees, injuring one of them badly enough to cost him four days of work and seriously harming the second. The second employee, a general helper, suffered two pelvic fractures, a winged scapula, a dislocated ankle, and internal injuries. He wound up in a convalescent home and was out of work for more than seven months. A settlement arranged by the Illinois Workers Compensation Commission gave him $65,700, a fraction of the $300,000-plus he racked up in medical bills.

USDA records never identified the elephant who launched the attack, but there is reason to believe it was Billie. The following January, USDA inspectors found Billie's face and trunk rife with new and recent wounds. Pink scar tissue had grown up over some of the injuries, but others, including a gash at the center of her trunk and a lesion near her mouth that appeared reddened and moist, were more recent. The employee in charge of the elephants told the inspector he thought the injuries occurred the previous November, and speculated that Billie and Nicholas had wounded each other while fighting through the enclosure bars. There was no indication that a veterinarian had been consulted about the injuries. Inspectors noted that Hawthorn's custodian of records lied when she told them no employee injuries had occurred in the past six months. Inspectors issued citations to Hawthorn, not for administering the wounds, only for failing to treat them.

⊷ ▰◆▰ ↢

Misty and Lota, the second and third Hawthorn elephants to relocate to the Sanctuary, settled into their new lives readily. Lota seemed fascinated by the automatic watering devices positioned out in the field, and fiddled with them repeatedly to make certain that water was indeed there for the taking. She and Misty roamed about the open space seemingly in wonder, soaking up the paths and devouring the produce and hay set out for them. Lota was unable to frolic, however. Her health was too fragile. She stood by and watched as, every now and then, Misty would circle her excitedly, charge up and down the hill and burrow into the mud. Caregivers often looked out to see Lota resting her thin frame on Misty's bountiful rump.

By late January, Lota's health took a bad turn. Tuberculosis had ravaged her lungs, making it hard to breathe. She lost what little appetite she'd had and despite hourly doses of oxygen she was clearly going downhill. She died at 3:00 A.M. the next morning with a caregiver and a visibly upset Misty by her side.

The Sanctuary celebrated its tenth anniversary in 2005, having amassed 50,000 supporters who eagerly tracked elephants' progress on the Sanctuary's Web site: elephants.com. But the anniversary was bittersweet. Two years had passed since the Hawthorn Corporation had agreed to place their elephants in new homes, and still the animals languished in their dark barn in Illinois. If anything, their condition was worsening. USDA inspectors noted that Billie, Sue, Frieda, and Queenie had gone without any foot care for nearly a year and a half.

The elephants weren't getting enough exercise; four had been taken off their chains only once in the past two months and four others had been untethered for just twenty minutes during that same period. The elephants were standing all day on feet beset with grossly misshapen nails that were so long they curved. One inspection report contained seventy-eight photos documenting their ailments and Billie was in thirty-one of the pictures, some noting the lesions on her trunk and her feet in bad need of care. Any warmth that had ever existed between Billie and Wade Burck seemed to have disappeared. A description of one photo, number fifty-two, said: "Billie—Wade Burck—whip/ankus and hot shot."

As the year progressed, inspectors cited the foot problems of Billie and her comrades once again. "Foot problems in elephants can lead to severe disability or death," the inspector warned.

The elephants weren't the only animals suffering. Inspectors cited Hawthorn for failing to document and treat hair loss, eye infections, and sores on four tigers. For nearly two weeks, eight tigers were kept in cramped transporting cages that measured just six and a half feet by seven and a half wide and four feet high. Hawthorn employees were also letting meat for the tigers thaw in direct sunlight, exposed to flies and open to contamination. And, as usual, the company was short of employees. Inspectors noted that the tiger trainer, Burck, had been put in charge of the elephants, too.

The time was long past to rescue the elephants. And the Hawthorn Corporation and Elephant Sanctuary officials had pretty much agreed that all but one of the elephants would go to Tennessee. They just couldn't agree on the details.

One of the sticking points had to do with the cost of caring for the elephants. Buckley asked whether Hawthorn would help pay the nearly $2 million she estimated the elephants would require over their projected lifetimes. The figure amounted to $125,000 a year for each elephant. It did not include any of the Sanctuary's capital expenses, including the cost of land, building barns or erecting fences.

A second issue was how quickly the Elephant Sanctuary could assume ownership of the Hawthorn herd. The Sanctuary had raised nearly $2.8 million in anticipation of accepting the elephants, but most of that would go for a new 16,000-square-foot barn to house the Asian elephants, which would make the original barn available for the Hawthorn girls. The new barn would take six months to build. Until it was finished there was no shelter for the elephants in Hohenwald. Elephants were strong enough to destroy temporary housing, and besides, the state of Tennessee, which licensed the Sanctuary, forbade it from keeping the elephants in a temporary facility.

In the meantime, Buckley wanted access to the elephants' medical records and the right to visit them in Illinois to learn more about their personalities. She was particularly interested in the three elephants labeled as aggressive: Billie, Frieda, and Sue.

(The Sanctuary had said no to just one Hawthorn elephant, Nicholas, because as a male, he would need to be kept separately. The PAWS sanctuary had offered to take Nic. The Elephant Sanctuary was prepared to take the remaining ten Asian elephants along with Joy, the lone African.)

Talk of money and a delay in the moving date plunged discussions into a tailspin. USDA interpreted Buckley's request for financial assistance from Cuneo as a deal-breaking demand. Three months passed before the federal government suddenly did an about-face and announced plans to send three of the elephants, and possibly two more, to Carson & Barnes's endangered breeding facility after all. The head of the foundation, Barbara Byrd, the daughter of circus founder Dorey Miller, said she hoped the three adult elephants would be able to have babies; if they did, the babies would be trained to become circus performers.

The decision incensed animal welfare activists, along with Buckley and Blais. USDA initially rejected the Endangered Ark Foundation as unsuitable for any of the elephants and consistently identified the Elephant Sanctuary as one of the best possible places to send them. The Sanctuary's barn would be finished in another three months. Couldn't the government wait that much longer to give the elephants the very best home possible? But USDA insisted there was no time to lose. The government planned to hand off the elephants the first week in June.

The prospect of losing them to circus-run facilities was too much. PETA, which had spent years monitoring the condition of the Hawthorn elephants, filed suit to stop the transfer. The federal judge overseeing the matter denied legal standing to PETA. Judge Paul Friedman of the U.S. District Court for the District of Columbia acknowledged that the footage of Tim Frisco attacking the elephants was troubling and showed conduct that violated the Animal Welfare Act. But Friedman ruled that animal welfare groups lacked legal standing to interfere with the transfer.

In an eleventh-hour decision, USDA did another about-face and determined that the results of three of the elephants' bloodwork introduced doubts about their tuberculosis status. The bloodwork of Joy, the lone African elephant, showed no problems, and she was sent off to Carson & Barnes's Ark Foundation. That left the Elephant Sanctuary the only entity willing to take the remainder of Hawthorn's female elephants, regardless of the state of their health. On November 28, 2005, Cuneo signed the papers agreeing to donate nine of the elephants to the Sanctuary.

HOLLYWOOD COMES CALLING

By 1900, New York alone had ten firms trading in wild animals, on top of the foreign dealers who shipped thousands of exotic animals to the United States. Nearly every large city in America was buying wild animals, and many rich Americans kept private zoos of their own. For decades traders disembarked their exotic animals in New York or Boston and shipped them inland to cities like Detroit and Chicago. It wasn't until the 1920s that a West Coast trader began to give Easterners a run for their money.

Born in New York in 1896, the son of a butcher, Louis Goebel moved to Los Angeles when he was twenty-three and worked his way into a job with Universal studio's zoo, which was operated by Carl Laemmle, a partner in the studio. Goebel eventually bought Laemmle out and moved the six lions in his possession to Ventura County, northwest of Los Angeles. On five lots off what is now Thousand Oaks Boulevard, Goebel built cages for his lions and, during the daytime, tied the animals to an oak tree. Within three years he had an entire menagerie of exotic animals, and Goebel's Lion Farm had started to make a name for itself. In time, it would become better known as Jungleland, a tourist attraction that lured thousands of families, until Disneyland, which opened in 1955, and other rival attractions eclipsed it.

Goebel boasted that he had more animals on his property than the three largest circuses in the country combined. (He purchased twenty-six elephants in a single transaction once, but turned around and sold them as soon as a new buyer came calling.) He rented out dozens of his animals to Hollywood, including Leo the lion, the famous MGM trademark; Tamba and Peggy, the chimpanzees from the Tarzan movies and *Bedtime for Bonzo*; and elephants Big Emma (from the 1954 movie *Elephant Walk*) and Bimbo, who starred in the television series *Circus Boy*. Goebel bought and sold hundreds of exotic animals, including scores of elephants over the years. In 1940 a fire ignited at Jungleland when a barnful of dry hay combusted spontaneously and raced through the complex, injuring a half-dozen Bengal tigers and two elephants. One of them, Sally, fell into a gulch after the flames burned her and had to be destroyed. Employees had to euthanize the other elephant, Queenie, after she suffered burns about her head. Attempting to escape the blaze, Queenie tripped over and broke a water main and then ran headlong into a tree. Her accident greatly hampered efforts to fight the fire.

Queenie had appeared in several Tarzan movies and was cloaked as a woolly mammoth for a Victor Mature movie called *One Million B.C.* When MGM later imported seven baby elephants from Siam to perform in the Tarzan movies, the head of the studio's advertising department, Frank Whitbeck, insisted that two of the elephants be named after Sally and Queenie. Only three of the baby elephants survived the journey; intestinal parasites killed the other four. The remaining three were seven years old when MGM stopped making Tarzan movies, at least temporarily. Whitbeck was convinced the young elephants would die of heartbreak if they were separated, so he, Goebel, and George Emerson, the boss animal man at MGM, bought them. The elephants went on to perform with the Pollock Bros. Shrine Circus.

THIRTEEN

+⊶≡◆≡⊷+

SETBACKS IN ILLINOIS

One obstacle remained before the Sanctuary could truck the remaining nine Hawthorn elephants to their new home. The state of Tennessee required blood tests on the animals. So late in 2005, Blais headed to Illinois, accompanied by veterinarian Susan Mikota and Sanctuary employee Lydia Scheidler, to observe and take back with them the blood samples collected by the Hawthorn team. They expected to spend two or three days completing the task.

Blais was astounded at the condition of the Hawthorn facility. At one point in its history the barn might have been spotless, but now it was a pigsty. Cobwebs lined the interior of the dimly lit building; the piercing, fermented smell of urine and elephant dung assaulted Blais's nostrils. Rat and mouse droppings were everywhere, including the grooms' bedrooms, which were located down a long hallway. Some of the handlers lived in trailers parked outside. If anyone flipped on the kitchen lights after dark, they'd be greeted by a roomful of eyeballs. Blais heard stories of previous grooms coming to work falling-down drunk, dropping a little hay at the foot of each elephant and walking away. Days might go by before anyone bothered to muck out the piles of feces.

Six of the elephants were on a picket line, chained by one front leg and one rear leg, facing outward, away from the wall. At one end, Debbie and Ronnie stood side by side. Debbie, thirty-five, was one of the herd's youngest elephants and, at 10,380 pounds, one of its biggest. She had a reputation for being dangerous. Ronnie, forty, was vocal and highly animated. She had performed for circuses since she was nine and at the age of twenty-seven had given birth to a son, Nicholas, the male elephant kept in protected contact. Debbie and Ronnie were best friends, forever caressing each other with their trunks. Next to them stood Gypsy, thirty-eight. Imported from the wild, she'd performed with Ringling and three other circuses before Cuneo bought her.

At the other end of the line was Queenie, forty-seven, the elephant Cuneo had purchased from Benson's Wild Animal Farm in New Hampshire. Next to her were Lottie and Minnie. Lottie, forty-three, was sold to Cuneo in 1995 at the age of thirty. Minnie was forty and enormous, weighing in at 11,130 pounds. Before she was sold to the circus she was believed to have been someone's pet. She and Lottie were tightly bonded; they stood as close to one another as they could get.

In the center of the line, stationed a bit apart from the rest, was puny Liz. At forty-nine, her trunk was partially paralyzed and she limped slightly from an infection between two toes on her right front foot. She was kept farther apart from the others to protect her rations. Given half a chance, the other elephants would devour Liz's share of hay.

With nothing else to do to all day, the elephants swayed back and forth. They seemed to welcome human contact and no one anticipated any trouble with their blood draws. There was more concern about the four elephants on the other side of the barn, in protected contact.

Billie, Sue, and Frieda were kept loose in their twenty-foot-by-twenty-foot pen originally designed for Nicholas's father, Tunga. None of the female elephants were tethered in place—the only chain was the loose one attached to Billie's ankle. Nicholas, considered aggressive by virtue of his gender, was kept in a similar-sized stall on the other side of the restraint chute. The isolation ward was so dark and gloomy and moist it reminded Blais of Hannibal Lecter's cell in *The Silence of the Lambs*.

Mikota, the Sanctuary's veterinarian, was struck by how constantly the Hawthorn grooms yelled at the elephants. The keepers didn't ask the animals to perform a behavior, they commanded them to do so. Yet the handlers were also capable of treating the elephants with some degree of kindness. Burck talked excitedly to the elephants on the picket line while he worked on their feet. Liz had an endearing *conk conk conk* noise she'd make when she was excited, and she made that noise with Burck. Burck also had a special fondness for Nic. Nic loved water: after the morning muck out, Burck would hand him the hose and let Nic play with it, standing on the hose and aiming the end of it up under his neck: he'd "squeal and chirp and act the fool, and twist himself into the goofiest Gumby poses you can imagine," Burck wrote later.

He felt no such affinity for Billie. Burck described her as extremely dominant and "probably the most dangerous animal I have ever been involved with." She'd come a long way from the days when Burck felt comfortable enough to let his three-year-old son walk alongside the Hawthorn Five.

Billie's ceaseless appetite annoyed the grooms. To keep her from eating the other elephants' food, Burck would separate the three females: he'd put Frieda into the crush, lead Sue outside, and leave Billie in the pen so he could keep an eye on the amount of grain each consumed. He would have preferred to put Billie in the crush, but after the beating she'd endured years earlier she refused to enter the crush again. In the wintertime, if it was too cold to take Sue out, Burck would leave her in the pen with Billie—which inevitably meant that Billie would steal some of Sue's food. Each winter, Sue lost weight and Billie would gain it. But Blais didn't understand why Billie should be held to blame. The elephants had been forced to share a space barely bigger than three parking spaces. How could they not wind up eating each other's food?

The grooms spoke nicely to Frieda and Sue, in spite of the elephants' rap sheets. They seemed to have forgiven Frieda and Sue their past transgressions. Not Billie. Billie was "the bitch," always the bitch, as far as her handlers were concerned. Each morning Blais heard the greetings: "Good morning, Sue. Good morning, Frieda. Hey, *bitch*."

There was an unforgiving attitude toward Billie, a callousness reserved especially for her. When Frieda stepped into the chute for her meals, the grooms would talk to her sweetly, and then turn around and be cold and short with Billie. They might take Billie outside to get her out of the way and leave her there for hours, even when temperatures hovered in the single digits, unacceptably cold for an elephant. The grooms would say, "Aw, just leave her there all day. She deserves it."

From what Blais could tell, Billie had done nothing to merit the mistreatment. She'd done nothing the day before, either, or the day before that. Billie's crime was that she wasn't willing to tolerate the confines of captivity, to accept her sentence passively. Maybe she'd figured out that if she did lash out, her keepers would leave her alone. Whatever her motivation, she seemed to be saying: *I don't want to make the best of it. This is not right.*

—❦—

Hawthorn's veterinarian opted to sedate Billie, Frieda, Sue, and Nic before drawing blood. Sue was first and seconds after she was darted, she began to collapse. The vet injected her with a reversal drug, but it wasn't enough. In an instant, what started as a routine procedure escalated into an emergency. The Sanctuary team rushed in to prevent Sue from crumpling onto her belly, which would have impeded her breathing. They worked around the clock to try to keep her from losing consciousness.

Over the next several days the forty-year-old elephant struggled to overcome the effects of the sedative, unable to stand without assistance. Team members took turns giving her fluids and administering a range of therapies, using forklifts, straps, and large tires to try to support her. They offered her fruits, vegetables, even peanut butter and jelly sandwiches—anything to try to revive her. They never left her side.

From a distance, the elephants on the picket line could see and hear the goings-on. The other elephants in protected contact—particularly Billie, who was in the adjacent pen—could witness the ordeal up close. Blais wondered how Billie might react to the frantic efforts on behalf of her friend. Of all the elephants, she was clearly the most traumatized. By day Billie was her usual defiant self, lashing her tail against a gate when her handlers passed by as if to say: *I'm still Billie, and I still don't like you.* But at night, when the Hawthorn employees were gone and the Sanctuary staff was still working with Sue, Blais began to notice something. Billie would step forward to the edge of her pen and watch the Sanctuary team at work, curious. Elephants are night owls; they average only about four hours of sleep. Between the hours of midnight and 3 A.M. Billie was awake and that is when she began to utter soft, sweet noises, little squeaks. She was trying to open up to these newcomers.

Blais recognized her as the same elephant he had seen a couple of summers at the African Lion Safari outside Toronto, the elephant who even then had been singled out for rough talk and gratuitous smacks. He began to see in Billie a strength of character, a determination not to surrender herself to the life she'd been conscripted to. Her amber eyes showed a wary wisdom, a look of knowingness. Blais sensed that she had catalogued and seared into memory every wrong ever done to her. Whatever had happened in her past, Billie hadn't forgotten.

In an environment so punishing, it took courage for Billie to express herself, to let even an inkling of her real self shine through. Blais was exhausted by the endless efforts to revive Sue, but every now and then he remembered to speak reassuringly to the elephant who was watching so intently.

"Hey, Billie, we're doing everything we can for your friend," he murmured. "We're trying to do right for her."

The days and nights passed. Volunteers stepped forward to help. Wisconsin residents Lisa and Larry Kane made several trips delivering supplies from the University of Wisconsin's Veterinary Medical Teaching Hospital in Madison. Nashvillian John Rippetoe drove a truckload of hay from the Sanctuary to the Hawthorn barn. Illinois supporter Harry Camn ran crucial errands on behalf of the team. PETA's Debbie Leahy spent many days delivering Pedialyte, fresh produce, and tools and equipment, including a rented forklift she managed to track down on a Sunday morning.

But each day that Sue was unable to stand, her prognosis diminished. Upset by her inability to hoist herself up, she bellowed occasionally, and each time she did so the other elephants trumpeted and squealed and struggled against their chains, vainly trying to get to her. Nic threw himself against the slats of his cage, the sound of the clanging steel reverberating through the barn.

Surprisingly, in the thick of the hubbub, Billie opened up a little bit more. There was plenty of produce for Sue, so the Sanctuary team began to share some of her fruits and vegetables with Billie, Nic, and Frieda. Billie, especially, seemed to accept the tokens as they were intended: a rare act of kindness, a gesture of trust. It was as though she was looking for an excuse to connect with the humans in her midst.

Right before she went to sleep, Billie began to let out a series of little squeaks, and members of the Sanctuary team encouraged her.

"Are you okay?" they'd ask after she emitted the first round of squeaks.

More squeaks.

"Okay. Good night." And Billie would settle in for a few hours' sleep.

Eleven days after Sue's collapse, the team tried one last measure: they brought in a float tank, lifted the elephant into it, and filled it with water. To their amazed relief, Sue began to splash about in the water with her trunk. Her muscles seemed to have gathered a bit of strength. How many years had it been since this elephant had had a chance to immerse herself completely in water, something elephants love to do?

Then, suddenly, Sue's trunk went limp. She was gone. Instantly the barn fell silent. The rest of the elephants knew they had lost one of their own.

Later, writing about those two weeks, Leahy wondered how differently things might have turned out if USDA inspectors had acted more quickly to rescue Cuneo's elephants. "Why wasn't Hawthorn shut down immediately in 1994, after Tyke killed her trainer and police shot her to death in Honolulu?" Leahy wrote. "Or in 1996, after Hattie and Joyce died of tuberculosis and the other elephants were quarantined? Or after Lota became emaciated as this highly contagious bacterial lung disease ravaged her system? . . . Or after a trainer was convicted of cruelty to animals in Norfolk? Or after the elephant Delhi was confiscated because she was in imminent danger from lack of veterinary care?

"Over the years, how could USDA inspectors see the same things that I was seeing—filth, neglect, abuse, emaciated elephants, sick elephants, dangerous elephants, neurotic elephants— and just leave those animals there to suffer?"

THE TALE OF BABY BOO

Hollywood was enchanted with elephants, the smaller the better. One of importer Frank Buck's toughest requests came from an animal dealer in Los Angeles who wanted him to locate a female baby elephant to work in the movies. The elephant needed to be shorter than three feet, which would make it the smallest elephant in America. Several years earlier Buck had brought back a tiny elephant named Mitzi, who became famous as part of the vaudeville act Singer Midgets. But she was three and a half feet high when Buck delivered her. The L.A. dealer wanted his elephant to be even smaller.

Buck traveled to Calcutta to collect a long list of other animals, and while there he checked out more than a dozen tips about tiny elephants. None panned out. A few weeks later, he and his assistant were in Sumatra when a local trader who had just swapped Buck a lizard for Buck's knife suddenly asked: *"Berapa ada kechil gaja?"* How much would you give for a little elephant?

Buck had just about given up on the idea of finding a tiny elephant, but the trader's offer prompted him to turn around. How big is the elephant? Buck asked the man. The man raised his hand four feet above the ground. Buck shook his head. Too big, he told him. The trader then insisted the elephant was really much, much smaller. He lowered his hand until it was just a few inches off the ground. Buck was ready to laugh off the conversation until the trader mentioned that the elephant had hair all over its body. Now Buck was willing to take him seriously: an elephant covered in hair was still a baby and might, in fact, be under three feet. Buck and his assistant walked for four hours with the trader to his village, to a tapioca garden at the rear of the village headman's shack. Standing there with a rope around its neck was the scrawniest elephant Buck had ever seen. He used a carpenter's rule to measure the calf at the shoulder and sure enough, the baby was just two feet ten inches in height. By Buck's estimate it could not have been older than ten or twelve days.

The elephant trembled and wobbled. She looked starved, typical of a baby elephant who'd been taken from her mother at such a critical stage. The elephant had no idea how to use her trunk, and when the trader repeatedly tried to wrap the end of her trunk around a banana, the banana dropped on the ground. Buck guessed that without food the elephant would die in a couple of days.

Despite the elephant's precarious health, Buck bought her and immediately sent his aide out to find a goat they could milk. They tried pouring some of the milk down the elephant's throat, but she clamped her jaws shut and refused to open her mouth. Buck finally hit on a solution. He cut off a piece of bamboo about nine inches long, leaving a joint at the bottom of the reed. Then he filled the bamboo tube with a concoction of rice boiled in water and mixed with goat's milk. Buck's assistant had to practically stand the elephant up on her hind legs to force the end of the bamboo tube between her jaws and tip the gruel down her throat, but he finally got it down. He followed it with two more tubes of gruel, then laid the elephant down and covered her with gunny sacks. The next morning the hungry elephant swallowed the gruel willingly. A couple of hours later, Buck and his assistant put her in an oxcart and hauled her the four hours back to town. From there they shipped her to Singapore, where Buck called the dealer in Los Angeles and offered her to him for $2,000. The dealer said yes. The elephant went on to star in several movies under the name of Baby Boo.

While one picture was filming, a scene called for Boo to run, but she refused. The director was frantic over her unwillingness to cooperate. Then her keeper remembered that Baby Boo had come with a "magic wand": a bamboo tube that had won her over in the past. The keeper pulled out the tube and called to Boo. When she spied the bamboo, she began to run toward him and the director got the shot he was looking for.

FOURTEEN

━━◆◆◆━━

CARAVAN TO FREEDOM

Two months later, on February 8, 2006, the morning of Billie's departure dawned sunny but freezing: the Midwest's notorious humidity made the thermometer's thirty-five degrees feel more like fifteen. Blais rolled up his bedding and shoved his belongings behind the passenger seat of the tractor trailer. He swept his fingers through his light brown hair and tried not to look as apprehensive as he felt. As soon as he could get the paperwork in order and load the elephants, he could loosen up. At least a bit.

Three times over the last couple of weeks the "Caravan to Freedom," as the media dubbed it, had made the 600-mile trip from the Hawthorn exotic animal barn outside Chicago to the Elephant Sanctuary, delivering a pair of pachyderms each time. Minnie and Lottie were the first to arrive, followed by Queenie and Liz, then Debbie and Ronnie. The elephants seemed to acclimate quickly. They headed out to explore the two hundred acres set aside for them, conferring with one another in squeaks and low rumbles and caressing one another reassuringly. Minnie was especially adventuresome and energetic. She reveled in her freedom to wander: crossing the creek, pushing on trees, digging holes in the earth, and wallowing with abandon.

Even at this stage, John Cuneo was making things difficult. He'd made known his contempt for the Sanctuary—the notion that elephants needed saving from circus work struck him as ridiculous—and days earlier his employees had delayed Debbie and Ronnie's departure by several hours. Blais worried that, even with just two elephants left at Hawthorn, Cuneo could change his mind and throw a wrench into the plans. For weeks now, for harmony's sake, Blais had smiled and nodded and acted deferential around Cuneo and his employees. Blais was exhausted from all the tiptoeing around. He couldn't relax until all eight elephants were in the Sanctuary's possession.

He headed to the barn to check on Frieda and Billie. Two months had passed since Sue had died, and Blais had no idea what frame of mind he would find Billie in. Despite Frieda's violent past, Blais sized her up as less of a problem. She was thousands of pounds underweight and seemed perfectly compliant. The Hawthorn handlers considered Billie more volatile by far. Blais hadn't seen that side of her, but he knew it could surface at any time.

As much as Blais respected Billie's resiliency, he needed her to work with him, to board the back of the semi. He'd spent weeks mulling over the best way to coax her inside the trailer, and how best to keep her calm once the trip got under way. Billie and Frieda would be riding together and Blais decided to board Billie first. It might take three minutes or three hours; however long she needed was fine with him.

The saga of the Hawthorn elephants was big news in the Chicago area and a CNN correspondent and camera crew were on hand to record the final road trip. A Hawthorn employee tried to block the camera's view of the barn. But to smooth the process, Wade Burck offered to remove himself from the scene. Blais had never seen Burck mistreat Billie, but he knew the trainer regarded the elephant as brooding and obstinate, and Burck's very presence in the barn caused Billie to bristle. "She hates me," Burck told Blais, and he wasn't exaggerating. Blais could tell from the way Billie planted herself so squarely, from the way she stiffened her trunk and hardened her gaze on Burck, that she really did despise him.

Once Burck moved out of the picture, the driver of the semi, Angie Lambert, backed the trailer to a ten-foot-wide gateway at one end of the barn and opened the rear doors. Billie's task seemed simple enough. From inside the barn, she needed to walk twenty-five feet to the ramp, step up the incline into the truck, and make her way to the front end. Getting on and off the circus trucks was never optional for elephants. They did it and they did it on circus time. Handlers prodded them with bullhooks, yelled at them to keep moving and, if that didn't work, they whacked them—hard.

This time, Blais *asked* Billie to walk up the ramp. For once she had the freedom to think about her actions, to take her time. She had a choice in the matter. Blais had learned from experience to let go of any expectations and just let matters unfold as they would. This was Billie's day and he would heed to her schedule.

He stood back to see what Billie would do. Of all the elephants, she was the most distrustful, the most insecure. She might balk at the very thought of leaving the barn. She might even turn violent. One false step and Blais could have a disaster on his hands. But it occurred to him that Billie might also be curious about the trailer—that she might wonder what it was doing there and why she had been asked to step aboard. If the alternative was to remain in her Hawthorn pen, Blais thought, what animal wouldn't welcome the chance to escape by whatever means possible?

Blais had dealt with reluctant elephants before. In past rescues, the Sanctuary had gone so far as to park a trailer near an elephant for a month just so the elephant could grow comfortable around a vessel that size. But in the case of the Hawthorn elephants, any delay was risky. If Billie balked, Blais had a plan B: he would grasp the chain around her leg, wait for her to step forward, then carefully tighten the slack in the chain, offer Billie a treat and try to slowly build her trust. She could stand still forever if she chose, but if she did decide to move, her only choice would be to move forward.

Worst-case scenario, Blais could use a winch to take up the slack, a safety measure that would prevent Billie from slapping anyone's hands. But he didn't want to resort to that. Getting Billie to board the trailer on her own would send a powerful signal—that, starting right now, her life was going to be different. Not just different, but better. Better than she could ever remember it being. For the first time in your life, Blais wanted to tell Billie, *you* get to decide.

He called for Billie to come forward. She stepped out of the barn. The minute she laid eyes on the trailer she waved her trunk and began sniffing. She moved about slowly, lifting her trunk to feel the sides of the fences that lined either side of the walkway. An elephant's trunk is one of nature's most remarkable inventions. At three hundred pounds, it's powerful enough to hoist a person high in the air and dash him down on the ground, but also sensitive enough to grasp the tiniest of objects and relay all sorts of information back to its owner. Its pliable tip acts as both nose and hand. Billie was using her trunk to investigate everything about this new scenario.

Blais thought about how different her past road trips had been: tens of thousands of miles in dark chambers, anchored in place alongside a half-dozen other elephants. Blais wouldn't blame Billie if she never wanted to step foot inside a trailer again.

The elephant made her way to the trailer's back end. She brushed her trunk first on one side of the ramp and then the other. She glanced up inside the trailer as if to study its open and airy interior. She had to know that six other members of her herd had already left the barn. Surely she could detect their scents inside the semi.

"It's okay, Billie," Blais said to her. "You can do it."

Suddenly, without hesitating, she walked up the ramp and entered the semi. Slowly, deliberately, she continued down the length of the truck until she reached the front compartment. Then she turned and faced Blais as if to say, *Now what?*

Blais glanced at his watch. Fifteen minutes had passed. He'd been prepared to wait all day and the next to get Billie on board, and she'd finished the job in fifteen minutes. Maybe she sensed that this was no ordinary journey—that here was her chance to turn her back forever on her wretched past and start a new life. In spite of her fear, in spite of all her memories of traveling in chains, she'd demonstrated a remarkable measure of faith, a willingness to take a chance. Blais had asked her to climb on board, he'd told her she would be all right, and she had done as he had asked. It was as though she was saying back to him: *Okay, I'm going to trust you on that.*

The inside of the trailer was six feet wide and ten feet long, narrower than any compartment Billie had entered in quite some time. The semi was white and odorless and sparkled with cleanliness. Slatted vents the size of small windows allowed fresh air to flow in on either side. The truck radiated with heat, too. On this frigid February day, no blustery breezes sliced through corner cracks, no bone-chilling temperatures seeped up through worn-out wooden planks. Billie stood on cushioned, warm floors.

She had the front chamber all to herself. She watched as Blais now asked Frieda to step up the ramp. The smaller elephant did not hesitate. She climbed the ramp slowly and came to a stop in the middle of the rear compartment. A set of bars separated the two animals, nothing more. All that space for just two elephants.

Blais waited a few moments for the elephants to settle in. Then he worked his way up a protected aisleway on the right side of the trailer, knelt in front of Billie and took hold of the steel chain dangling from the bracelet clamped around her front left ankle. Quietly reassuring her, he slowly produced a pair of bolt cutters and clasped the tail part of the chain. He paused for a moment and then, heart pounding, he snapped that part of the chain in two. In one swift move he'd managed to lop off four of the eight feet. He could have snipped off more if he'd been able to get closer, but it was a start.

Billie watched him intently. She paced back and forth, up and down the ten-foot-long enclosure, testing her boundaries, what was left of her chain jangling beside her. She turned and once again glanced at Blais sideways with a look of concern, a look that said, *Don't push my limits.* But she seemed to also be registering the fact that no one had raised his voice to her or struck her from behind to force her inside. Blais had stood back and let Billie enter on her own time. Elephant time.

Blais ran down a final checklist with Hawthorn employees. It was midday when he climbed in the passenger side of the cab and Lambert pulled the tractor trailer out of the Hawthorn complex. The semi snaked its way on to Interstate 65, the CNN crew following behind. For the next seven hours the semi rumbled south through America's heartland, from Chicago to Indianapolis, stopping occasionally to feed and water the elephants.

"I don't think many folks at the truck stop in northern Indiana had any idea that when Blais was pulling a hose up to his truck, he was giving two elephants a nice big drink of water," CNN reporter Keith Oppenheim told viewers at one point.

Every couple of hundred miles Lambert pulled over so Blais could hop out and check on the elephants. The trailer had a large set of side doors, adjacent to Billie, that enabled Blais to work with them from the outside. He'd greet Billie first with soothing words and a treat: a couple of apples, a handful of peaches, a bunch of carrots, then make sure Frieda was doing well, too. If either animal had any fears about traveling, Blais wanted to quell them. But the elephants behaved calmly. To Blais's surprise, Billie seemed especially relaxed. She'd spent time in his company off and on for several weeks now and seemed to have sized him up as an ally, someone she could count on to treat her compassionately. Not once had she spied a bullhook in his hand.

A few miles north of the Kentucky-Tennessee border the driver pulled over for the night. Blais gave the elephants a final meal of the day of carrots, apples, bananas, and hay before he fell asleep a few feet away, propped against some hay bales at the front of the trailer. From time to time Billie and Frieda paced about. Shortly before seven o'clock the next morning Blais awoke, fed and watered the elephants, and then climbed into the cab next to Lambert for the last two hundred miles, bypassing Nashville and heading south. At noon they turned onto a gravel lane, negotiated a series of curves, then backed up. The truck moaned to a halt.

Word spread that the final truckload of elephants had arrived and the Sanctuary staff gathered to greet the new inhabitants. Blais was too exhausted to celebrate the milestone. For two weeks he'd been on the road, back and forth to Illinois, nearly 5,000 miles in all. He was bone tired. He wanted nothing more at that instant than a steamy shower and a single night's uninterrupted sleep in his own bed.

He stepped down from the cab, talked briefly with the staff, then strode to the back, unlatched the heavy metal doors and swung them open. The elephants stood silently. Blais beckoned to Frieda to disembark and she did so without any fuss. Moments later he returned for his final passenger. "Come on out, Billie," he said to her. "It's okay."

The elephant paused for a moment and flapped her ears. The tip of her trunk touched the inside wall of the trailer as if she debated whether to leave this clean, safe chamber. For the first time in her life she had ridden in a trailer with fresh air, plenty of room, and an abundance of hay and produce. But Blais was calling her to step out.

Carefully she moved backward, one enormous hind foot followed by the other. The four-foot-long chain hanging from her front leg clanged loudly against the metal floor as she made her way to the ramp.

"Very good. There you go," a second voice said.

Billie paused. She didn't recognize Carol Buckley's voice. "Take your time," Buckley said as Billie felt her way to the back of the truck. "What a *good girl*."

The elephant edged back the way she'd done so many times in her past. A gust of cold air gripped the tuft of hair at the end of her long tail, her leathery backside and finally her broad, impassive face. Once she stepped off the ramp she turned toward the barn and immediately stepped indoors again. Caregivers crowded nearby, clapping quietly, beaming. They didn't want to startle her, but the significance of the moment left them gulping with emotion. Billie had finally escaped her awful past. After decades of confinement she was about to experience a return to nature she could never have imagined.

She didn't know that, of course. All she knew was that she was standing in a warm building bathed in light, a barn filled with the aroma of fresh hay and the familiar smells of her fellow elephants. And next to her was the man with the soothing voice who had brought her to this new place. He was speaking to her now. She might not have understood what he was telling her, but she recognized the sound of her name, and the tone of his voice was clear.

"Billie," he was saying to her. "Welcome home."

BIG MARY'S TRAGIC FATE

If the victim of an elephant's wrath was a spectator or a zookeeper, the elephant usually paid with his life. But if the injured party was a mere bull man, circus owners tended to overlook the incident. It was easier to hire another roughneck than to replace a costly elephant.

Circuses typically had one groom for every two or three elephants; the men led the elephants back and forth to the lots, fed and bathed them, and shoveled their manure—about two hundred pounds a day for each elephant. It was hard, dangerous work and the men who filled those jobs were as rough as they came. When they weren't walloping elephants with bullhooks, they were apt to turn the weapons on each other. In the early days, circus owners were known to carry sturdy canes around the lot to whack handlers in the head just to remind them who was in charge. It wasn't uncommon to see a bull man lying in the dirt, bleeding and out cold.

Handler Red Eldridge suffered a far worse fate. Eldridge, a transient who rode the rails, signed on as a bull man with the Sparks Circus when it came through the tiny town of Saint Paul, Virginia, in the fall of 1916. Following its performance the circus traveled by train to Kingsport, Tennessee, its next stop. The circus had several cages of wild animals, camels, clowns, about a hundred and fifty horses, various human performers and five elephants. The star was Big Mary, billed as "the largest living land animal on earth, six inches taller than Jumbo" and weighing more than five tons. Mary's reputation for violence was just as big as her talent in the ring: she was said to have killed more than one person and as many as eighteen. But she was enormously popular. The circus claimed that she could play twenty-five tunes on the musical horns "without missing a note." The circus's climactic scene was a baseball game acted out by the elephants, with Mary in the leading role. The other elephants wore oversized uniforms, masks and gloves for their parts as pitcher, catcher, umpire, and fielders; Big Mary was the batter. The showstopper came when Mary gripped the bat with her trunk, connected with the ball (a stunt she almost always pulled off), and then ran from one base to another, finally sliding in to home.

After the performance, the circus paraded its participants down Center Street, intending to stop at the town pond so the animals could bathe and get a drink. Mary was leading the elephants single file when she spied a watermelon rind and stopped to check it out. The accounts of what happened next vary. According to the best-known version, Eldridge poked Mary to keep moving. When she ignored him he poked her harder—a fatal mistake. Mary hoisted up the novice with her trunk and hurled him against a wooden soft-drink stand. To show she meant business, she walked over to Eldridge and crushed his head with her front foot. Spectators began to flee. Mary backed away from the scene and the other four elephants, reacting to the chaos, began to trumpet frantically. Once the circus got the elephants under control the crowd amassed again, this time yelling: "Kill the elephant!"

The circus managed to hustle the animals onto the train and travel thirty-seven miles east to its next stop, the town of Erwin. By now rumors were rife that a lynch mob planned to lug a Civil War cannon out of retirement and aim it at Mary. If anyone was going to kill his lead elephant, Sparks decided, he would do it himself. At the following day's performance he announced that Mary would be hanged from a derrick car at the Clinchfield Railyards. A crowd of more than 2,500 gathered to watch the spectacle. Sparks walked the other four elephants down to the railyards, trunk to tail, behind Mary, supposedly to help calm her. Bull men draped a chain around Mary's neck and led the other elephants away. Authorities latched the boom of the crane to the chain and began to hoist Mary up. They'd barely raised her off the ground when the chain broke and she fell into a sitting position, breaking one of her hips. The crowd ran in fear until one of the locals sprinted up Mary's back and fastened a sturdier chain. The hanging succeeded the second time around. Sparks kept Mary dangling a good half hour before she was dropped into a grave the railroad had dug with a steam shovel several hundred feet down the tracks.

FIFTEEN

―+―⊨◈⊨―+―

THE START OF A NEW LIFE

Blais slumped with relief. It had taken years of years of wrangling with USDA, followed by weeks of schmoozing with John Cuneo's Hawthorn staff, to pull off this feat. But the struggle was worth it. The Sanctuary had landed eight new elephants at once—an unprecedented coup. Blais had postponed moving the least predictable of the animals until the very end and now, at last, Billie was here. Despite all the warnings, she hadn't given him a speck of trouble.

Blais followed from behind as Billie heeded Buckley's calming voice and maneuvered her massive bulk down a wide aisle inside the barn. In front of her was a giant set of scales. She stepped on them and paused long enough to let a caregiver record her weight: 8,450 pounds. Five of the Hawthorn elephants were playing in the creek when the truck arrived, but they quickly lined up along the fence to see what was happening. Billie stepped out into the barnyard and ambled over to the fence where Lottie, Minnie, Queenie, Ronnie, and Debbie greeted her with the kinds of caresses elephants bestow naturally in the wild, a swarm of touching Billie hadn't felt in decades.

If she was disoriented it was understandable. In the space of two days she had gone from a dim stall barely big enough to turn around in to a light and spacious barn with radiant-heated rubber floors to warm her feet and the sudden company of seven other elephants. Her longtime companion Sue was gone and Gypsy and Nicholas were missing (they eventually wound up at PAWS), but everyone else was here, and they were moving about freely. The only chain in sight was the one wrapped around Billie's left ankle, the one that jangled each time she took a step.

For the rest of that first day and night the Sanctuary staff put Billie and Frieda in separate stalls, careful not to overwhelm them. It was eight thirty the following morning, the sun peeking over the tree-covered hills, when two caregivers slid back an inside door, rolled in a cart brimming with vegetables, fruits, and grains and deposited the food in front of each stall. The elephants moved forward to start eating, and Billie immediately dug in. The caregivers waited another hour and then raised the slatted metal barn doors and beckoned the elephants outdoors into a chilly but luminous day.

Minnie and Lottie exited the barn right away. The first to arrive a week and a half earlier, they had already settled into a routine and were eager to investigate. Most of the elephants ambled after them, but Billie, Liz, and Frieda stayed behind. The Sanctuary was all about choice, about letting the elephants do what felt comfortable. If these girls preferred to stay inside, that was fine. Still, one of the caregivers tried to coax them outside into the barnyard. These animals needed to experience the wide-open sky. Discover the meadows and trees. Breathe in the unsullied air.

Frieda and Liz dawdled. They were thousands of pounds underweight and struggling with health problems: Liz had her partially paralyzed trunk and that infection on her right front foot, which caused her to limp slightly. Frieda was also hobbled by an infected foot. Perhaps they sensed a mutual vulnerability in each other. Or maybe it was just too cold outside. They huddled together, unwilling to explore. Billie, though, responded to the caregiver's encouragements. She followed her beneath the rolled-up metal door and out into the barnyard.

The chilly air may have stopped her. Or maybe it was the view. Before her spanned a gently curving meadow bordered by endless acres of forests, an ocean of green that stretched so far it seemed to blend into the sky. To her left, a pond the color of champagne glimmered in the morning light. In the distance she could see five of the Hawthorn elephants making their way down a dirt path toward the trees. The air smelled bracingly clean, the fresh scent of pine trees slicing through the cold. All around her was a calming stillness: no circus clangor, no announcers bellowing, no brassy music blaring. The only sounds piercing the air were the gentle voices of the caregivers and the chirps and whistles of the other elephants. Otherwise, sweet silence.

Overnight Billie's world had been transformed. Instead of a tiny corral barely large enough to turn around in, she would spend the rest of her life in a veritable Eden—two hundred acres of natural habitat filled with pine and hardwood forests, dirt trails to meander, ponds to soak in, and most of all, space. It was almost unimaginable, the vastness of space that was suddenly available to her. Space to wander, to lose herself in. Enough space to heal spiritually and reclaim her untamed self.

Billie seemed immobilized. She stared, unblinking, at the expanse of nature before her. Minutes passed as she drank in the view. Then she turned her back to the vista before her and faced the barn again. She milled about the barnyard the rest of the day, within sight of Frieda and Liz but some distance away from them. In the face of this brand-new world, she seemed to want the company only of herself.

Billie's behavior baffled her caregivers. Liz and Frieda were hanging back, but that was understandable; they weren't feeling well. But the rest of the elephants had assimilated right away. No one had to explain to them that, finally, here was a place where they could eat what they wanted, gather together with the companions of their choosing and decide for themselves how to while away their days.

Since arriving, Lottie had partially claimed the role of top elephant. Somber and unruffled, she acted as the Sanctuary's Welcome Wagon, greeting each elephant who arrived after her. Now that all eight elephants were there, Lottie had begun disappearing to some untrammeled part of the Sanctuary, then trumpeting for her friends to follow suit, and most of them did so.

Because she was Lottie's best friend, Minnie enjoyed the influential role of her daughter. Queenie dutifully tagged along behind Minnie and Lottie. Ronnie was animated and blessed with a voracious appetite. She was one of the first to bound up to a four-wheeler for a snack. She paired up with Debbie, one of the herd's youngest elephants. Caregivers dubbed the gregarious elephants the Fabulous Five and watched with relief as they bolted about in wonder, as if at any moment their newfound paradise might be snatched away. The elephants meandered down the dirt roads crisscrossing the property and vanished into thickets of trees in search of berries and branches. They ladled handfuls of dirt with their trunks and tossed them over their bodies, coating themselves to protect their wrinkly skin from insects and the sun. When rains came, the girls basked in the cool tingle of the pelting drops.

But Billie, Frieda, and Liz stayed close the barn, Billie at one end and Frieda and Liz at the other. The elephants' day began early, before 8 A.M., with a breakfast of vegetables, fruit, grain and dietary supplements delivered to each stall. Afterward came a warm water hose-down and, if necessary, a foot trim. In warmer weather Billie and the other elephants could choose to remain outside overnight; the caregivers would deliver their meals on a four-wheeler filled with hay and produce. But in winter months the animals spent their nights in the barn. At 9 A.M. caregivers raised the barn doors and the elephants were free to roam. As soon as the girls made their way into open pasture, the caregivers would head back to the barn to shovel manure and pressure-wash the floors and rubber mats. The remaining two meals of the day came much later: lunch was laid out at 6 P.M. and supper was delivered around 10:30 P.M., a smorgasbord of hay, mixed grains, vegetables, and fruit.

--- ❦ ---

That first couple of weeks the elephants behaved splendidly: they treated one another with respect and seemed to go out of their way to give each other a little space. They had plenty of room to explore. Wandering the Sanctuary grounds, they could supplement their meals with grass, leaves, branches, root plants, blueberries, blackberries, and persimmons. Unlike the African elephants one pasture over, these Asian girls were 2,000 pounds smaller and more docile. They genuinely appeared to enjoy one another's company.

No one was prepared when, a couple of weeks later, the honeymoon suddenly ended. The Fabulous Five were splashing about in the pond when two of them, Minnie and Lottie, suddenly teamed up to block Debbie from climbing out of the water. As Queenie and Ronnie ducked out of the way, Debbie tried to circle around her playmates and gain a foothold on the slippery bank. No sooner had she managed to pull herself out of the water than Minnie and Lottie followed her, and back on dry land they jostled her heatedly. Minutes later a caregiver motored up on a four-wheeler full of snacks, and the scuffle ended. But over the next several weeks, more clashes ensued. At the slightest provocation the elephants roared loudly, lifting their trunks in agitation. Often when caregivers passed near them, the girls would swing their trunks back and forth and kick their legs out menacingly. Inside the barn, a pair of elephants might hurl trunkfuls of hay and sticks across the room. The staff was taken aback by the meltdowns. The elephants seemed to be adjusting so well. What could possibly have gone wrong?

The elephants were mired in confusion. Always before, a new arrival to the Sanctuary would pair up with a long-term resident, an elephant accustomed to the open environment, who could introduce the newcomer to her new world and help her settle in. Housed separately from the rest of the Sanctuary herd, the Hawthorn elephants had no seasoned veteran to show them the ropes. They'd been cooped up for years, chained so tightly they had no chance to interact with one another. Now that they were unmoored, the girls weren't sure how to behave. They were free to express their euphoria, but they were also able—for the first time—to let vent the rage built up from all those years of captivity.

The elephants had plenty of anger to release, as it happened. The Sanctuary needed to separate them before they caused one another harm.

Billie shied away from her boisterous companions; the roughhousing unnerved her. She was especially frightened of Minnie, whose assertiveness frequently morphed into bullying when other elephants tried to deflect her invitations to play. Minnie and Debbie liked to single out Billie, and to get away from them she cowered in the trees. Blais was haunted by her guarded demeanor, that faraway look in her eyes. She was full of fear—such a difficult emotion to control and overcome.

For the next three months, Billie practically Velcroed herself to the outside wall of the barn. She could look down the verdant green pastures into the woods beyond, but she refused to venture out into them. Always, she kept to herself. It was as if she needed time to process all those memories, the years of traveling the highways in the back of a semi, of shifting her weight constantly to stay balanced. Gone were the cranked up sounds of rock and roll and the glaring lights that bore down on her when she entered the ring. Gone, too, were the handlers who didn't even like elephants—or, at least, didn't like her—who were forever pummeling her with their hands or their bullhooks.

At the Sanctuary, finally, Billie could cocoon herself in solitude. Even when she began to explore she went solo, tentatively investigating each downed branch she came across, each rock, each forested nook. As springtime neared, caregivers began to spot her at the crest of the nearest hill, standing alone amid the trees. Sometimes she busied herself collecting fallen hickory branches or rooting for berries. At other times she rested quietly in the dappled sunlight. The hilltop behind the barn became her favorite refuge. From her vantage point she could look down on the other elephants as they congregated in a loose circle, tossing dust on their backs and rubbing each other's trunks. As long as she was at a distance she could enjoy her companions' pursuits vicariously, without any emotional risk.

It's entirely possible that, in spite of the distance, Billie was communicating with the other elephants. Elephants chirp, squeak, and roar, using a series of vocalizations the rest of the world can hear. But they also rely on low-frequency rumbles—sounds produced by expelling air over their lungs, causing the vocal cords to vibrate, audible for several miles, but only to other elephants. Elephants also use the tips of their trunks to pick up low-frequency vibrations. In the wild the seismic signals likely tell them if another herd is fleeing a water hole, which might mean that predators are lurking, or that authorities are culling another herd. Or, in the case of Billie, that Minnie was getting close.

Some days, if Billie could see Minnie from the barnyard, she would escape up the hill and hide. The staff erected a hot wire to protect the elephants inside the barnyard, but one day Minnie took the hot wire down and she and Lottie entered the yard where Billie stood. Billie opened her mouth and let out a roar so loud it sounded prehistoric. The staff dubbed it her dino roar. Minnie left Billie alone that day, but the mere fact that she was in close proximity had Billie petrified.

There were unexpected delights, too. In midspring, Billie discovered the pond, a muddy four-foot-deep watering hole a hundred feet from the barn. She ambled down the bank, waded in and dunked her head. It had been years since she had savored the luxury of immersing herself entirely in a body of water. Caregivers watched as she suddenly hoisted her trunk out of the murky pond and showered her face with a forceful spray. She plopped down in a sitting position, dipped her trunk into the water and thrust it out again. Over and over she submerged her trunk, in and out, in and out. She seemed mesmerized. Despite the cold temperatures she spent hours amusing herself in the pond's shallow depths.

The pond quickly became her favorite destination. On good days, Billie might race into the pond, spank the water vigorously with her trunk, then tear out, dripping wet, toward the sand pile, then return to the pond again. She would sit on her hind end while Angela Sherrill, a caregiver, sprayed her with a hose, catching the water in her trunk. One afternoon a Sanctuary "ele-cam" captured Billie dashing from the pond to a gate, which she banged open and shut over and over, reveling in her own little symphony.

The big grassy field beyond the barnyard was more intimidating. Months passed before Billie worked up the nerve to venture out into it. Even after Liz and Frieda started to explore the large pasture, Billie would accompany them a short way and then head back to the barn. "She was not okay being away from those girls and she was *not* okay being first," Sherrill recalled. The day Billie meandered out into the sprawling pasture—her big butterball self a good hundred yards from the barnyard—was a milestone. Sherrill watched her, stunned.

At forty-four, her skin was a bit lighter in color than her herd-mates', almost silver, and her ears had unusually scalloped edges. She was heavy-built, a tank. Her big round belly swooped so close to the ground the staff nicknamed her Low Rider. More than anything, she was the lonely elephant, apart from the herd. Some days she was so reluctant to come back down from the top of a hill that at night a couple of caregivers would fan out, scanning the woods with flashlights, to try to sweet-talk her into returning to the barn. They could have let Billie stay outside, but they felt bad about leaving her out there, glued in place by fear. Left in the wild, she would have spent her days close by her matriarchal family. It didn't seem right that she would feel so ill at ease in the company of the other elephants.

Summer finally arrived. Middle Tennessee's rising temperatures and humidity ushered in long, warm days and gradually Billie began to settle in. She now sought out the company of Frieda and Liz. Caregivers soaked Liz's foot in apple cider vinegar, a treatment that had remedied other elephants' infections, and weeks of extra servings of grains and hay strengthened the underfed elephants: in a matter of weeks Liz gained 500 pounds and Frieda added a whopping 800 pounds to her once-gaunt frame. The real chowhound, though, was Billie. She came running at mealtime, her front legs galloping in front of her, her hind legs bouncing along like humongous pogo sticks. Bananas were her favorite treat. She'd wrap her trunk around a bunch at a time and gulp them, peels and all, her enormous molars making quick work of the mushy, pliable fruit. She couldn't seem to get enough food—she ate anything that was put in front of her. The rest of the elephants got by on 150 pounds of food a day. Billie devoured 200 pounds.

She continued to trek up the hill by herself, but in time she cut short her solitary sojourns and moseyed back down to graze alongside Frieda and Liz. There's a saying that when it comes to elephants, two is company and three is a crowd, but Liz and Frieda seemed accepting of Billie's presence. One afternoon a couple of the staff spied all three elephants frolicking in the pond, splashing about with complete abandon. Billie had managed to lure Liz and Frieda beyond their comfort zone to her treasured watering hole. Blais was thrilled. The elephants were bonding, developing the kind of closeness necessary to restore their emotional health, just as he'd hoped they would do.

Gradually Billie began to relax around some of the other Hawthorn elephants. Two of them, Ronnie and Lottie, approached her one afternoon and whiled away several hours in her company, and their presence did not jar her the way it once would have. Despite her trepidation, she even appeared to enjoy the attention of caretakers. Weeks passed without a hint of hostile behavior from this so-called dangerous elephant. Far from being aggressive, Billie seemed more like a four-ton teddy bear—frightened of many things, most of all the humans around her. For so much of her life, Billie had been manhandled regardless of how she behaved. "If she blinked they would hit her," Blais said. "If she breathed they would hit her." The attitude toward Billie was "if you so much as breathe before you're told to, you're going to get smacked. She just wasn't given any slack."

Little wonder she'd lost any ability to trust the people around her. She was too busy waiting for the other shoe to drop. She seemed to be asking: *Are you being nice to bait me into something? Are you coaxing me over to follow up with something negative?*

Frieda and Liz were different. Billie could shower on them all the affection she'd withheld for so long. Former caregiver Kat Haselau was struck by the look on Billie's face when she was in the company of Frieda and Liz. "She has one of the sweetest, softest smiles I've ever seen on an elephant," Haselau recalled. "It was always when she was with her sisters. It was never during any human interaction. When she saw Liz or Frieda and she would run over to them, her eyes would get super-soft."

Beneath Billie's foreboding was a playful animal who yearned to communicate. Blais was sure of it. He'd glimpsed it inside the Hawthorn barn in Illinois when Billie had chirped to him late at night, after her handlers had gone for the day. At the Sanctuary, Billie could act guarded and wary one minute then suddenly start squeaking and rumbling with pleasure. Billie epitomized fear-based insecurity, the kind that could lead to aggression.

The Sanctuary's nurturing atmosphere had never failed to turn a neglected elephant around. It was conceivable, Blais supposed, that Billie might prove to be too damaged emotionally to blossom. But he refused to dwell on the possibility. It was too upsetting.

He decided to act cautiously around Billie, to let Billie set the tone for their encounters, and his willingness to give her space began to pay off. One day about a month after her arrival she watched from a distance as Blais set out into the pasture to deliver an afternoon treat. For a moment Billie turned away from him, as if she were debating whether it was safe to follow. Eventually she worked up the nerve to catch up to Blais, the clanking chain around her ankle announcing her approach. Her appetite trumped her shyness.

Every once in a while she also consented to let Blais pat her quickly on her trunk or her forehead. Her comfort level fluctuated from day to day, even from hour to hour. Billie's mood could reverse itself based on factors that might seem subtle, even invisible, to the humans around her. The changes weren't subtle to Billie.

Inside the barn she would lean into the steel-slatted wall of her stall and let Blais scratch her trunk from the other side of the bars. Encouraged by her growing tolerance, Blais began stopping by Billie's stall in the morning, reaching between the slats of the steel wall and scratching a tiny patch of the wrinkled, gray skin on the other side. "Lean in, Billie," he murmured. "Lean in." The first time he tried it, the elephant shifted her weight and rested into the wires and Blais praised her for cooperating. "*Good girl.*" Still scratching her with his right hand, he circled his left hand through a slat and delivered a carrot to Billie's trunk. He tried it again. Once more, Billie leaned into the fence at Blais's instruction, and once more he rewarded her.

All this time, Billie had been too timid to let caregivers get close. Of all the elephants at the Sanctuary, she'd suffered the deepest emotional hurt. Her heart had clamped shut. Now, finally, she was starting to connect, to understand that it was okay to let herself trust the soothing voice on the other side, to relax into the tender scratches. Once the elephant let go of her fears, Blais hoped to accomplish something he'd been yearning to do: remove the dull steel chain adorning Billie's front ankle.

The third time Blais tried to coax Billie into leaning, though, her demeanor changed; she stepped away from the fence and turned to face him dead on. *Don't try to be nice to me,* she seemed to be saying. *I won't fall for it.* She avoided him after that and Blais, determined to respect her wishes, stopped trying to make contact. In the only way she knew how, Billie was telling him to back off. She didn't trust anyone to reward her without expecting something in return. The elephant's misgivings were too pervasive, the psychological damage too deep. In spite of everything Blais had done to win her over, Billie was clearly telling him, *No, you'll just have to earn it more.*

THE SHORT LIFE OF BABY HUTCH

The first American-bred baby elephant was Hutch, born in 1912 to a Sells-Floto Circus elephant named Alice. Hutch was twenty-eight inches high with a foot-long trunk and covered with coarse black hair. His mother tried repeatedly to lunge at him, so his handlers took him away and fed him with a bottle. Twice a day they put Hutch in the circus's former glass "snake den." While the band played "Mammy's Lullaby," another elephant pushed the cage around the Hippodrome track wearing a blanket that said "This is my baby!"

Audiences loved the tiny elephant. Baby Hutch generated $1,000 a day for Sells-Floto. Ringling Bros. got wind of the stunt and ordered six elephant baby buggies to outdo the competition. But on a trip to California, the stock car next to Hutch's private rail car caught fire, filling his car with smoke. When the engineer slammed on the emergency brakes, Hutch was thrown from one end of the car to the other. The damage to his lungs and his bruised body were too much: he died shortly before noon, malnourished and just six weeks old. The circus had him stuffed and continued to display his taxidermied self in the snake den.

◄ ◆►

SIXTEEN

THE CONUNDRUM WITH ZOOS

T he idea seemed laughable, even to officials at other zoos: To provide a means of exercise for its only elephant, Maggie, the Alaska Zoo in Anchorage installed a $100,000 custom-made treadmill. One big enough to accommodate Maggie's 9,120 pounds.

Orphaned when her herd in Zimbabwe was culled, Maggie had spent twenty-four years at the zoo, in a climate often so dark and cold—a complete contrast to her native land—that she was forced to spend much of her time indoors. Moreover, she spent it alone. She'd lost her only elephant companion eight years earlier, when Annabelle died of a foot infection at the age of thirty-three.

The zoo recognized that Maggie needed better care, so it doubled her indoor and outdoor space, replaced her concrete floor with radiant floor heating, hoisted feeding stations high up so she would have to reach up for her food, and hid treats for her to track down. The extra activities and a new diet helped her trim a thousand pounds. But the treadmill was a no-go. Maggie refused to use it. Critics demanded the zoo give up trying and send Maggie to a sanctuary instead, saying "America's Ice Box" was no place for an elephant.

The battle over Maggie's fate was exactly the kind of public relations debacle the zoo world did not need. For two decades activists had protested living conditions for elephants in captivity, saying the intensely confined conditions were causing debilitating foot disease and arthritis, problems with infertility, and acute psychological distress from being swapped around from zoo to zoo and stuck in small spaces with nothing to do.

Zoos had come a long way from the early days, when animals were captured from the wild, often brutally, and kept in barren cages. They'd moved beyond the windowless concrete buildings that could easily be bleached and hosed off (preventing the spread of disease). Zoos began to create exhibits that looked more natural, giving spectators at least the sense that they were watching animals in the wild.

But animal lovers were just starting to turn up the heat. Groups like PETA and In Defense of Animals protested the stringent routine zoos imposed on elephants when it came to meals, baths, and checkups. Even if their enclosures looked more natural, elephants were still being denied the simple pleasures of foraging for twigs and leaves, stripping bark off of trees and carrying branches around in their mouths, the kinds of activities they would engage in on the savanna or in the jungle. Zoos couldn't begin to provide elephants the rich social life they would have experienced in the wild, and their enclosures offered a fraction of the space that would enable an elephant to exercise properly. Elephants needed to be able to walk at least seven miles a day.

Male elephants suffered the most in zoos because they are powerful, unsafe, and extremely fickle, and tend to roam solo in the wild—which means that, in zoos, they have to be kept isolated. "They end up living in miserable conditions," Catherine Doyle of In Defense of Animals said.

Many elephant keepers adored their elephants and worked tirelessly, and at very low pay, to care for the animals and try to give their lives some meaning. But interacting side by side with an elephant works only if the elephant understands that the humans are in charge. Handlers often resorted to beating the elephants to drive that message home.

The campaign to improve the lives of zoo elephants started in earnest in 1988. That year, trainers transferred a nineteen-year-old elephant named Dunda from the San Diego Zoo, where she'd spent most of her life, to the Wild Animal Park, where they hoped to breed her. When Dunda acted out in her new setting, zookeepers conducted "disciplinary" sessions in a barn, according to reports, chaining the elephant, bringing her to her knees and striking her relentlessly about the head with axe handles in several sessions over two days. One keeper described the blows as "home-run swings." Leading the sessions was elephant superintendent Alan Roocroft, who was a big believer in corporal punishment. He co-wrote a manual, *Managing Elephants,* in which he explained that disciplining needed to be "fairly forceful"—solid blows delivered with a "fairly heavy implement."

"The handling of problem elephants requires a well-drilled team, a crew of at least eight, preferably ten, in order to ensure sufficient muscle," Roocroft wrote.

Later, at a public hearing over the matter, he defended Dunda's punishment, saying her head was only superficially damaged and her skin was never broken. He said the serrated chunks of peeling hide were caused by cracks that developed as the result of swollen bruises, that Dunda was now socializing well in the herd and that the beating was "the most effective way to bring a violent animal under control." But elephant keeper Lisa Landres, who'd spent a decade caring for Dunda, said that when she spied the elephant after the beating, Dunda's head was so swollen and she had so many gaping wounds that Landres didn't recognize her. A veterinarian told Landres the beating was the worst he had ever seen.

USDA fined and reprimanded the San Diego Zoo over its treatment of Dunda. The Association of Zoos and Aquariums, a private, nonprofit accrediting organization financed by member dues, decided against citing the zoo for any ethics violations, but formed a task force to study the handling of elephants.

Soon afterward, a video surfaced showing trainers at the Milwaukee Zoo using block and tackle and bullhooks to teach an elephant named Annie to lie down and roll over on her side for baths. An anonymous whistle-blower leaked the video and animal lovers were outraged at the sight of the twenty-nine-year-old elephant writhing and bellowing as trainers dug their bullhooks into her legs and back. As result of the furor, the zoo retired Annie and another elephant, Tamara, to Pat Derby's PAWS sanctuary in California.

It took more than a decade, but in 2001 the AZA came forth with guidelines for handling elephants, which in part limited excuses for striking them. A keeper could hit an elephant on the side of a leg to get it to move, the AZA said, but physical discipline was forbidden. Yet most zoos continued to handle their elephants using free contact, absent any barrier between handlers and elephants. The very nature of that system requires keepers to dominate an elephant every moment, using negative reinforcement to remind the elephant who is boss. (What's more, the free contact system is unquestionably dangerous: Since 1990, elephants in accredited zoos have seriously injured twenty-three keepers and killed six.)

The AZA's new policy did not apply to the thousands of non-accredited wildlife exhibitors in the United States. Absent enough federal investigators to monitor minimal standards for treatment of elephants, those elephant owners could do as they damn well pleased, as the Humane Society of the United States' Richard Farinato put it.

Disciplining zoo elephants was one controversy. There was also the matter of their feet. All that walking on hard surfaces was having a deleterious effect on their spongy soles. Federal agencies took note of the depressing statistics and began to cut back on the number of elephants zoos could import into the States. With the help of a crisis-management firm, the AZA launched a public relations campaign asserting that zoo elephants were in fact flourishing. The organization blasted animal welfare groups as extremists and commissioned polls showing the public supported zoos' elephant programs. Proponents claimed that zoo elephants actually were safer and healthier than elephants in the wild because they didn't have to trek for miles during dry months in search of water and food or compete for sustenance; wild elephants were sometimes poisoned or electrocuted for trampling villagers' crops, or they were shot to death for their ivory. Calves born in the wild faced the very real risk of being orphaned, and when that happened they frequently died unless humans interceded, the AZA said.

Don Moore, the National Zoo's then-associate director of animal care sciences, argued that animals in zoos had great lives: regular food, social management, no diseases or parasites, no predators and plenty of food. "If I'm an animal, I guess I'd rather be in a zoo, where I'm a lot more comfortable," he said.

The pushback worked. Legislation to ban elephants from zoos in Chicago later died and efforts to curtail elephants in captivity in California and El Paso, Texas, were similarly shot down.

Still, criticism kept mounting. In Defense of Animals began issuing a list of Top Ten Worst Zoos in America. (One of them was Southwick's Zoo, where an elephant named Dondi danced, gave rides to children, and spent time in a barren exhibit absent the company of other elephants until she died at thirty-six.) Even former zoo officials joined the criticism. In a letter to the editor of the *Los Angeles Times,* Les Schobert, a retired curator of animals at the L.A. Zoo who worked with elephants for more than thirty years, wrote that "unless elephants can be kept in a way that addresses their spatial, social and psychological needs, there is no ethical basis for keeping them in zoos."

For three years in the early 1980s, the South African government had permitted 3,200 elephants to be slaughtered and their
calves captured and shipped overseas. Schobert acquired a number of the calves for his zoo, but he felt terrible about it. "The
only way you could do it was to kill the mother first," he recalled
later. "You couldn't get a baby elephant away from its mother in
any other way." One-fourth to one-third of the babies died within
four months of arriving in the United States.

David Hancocks, a zoo consultant and former director of the
Woodland Park Zoo in Seattle, also experienced a change of
heart. Zoos really hadn't changed much from the old days, Hancocks said. The natural-looking habitats were "just an illusion
created to enhance the visitors' experience," he said. "From the
animals' point of view they are no better than they were when
they were in cages. It's all done for theatrics."

In 2006, USDA's Animal and Plant and Health Inspection
Service sought advice from the public on how to counter foot disease in captive elephants, which was killing them. One of them
was an Asian elephant named Toni, who had been brought from
the wild to the National Zoo in Washington, D.C. Her feet became so cracked and infected from standing on concrete that she
lost more than 900 pounds and had to be euthanized at the age
of thirty-nine. At the Oregon Zoo, an elephant named Pet suffered such severe degenerative joint disease that she was forced to
wear sandals and use her trunk to support her weight. The zoo
put her down at the age of fifty-one.

Reluctant to have the federal government tell it what to do, the
AZA drew up its own set of guidelines. Member zoos needed to
build bigger barns to house their elephants and also provide them
company, or else get out of the elephant business altogether. By
June 2010, eighteen zoos across the country had closed their exhibits or announced plans to shut them down. Others decided to
invest in larger exhibits. The Oregon Zoo in Portland passed a

$125 million bond issue measure to expand its elephant habitat. Cleveland's Metroparks Zoo opened its new African Elephant Crossing. St. Louis Zoo cut the ribbon on its own ballyhooed exhibit.

The changes have made some difference. The Phoenix, Arizona, zoo's three elephants previously quarreled so much they had to be separated, which meant that only one elephant was visible to the public at a time. Visitors assumed the zoo had only one elephant because they never saw the other two. With the help of Alan Roocroft (the same consultant who advocated corporal punishment for elephants), the zoo stopped feeding the elephants in bulk and instead installed elevated feeders that enabled the elephants to browse leisurely. The zoo added a two-foot layer of sand to the floor of the holding area, created a new wallow and scratching post and sandstone boulders for the elephants to rub themselves against. Large mounds of dirt were brought in to create barriers the elephants could walk around. The zoo stopped having the elephants perform front and hind leg stands for visitors and instead exercised the animals by having them walk from one part of the exhibit to the other. The zoo also instituted a better standard of foot care.

The AZA's new standards require member zoos to provide at least 600 square feet indoors each for male elephants, 400 square feet each for females, and 5,400 square feet outdoors for each elephant. Some elephant exhibits now vastly exceed that amount. The Oakland Zoo has set aside six acres for its fifteen elephants. The Oklahoma Zoo's Asian elephant zoo exhibit is the largest in the country, with 9.5 acres of elephant yards, a demonstration pavilion, a barn with eight stalls, and a common area covered with sand. The exhibit is fourteen times the size of the elephants' old enclosure, big enough to hold six elephants. Zookeepers can suspend food and games from the pavilions, the elephants have old tree trunks to play with and new areas to explore.

Yet sometimes even when a zoo spends a lot of money on a new exhibit, there isn't much to show for it, at least for the elephants. In 2012 the Denver Zoo opened a $50 million Toyota Elephant Passage, a ten-acre habitat that winds around other exhibits housing hippos, rhinos, tapirs, and gibbons. Steel-cable fencing enables visitors to see the elephants meandering two miles of paths, an aerial bridge, and a series of channels and pools. But the elephants aren't free to wander the entire exhibit: before they can move from one area to another, a zookeeper must open one or more gates. And the elephants derive no pleasure from the battered hut outside the exhibit that replicates the damage an elephant can cause. One newspaper said the special effects felt like a miniature golf course.

Woodland Park's exhibit in Seattle consists of a single acre for three elephants. The Honolulu Zoo's new $12 million exhibit is 1.4 acres for two elephants—seventeen times the size of its old one, but not nearly big enough, advocates say, when you consider that female elephants have to be kept separate from the males. Nearly half of the forty-plus elephants born in zoos since 2004 are male.

In 2010 the National Zoo opened phase one of a much-heralded $52 million exhibit: a 5,700-square-foot barn, a quarter-mile-long walkway through trees and two new yards, one of which has a pool. The changes were huge for the elephants, especially sixty-two-year-old Ambika, who had spent decades in the zoo's old elephant house. But a former zoo curator, Peter Stroud, was dismayed to see that the new exhibit offered a total of just 1.9 acres for its four elephants. Stroud saw broad green lawns and a shallow-looking pool, but little shade or shelter, no piles of loose earth or sand for the elephants to wallow in, no scratching posts, boulders, or logs that could entertain the inhabitants. A new indoor area does offer some enrichment. But the zoo's walking trail is paved with asphalt—the very kind of hard surface that has proven so detrimental to elephants' feet.

The Dallas Zoo faced a particularly vexing challenge with its African elephant Jenny, who arrived after years of performing for and being abused by a circus. After twenty-two years at the zoo, she still suffered from depression and post-traumatic stress disorder. She crashed her head into walls and mutilated herself with her tusks. Zookeepers had to sedate her heavily. Weary of handling her, the zoo announced plans to pass Jenny off to a wildlife park in Mexico. When animal-welfare activists decried the move as an abandonment of a suffering animal, the zoo thought better of its plans. It kept Jenny, brought in a companion for her, Gypsy, and began upgrading its exhibit. The zoo opened a $40 million Giants of the Savanna habitat and added four female African elephants to join Jenny and Gypsy.

The new exhibit boasts a 10,000-square-foot elephant house with padded, heated floors and a communal area with a seven-feet-deep floor of sand. Outside is a six-acre meadow with man-made "wobble trees" that can drop down food when elephants rub up against them. The elephants can shower any time they like by pulling a shower cord. A second cord wets down children visiting the zoo on the other side of the fence. Jenny slowly began to get used to her new companions and within a year she was spending 90 percent more time exploring her environment. Yet she still suffers from PTSD and probably always will.

At the Los Angeles Zoo, Billy, a twenty-five-year-old Asian male, had spent nearly his entire life isolated in a small enclosure, beaten with bullhooks and subjected to hot shots by his keepers. Advocates sued the zoo on Billy's behalf. In the meantime, the city council authorized a $42 million new six-acre elephant exhibit and moved in two female elephants, Tina and Jewel. They were the first elephants Billy had laid eyes on in four years. The lawsuit still went to court. In a 2012 decision, L.A. Superior Court Judge John L. Segal said he found no evidence that zookeepers were abusing the elephants, but in spite of the improvements, it was clear Billy and his comrades were "neither thriving, happy, nor content." The judge said he found it especially troubling that the senior elephant keeper tried to dismiss Billy's head-bobbing as a sign of contentment. The judge ordered the zoo to exercise the elephants at least two hours a day and rototill the ground they walked on to avert foot injuries.

With the number of captive elephants on the decline—by 2013, just 288 elephants lived at seventy-eight accredited facilities in the United States—zoos have turned their focus to breeding. Zoos used to mate elephants the old-fashioned way, but that's expensive and risky. Clyde Hill, the former curator of mammals for the San Diego Zoo, once wrote that he lay awake at night troubled by the very real danger of bringing in a male elephant experiencing musth to mate with the zoo's female elephants. "I am worried about keepers and other people being hurt or killed and male elephants are so destructive to themselves, breaking tusks and battering themselves about," Hill wrote in a 1975 letter to elephant enthusiast Chang Reynolds. "So far I am having a hard time convincing (the board) of the seriousness of the problem and the necessity of building humane and safe quarters."

The modern-day solution involves taking blood samples of a zoo's elephants, collecting semen, and attempting to artificially inseminate the females, something AZA members are required to do. Nothing about this is natural. The Woodland Park Zoo spent two years conducting mock artificial inseminations on its elephant Chai by putting her in short chains—tethering her so tightly she could barely move—and inserting a lengthy hose into her reproductive tract. When elephant sperm finally arrived, the zoo inseminated Chai ninety-one times over four years, often twice a day. She failed to get pregnant, so in 1998 the zoo trucked Chai two thousand miles to the Dickerson Park Zoo in Springfield, Missouri, to be bred there. Normally timid and bashful,

Chai turned rebellious at her new home, and witnesses reported seeing handlers beat her repeatedly over two days. The USDA fined the zoo $5,000 over the beating. Chai's problems weren't just with her handlers. The rest of the herd bullied her, even biting off the tip of her tail. Handlers tranquilized her to get her to calm down.

Artificial insemination racks up more misses than hits. More than half of the resulting pregnancies have ended in miscarriages and stillbirths. And mother elephants kept in zoos often reject their newborns or even kill them. (By contrast, infanticide almost never happens outside of captivity. Researchers at the highly regarded Amboseli Trust for Elephants in Kenya, a nonprofit research and conservation concern, observed 1,500 elephant births in the wild, and not once did they witness a mother rejecting or killing her baby.) To protect a baby from injury, zookeepers typically chain all four of the mother's legs, sometimes days or even weeks in advance, and remove the calf immediately from her reach the moment it is born.

Chai finally succeeded in getting pregnant, but the price was high: she brought the elephant herpes virus back with her to Seattle. To the heartbreak of Seattle-ites, her beloved calf, Hansa, died of the virus at the age of six.

In a groundbreaking series published in 2012, *The Seattle Times* found that the infant mortality rate for elephants in zoos is a whopping 40 percent, almost triple the rate among wild elephants. The herpes virus has surfaced in a dozen zoos, spread as zoos have loaned elephants back and forth to attempt to produce calves. Experts don't know how the disease is transmitted and blood tests don't reveal its existence; calves may be at greater risk of contracting the virus because their immune systems aren't yet fully developed. The virus comes on quickly, infecting the cells lining the blood vessels and causing internal bleeding. Victims die mere days or weeks after their veins collapse. The only treatment is prevention—medications and a daily inspection of a calf's tongue to make sure the baby is not suffering an attack.

Even after she gave birth to Hansa, Chai continued to be artificially inseminated. By December 2011, the thirty-two-year-old elephant had undergone the procedure 112 times.

Baby elephants that somehow survive the odds aren't exactly home free. The *Times* discovered that Lily, a baby elephant born at the Oregon Zoo in 2012, in fact belonged to Have Trunk Will Travel, a California company that rents elephants out for entertainment, commercials, and private parties. In exchange for using the siring services of Tusko, a male elephant owned by Have Trunk Will Travel, the zoo agreed to give the company the second, fourth, and sixth babies born to the zoo's Rose-Tu. Have Trunk Will Travel, owned by Gary and Kari Johnson—the stepdaughter of trainer Smokey Jones—has a history of using chains, bullhooks, and electrical hot shots on its six elephants, even its star, Tai, who portrayed an abused elephant in the 2011 movie *Water for Elephants*. A videotape secretly shot for the animal-welfare group Animal Defenders International seven years earlier showed handlers striking the elephants hard and subjecting Tai to a hot shot as she attempted a headstand. The Johnsons said the footage was taken out of context but didn't deny what the videotape showed.

The outcry over Lily pressured the zoo into buying the elephant and her father, Tusko, from the Johnsons for a sum of $400,000. But the Oregon Zoo wasn't the first to do business with Have Trunk Will Travel. The Los Angeles Zoo turned two calves over to the company, which wound up handing them off to a third party. Several of the twenty-eight calves born at the Oregon Zoo were also sold to circuses.

The *Times* also analyzed 390 elephant deaths at accredited zoos in the United States over the last half century and identified the culprit as long-running foot problems caused by standing on hard surfaces and musculoskeletal illnesses associated with having been confined for days, even weeks on end. The elephants in question should have lived to be fifty or sixty years old. Instead, nearly half had succumbed by the time they were twenty-three.

Zoos are still trying to upgrade their image. Seventy-three accredited zoos have collaborated to create a National Elephant Center in Fellsmere, Florida, a hundred miles southeast of Orlando, where aging elephants and elephants who have been passed from one zoo to another will be able to spend time. It's unclear how sanctuary-like the center will actually be. Officials have said they won't use bullhooks there, but the original site for the facility was moved from St. Lucie County, Florida, after local authorities stipulated that the use of bullhooks would be banned.

The AZA has also given its members until 2016 to stop working in the same space as their elephants, meaning that, unless they're administering medical procedures or breeding the animals, handlers must separate themselves from their elephants by mean of bars or other restraints. Zoos in San Antonio, Texas; Detroit, Michigan; Ashboro, North Carolina; and Oakland, California already use protected contact, relying on positive rewards to entice their elephants into cooperating—otherwise the animals are free to simply walk away. But many zoos that claim to have converted to the new system continue to use bullhooks, which means the old system of human dominance still rules. The Elephant Managers Association, an organization comprising zoo and circus keepers, has gone on record in favor of continuing to work around elephants absent any barriers.

Every now and then a hopeful story emerges. Maggie, the elephant who refused to step on her treadmill in Alaska, finally got a reprieve from her cold and lonely existence. In the fall of 2007 the zoo bowed to protests and let her go. Maggie was crated up, flown to California, and trucked to the PAWS sanctuary, where she spent her first day taking a long, hot bath, dusting herself, eating treats, and exploring the wide open meadows of her new home. She ended the day with a loud trumpet, and in the years since has bonded nicely with her new family. The Sanctuary expects her to enjoy her relative freedom for many years to come.

THE PLIGHT OF ZIGGY

One of America's most famous elephants was Ziggy, a male born around 1917, who was first owned by Ringling Bros., then by Broadway impresario Florenz Ziegfeld, who purchased the elephant for his son. Eventually Ziggy was sold to the Singer Midgets, where he learned to play "Yes Sir, That's My Baby" on the harmonica, smoke a cigarette from a long holder, and dance on a steel drum.

After Ziggy escaped from a new handler, the circus sold him to Chicago's Brookfield Zoo. He'd been there five years when he attacked his keeper, Slim Lewis, and nearly killed him. Lewis implored the zoo to spare the elephant. Instead Ziggy was sentenced to a concrete bunker by himself. For three decades he was chained in solitary confinement in a thirty-five-by-fifty-foot stall, without even a window to break the monotony.

Lewis defended Ziggy's cell as spacious, with floors designed to accommodate an elephant and big skylights that kept his stall "as bright and cheerful as the out-of-doors." But in 1969, after the *Chicago Tribune* revealed Ziggy's plight—the fact that his six-foot tusks were now broken and decayed and that he spent his days facing a wall, his back to visitors who threw food at him—readers demanded that Ziggy be allowed to go outside.

The zoo began raising money for an outside enclosure. But first, the zoo gave Ziggy a test run. Keepers installed a wooden ramp from his stall to the outdoor yard. Lewis spread a pitchfork full of Ziggy's dung just outside the door to his stall, and beyond that he scattered a bushel basket full of fresh carrots, bananas, and apples. But the elephant was too timid to leave his concrete cell. He approached the open doorway, reached out his trunk and hesitated.

"Go on, Ziggy, go on outside," Lewis called to him.

Several times the elephant stepped forward at Lewis's encouragement, only to retreat. Half an hour passed. Lewis felt defeated. Instead of urging Ziggy to step forward, the trainer commanded him to come. "Pick up your foot, Ziggy, pick up your foot," Lewis told him.

Ziggy did as he was told. He stepped up onto the ramp, walked down it and seconds later appeared in the bright sunlight. As news cameras flashed, the massive elephant strolled over to a wall of rocks at one end of the yard, scratched his shoulder against one of the boulders, and reached up with his trunk to grab a handful of grass. When a reporter asked Lewis how it felt to see Ziggy outdoors again, the trainer's eyes welled with tears.

For the next four years Ziggy remained a big attraction at the zoo. He also remained volatile. In the spring of 1975, while temporarily housed in his old enclosure, he stretched out across an empty moat to try to strike a keeper on the other side, lost his footing, and fell headfirst into the eight-foot-deep ravine. He lay on his side for hours before the zoo brought in a tow truck with a chain strong enough to attach around the back of his head and his front legs. The winch slowly hoisted Ziggy high enough to let him stand on his front legs, but he was still stuck in the moat. The following morning his rescuers created an incline of gravel—1,580 wheelbarrows full—so Ziggy could walk out of the moat on his own. But the blow he'd suffered from his fall eventually caught up with him. A few months later his appetite diminished and he began losing weight. He died at the age of fifty-eight.

SEVENTEEN

SPOTLIGHT ON ABUSE

By the mid-1980s, animal welfare groups had ramped up their scrutiny of circuses' treatment of wild animals, especially elephants. Organizations collected whistle-blower accounts, taped undercover videos, and chronicled incidents of circus elephant abuse—of handlers striking elephants with bullhooks, brooms and pitchforks, even pinching baby elephants with pliers. Activists urged circus-goers to understand that the only reason elephants scrunched their feet up on tubs and stood on their heads was because they were frightened and intimidated into performing—and that the majority of their lives were spent riding in the backs of semis and/or chained in place. That animals as regal as elephants deserved a better life than circuses could give them.

The protests made some inroads. In 1989 the Acme Boot Company of Clarksville, Tennessee, the world's largest boot manufacturer, announced that it would no longer make boots from elephant skin. In 2001, *Time* magazine cast a skeptical eye on circuses. "Mixing hokum with the perception of brutality, the traditional circus seems uncomfortably out of place in today's entertainment market," the magazine said. "It's the interspecies version of a minstrel show."

A number of countries around the world banned the use of wild animals in circuses, among them Austria, Croatia, Greece, Hungary, Ireland, Poland, Argentina, Bolivia, Colombia, Costa Rica, Paraguay, and Peru. In the United States, thirty-five municipalities have imposed partial or full bans on circus animals. Twenty-seven jurisdictions in Canada have enacted similar bans.

Circuses in the United States fought back, hard. If a circus was making money off an elephant, they said, why on earth would handlers mistreat it? Ringling Bros. and Barnum & Bailey insisted that wild animals in the circus were better cared for than they would ever be in a natural setting, even in zoos, because performing about the country provided them regular exercise and a constant change of scenery. To critics who questioned the human dominance that ruled the lives of circus animals, Ringling spokesmen insisted that beatings were infrequent but necessary if trainers were going to work around animals, and also completely natural: in the wild, they said, every animal felt pain from time to time. The circus couldn't possibly abuse its elephants because if it did the animals would become dangerous and then no one would be safe: not the trainers, the handlers, or the audience.

The pro-circus arguments seemed endless. Circuses claimed that by taking in exotic animals they were really doing the world a favor because there was less natural habitat for the animals in the real world. Seeing elephants up close helped educate the public about their fellow creatures and made them more likely to support conservation efforts.

Circuses further argued that elephants were only asked to perform stunts they would carry out naturally on their own—something elephant experts disputed. Cynthia Moss, a research director with the Amboseli Trust for Elephants, one of the world's top experts in elephant behavior, said elephants might kneel down and touch the ground in the course of play, but they would never stand on their heads.

In 2007, a host of elephant experts joined Moss in refuting circuses' reassurances about performing elephants. "The totally unnatural existence of captive elephants in a circus, which includes significant physical and emotional suffering, is a travesty," the experts wrote. "To allow this practice to continue is unjustified and unethical," not to mention unsafe. Elephants have extraordinary memories and don't forget when they've been treated roughly by their handlers, the experts said. "Consequently, they can pose an unpredictable and abiding danger to the public, to their handlers, and thus to themselves."

But circuses were determined to win the public relations battle. Circus employees began referring to bullhooks as less-menacing "guides." A spokeswoman for Ringling, Catherine Ort-Mabry, tried to claim the instruments were intended to mimic the shape of an elephant's trunk. By using them, she said, keepers were simulating how a mother elephant would pull a baby closer to her side. Yet under the glaring lights of a circus ring, trainers began to conceal the instruments up their sleeves or they carried smaller versions, wrapping the hooks with black tape to deflect attention. Earlier in his career, Gunther Gebel-Williams, the dashing blond trainer credited with helping revive the circus, did not try to hide the fact that he disciplined his elephants, even the babies, with bullhooks and whips. Now Ringling Bros. began to depict Gebel-Williams as a softhearted animal lover who handled his charges with affection and respect.

No one defended the status quo more vehemently than Ringling Bros. and Barnum & Bailey owner Kenneth Feld. Feld's father, Irvin Feld, and two partners had purchased Ringling from John Ringling North in 1967 after the elder Feld spent a decade as the booking agent for the circus. Irving Feld injected new life into Ringling Bros.: he eliminated the big top and moved performances to indoor arenas. He sent two separate circuses, the Blue Unit and the Red Unit, on the road, each traveling different circuits for two years at a stretch.

Feld's son, Kenneth, took over in 1984 and, determined not to let anyone besmirch the company's image, he spent millions of dollars spreading the message that wildlife, especially elephants, were willing performers. A key component of Ringling's strategy was to keep regulators and protestors too far away to cause trouble. In 1992, when a committee of Congress scheduled a hearing to explore the mistreatment of circus animals, Ringling Bros. blasted the witnesses as "a handful of political radicals" and complained that they were leading a "harassment campaign."

Feld didn't hesitate to go after anyone who stood in his way. Eight years after a freelance writer, Janice Pottker, wrote a 1990 piece on the Feld family for *Regardie's*, a Washington, D.C.–area magazine, she learned that Feld had retaliated by hiring people to spy on her, infiltrate her life, and do everything possible to ruin her. Feld was said to be incensed that Pottker had mentioned the bisexual preferences and reportedly dubious parenting skills of his father, Irvin. To oversee his vindication, Feld hired Clair George, former deputy director for operations of the Central Intelligence Agency. In a sworn affidavit filed in 1998, George admitted not only to spying on Pottker, but that he arranged for a publisher to publish another of Pottker's proposed books to deflect her attention away from Feld. According to reports, cronies even brainstormed ways of destroying Pottker personally by hiring "a bodybuilder type" to try to seduce her and shatter her marriage.

To combat animal rights groups, Feld created a Long Term Animal Plan Task Force that met for a week to discuss ways of infiltrating and undermining them. From here on out, the company would become "exceedingly proactive" whenever criticism was raised, turn the tables and accuse the critics of lying. A full-page ad published in *The New York Times* in 2002 claimed that animal rights groups should not be trusted because they were linked to terrorist organizations. "It's important to know that the criticism comes from the small group of people who have an extreme agenda promoting complete separation of animals and humans," the ad, signed by Kenneth Feld, said. "I want to ensure you that at Ringling Brothers [there are] 400 animals we care for around the clock 365 days a year, with safe, stimulating and healthy lives."

Feld Entertainment had too much at stake to risk losing the public's support. Of all the enterprises Feld owns—Monster Jam, Disney on Ice, Disney Live—the circus and its elephants are the biggest moneymakers. They rake in more than $100 million a year.

But the federal government couldn't ignore the evidence forever. In 1998, USDA charged Feld Entertainment with two willful violations, claiming the circus forced a three-year-old elephant named Kenny to go out into the ring even though he was seriously ill.

Kenny was one of Ringling's star performers: he could balance atop a tub, kick a beach ball, turn circles, and wave goodbye to the audience with a handkerchief in his trunk. When he became noticeably ill—he was lethargic, was experiencing diarrhea and had begun bleeding from his rectum—a veterinarian prescribed antibiotics and recommended excusing him from that evening's show. But Ringling's Gebel-Williams sent Kenny out into the ring anyway. The baby elephant was too ill to carry out any of his tricks; he just stood there. Afterward his handlers gave him fluids to rehydrate him and left him chained to a concrete floor. Less than two hours later they found him collapsed, dead.

Protestors demanded USDA file charges against Ringling Bros., and were stunned when the department did so: for once, it seemed, the circus was being held accountable for its actions. The year before, USDA had fined King Royal Circus, a small family operation, $200,000 for allowing an African elephant named Heather to die in a poorly ventilated trailer where the temperature reportedly soared to 120 degrees Fahrenheit. But up to now Ringling always seemed to escape scrutiny.

The jubilation was short-lived: a few months after Kenny's death, USDA cleared Feld Entertainment of any wrongdoing. The circus agreed to donate $20,000 to elephant causes, and the government left it at that. Animal welfare advocates were dismayed. Despite what seemed a clear-cut case of neglect, still USDA would not act.

Later that year, two elephant keepers traveling with Ringling's Blue Unit quit their jobs when the show got to Huntsville, Alabama, and called local animal welfare officers to complain that the circus was mistreating the elephants. The men wound up talking with Pat Derby, the Hollywood trainer turned Sanctuary owner. Derby had badgered Ringling for years, helping instigate protests outside performance arenas and gathering hidden videos of trainers striking elephants. Lawyers for Derby deposed the two workers, Glenn Ewell and James Stechcon, who said that during their three months on the road they'd seen handlers regularly abuse and beat the elephants. Stechcon was particularly upset to see a handler beat Benjamin, a baby elephant, "forcefully and repeatedly." Benjamin's crime: after a brushing, he'd thrown a trunkful of sawdust on his back, something elephants do instinctively in the wild. "It was not pretty," Stechcon said of the punishment Benjamin received.

Pat Harned and the other keepers identified by Ewell and Stechcon heatedly denied the allegations of abuse. Appearing with Benjamin on NBC's *Today* show and CBS's *This Morning*— where Benjamin demonstrated that he could shoot hoops, pedal a tricycle, play musical instruments, and prop himself up on a wooden barrel—Harned said he rewarded the baby elephant with loaves of bread and bunches of bananas. Feld's corporate counsel made sure USDA knew that one of the whistle-blowers, Ewell, had been charged with harassment by a third party and the other, Stechcon, had been arrested twice for fighting. USDA's counsel, Kenneth Vail, recommended the agency drop the case and Animal Care's Ron DeHaven did so.

A year later, Benjamin drowned in a pond in Texas. He had been wading in the pond with another elephant, Shirley, on the morning after an overnight stop on their way from Houston to Dallas. When it came time to go, Shirley responded to Harned's call to get out of the water but, according to Harned, Benjamin dived underwater and died. Feld authorities concluded the elephant must have suffered a heart attack, but witnesses told a senior USDA investigator that Harned walloped Benjamin with his bullhook while the young elephant was playing near the bank, and that Benjamin swam toward deeper water to escape him. Despite their accounts, USDA chose not to cite Ringling over the incident.

At least one USDA inspector, Peggy Larson, later confirmed that the federal government provided almost no oversight to animal acts. She said she and her colleagues were under considerable pressure to go easy on citing circuses, to avoid disrupting their operations. The hands-off arrangement was a problem, Larson said, because circuses knew the inspectors had no teeth and "they just more or less thumb(ed) their noses at USDA."

DeHaven failed to act in yet another instance involving Ringling. On a tour of the company's Center for Elephant Conservation, its breeding and training barn, two USDA veterinarians came upon a pair of baby elephants roped and chained so tightly they could scarcely move. Doc and Angelica, both eighteen months old, had fresh lesions on their legs caused by the restraints. The veterinarians could also see scars from previous wounds. The head of the center, Gary Jacobson, later described how cavalierly Ringling separated baby elephants from their mothers: "We just grabbed them and tied them up." The elephants were unloosed for forty minutes of exercise a day, but other than that they remained tethered—one for ten days at a stretch and the other for four months.

DeHaven agreed that the evidence was sufficient to show unnecessary trauma, stress, physical harm, and discomfort. But instead of taking action, he told Feld officials he was certain they could address the matter "to ensure that it does not reoccur." Feld Entertainment objected so vigorously even to that that De-Haven ultimately downgraded the incident from an investigation to a "fact-gathering process."

The government's handling of these matters exposed the inadequacies of the Animal Welfare Act. It does not ban the use of bullhooks, and circuses argue there is no way to control an animal the size of an elephant without them. Moreover, the law gives the secretary of agriculture sole authority to suspend or revoke the licenses of elephant exhibitors. Private parties have no legal right to file suit requiring the government to enforce the law or insist that circuses obey it.

The Endangered Species Act allows private parties to file civil suits to stop people from harming or harassing animals listed as threatened or endangered, and Asian elephants are listed as endangered (African elephants are listed as threatened, a less stringent designation). But lawsuits against private parties typically aren't allowed if a federal agency has permitted the "taking" of a species—any action that constitutes harassment or harm, hunting, shooting, wounding, or other means. (Takings usually involve cases where animal habitats are also being used for other purposes. The northern spotted owl, a threatened species that resides in the Pacific Northwest's forests where timber companies want to log trees, is one example.)

The issue of standing creates an almost insurmountable

obstacle for private parties looking to protect animals. In court, human beings must somehow prove that they themselves have been harmed as a result of animal suffering, which is extremely difficult to do. An earlier effort by Derby's PAWS organization in 1996 to require USDA to enforce the Animal Welfare Act as it pertained to elephants wound up being dismissed in court in part because PAWS's founders were said to lack standing.

In 2000, Tom Rider, an elephant keeper who had spent two and a half years with Ringling Bros. and Barnum & Bailey's Blue Unit, stepped forward to complain about the mistreatment of the circus's elephants. Rider submitted a seven-page sworn affidavit to a USDA investigator in which he recounted twenty-five incidents of abuse. On Rider's behalf, Derby and her partner, Ed Stewart, hired Katherine Meyer who, with her husband, Eric Glitzenstein, ran a prominent public-interest law firm in Washington, D.C. Meyer and Glitzenstein had already won a series of animal rights battles and knew the ins and outs of the laws better than anyone. Meyer suggested Derby capitalize on a clause in the Endangered Species Act that authorized lay citizens to sue violators. Never before had a citizen lawsuit been filed in the case of a captive animal, but it was worth a shot.

The case took an unusual twist. Several months after the lawsuit was filed, a pair of private eyes paid a call on Derby. They'd been hired by a Feld executive who was subsequently fired by the company, who wanted the investigators to amass evidence of Feld's attempts to spy on animal welfare groups. When the fired executive refused to pay the investigators their fee, they offered the bounty to Derby: twenty boxes' worth of records. Among the wealth of material was evidence that spies for Feld had pretended to be volunteers in order to worm their way into PAWS. Spies for Feld had also infiltrated PETA and the group Elephant Alliance.

Derby suddenly had new ammunition to use against Ringling

Bros. and Barnum & Bailey. She sued its parent company, Feld Entertainment, claiming Feld had infiltrated PAWS, spied on its operations, and filched documents to try to damage PAWS's reputation. Feld's attorneys quickly offered to settle matters. In exchange for Derby's willingness to drop the suit and stop criticizing Ringling, they offered to give PAWS at least two elephants and an undisclosed sum of money. Derby agreed to the terms. She used the settlement to buy 2,300 acres in San Andreas, California, to accommodate PAWS' elephants. Now, along with the Elephant Sanctuary, there were two large refuges dedicated to needy elephants.

A month after Derby filed her lawsuit, Katherine Meyer sued Feld Entertainment in federal court in Washington, D.C., on behalf of a coalition of animal welfare groups: the American Society for the Prevention of Cruelty to Animals, the Fund for Animals, and the Animal Welfare Institute The plaintiffs wanted Ringling to be held accountable for its treatment of elephants.

The judge in the case, U.S. District Judge Emmet Sullivan, threw out the suit on grounds that none of the persons involved had sufficiently alleged that they personally had been harmed by Feld Entertainment's actions. The appeals court disagreed and said Rider's allegations were strong enough for the suit to move forward. Rider was unlikely to work with the elephants once he left Ringling, but he could see them any time by buying a ticket to the circus, and he would be able to detect signs of abuse that could continue to injure him aesthetically and emotionally, the appeals court said. Even though the circus's records showed that all but two of Ringling's fifty-two elephants suffered from foot problems, the trial would focus on the conditions of just seven.

Nearly a decade passed before the case against Ringling finally went to trial. In the meantime, circuses continued to duck charges of elephant abuse. USDA fined the Clyde Beatty–Cole

Bros. Circus $10,000 after determining its trainers had mistreated four of its six elephants with bullhooks (the circus claimed the injuries were caused by ingrown hairs). But the government waived the fine after the circus agreed to spend $10,000 to hire an elephant-handling consultant.

The following year, authorities charged Mark Oliver Gebel, the son of Gunther Gebel-Williams and a trainer for Ringling Bros., with gouging the left front leg of an elephant when she failed to respond quickly enough to his commands as Gebel led her into the San Jose, California, arena. The charge was a misdemeanor subject to up to six months in jail and a $1,000 fine and the trial lasted a week. The jury acquitted Gebel. They faulted witnesses to the alleged abuse for waiting until after the elephant's performance to check her for wounds, which made it harder to prove that Gebel caused the injuries.

In 2004, another incident raised flags. Ringling officials had to euthanize an eight-month-old elephant, Riccardo, after he fell off a tub and broke two legs. Riccardo was the son of Shirley, the elephant who had gone wading into the pond with Benjamin, the baby elephant who drowned. (Ringling had bred Shirley when she was just six years old, half the age of elephants in the wild when they begin to have calves.) Trainers began teaching Riccardo when he was just three months old. On the day he broke his legs, they'd tied a rope to his trunk and prodded him to climb a nineteen-inch-high tub.

A couple of weeks later, an animal welfare advocate videotaped a Ringling handler beating a chained elephant with a bullhook. The elephant was Angelica, one of the two elephants who'd been found tied up and wounded five years earlier at Ringling's Center for Elephant Conservation. USDA inspectors recommended fining the company $11,000, but the department's lead counsel, Kenneth Vail, refused to act.

USDA's own inspector general faulted the department's Animal Care unit for letting violators get away with their misdeeds. Animal Care's DeHaven said the agency was spread too thin to do the job adequately: it had a yearly budget of just $16 million and only 111 employees responsible for overseeing nearly 9,000 breeding, research, and animal entertainment businesses.

It was left to former employees of Ringling to sound the alarm. Several were brave enough to do so. One of them was Jodey Eliseo, a dancer who toured with Ringling Bros. for two years. Backed by PETA, Eliseo said she saw Ringling trainers beating elephants often for tripping up in the ring, including a young elephant named Sophie who was punished so frequently she was covered with wounds and a baby elephant who was severely beaten when he crashed through a wall in an attempt to escape. Eliseo led a protest outside the US Airways Center in Phoenix, Arizona, her hometown, holding a bullhook in one hand and a can of "wonder dust"—the gray powder trainers use to conceal bullhook wounds on elephants—in the other. "I saw how animals in the circus are routinely beaten," Eliseo told the crowd. "They live in constant fear. For them, the circus is a real-life horror show."

If there was any doubt about the brutal lives circus elephants were forced to lead, Sammy Haddock's account should have dispelled them. Haddock had worked with Ringling Bros.' elephants on and off from 1976 to 2005. He eventually left his job to care for his wife, Millie, who was dying from complications of diabetes. Millie never liked the conditions the elephants endured, especially the babies, or that Haddock was caught up in the abuse. Before she died, she told him, "Sammy, I know you'll do the right thing." Four years later, Haddock decided to honor his wife's request. He contacted PETA's Debbie Leahy, the same woman who had helped deliver supplies to the Hawthorn barn just before Billie and the rest of the herd were rescued. Haddock turned over to Leahy a raft of photos showing Ringling's baby elephants undergoing the rigors of training, and he unloaded decades' worth of details about the violent methods used to co-erce baby elephants into performing tricks. Leahy spent hours helping Haddock draft a fifteen-page statement, which he signed and notarized on August 28, 2009.

The baby elephants at Ringling's Center for Elephant Con-servation are taken early from their mothers and spend about twenty-three hours a day restrained, Haddock wrote. They are never turned loose outdoors to play because that would defeat the purpose—all of their movements are controlled by trainers. Training sessions take place behind a solid fence so no one can witness what's happening. Rock-and-roll music blares constantly to familiarize the babies to the noise and also drown out their screaming.

Trainers start the process by running a "snatch rope" over the baby's back and under its belly, fastening it to the elephant's left hind leg and then tying it to stakes. "After the initial training ses-sion the babies fight to resist having the snatch rope put on them until they eventually give up," Haddock wrote. Once the ele-phant is restrained a crew works with it for an hour and a half to two hours, twice a day, "until they get it right." The elephants are taught to lie down, sit up, perform a down-salute and turn in cir-cles while one foot is propped up on a spindle.

The training methods are violent, Haddock wrote: trainers tie ropes around all four of a baby elephant's ankles as well as around her trunk, waist, and neck. As many as four men will pull on one rope to force the elephant into a certain position. Other trainers use bullhooks and hot shots to prod the young animal into compliance. Training a baby to lie down involves stretching out all four of its legs, dropping it to its hindquarters and then slamming it down, one trainer pulling the elephant's left leg un-derneath it at the same time the head trainer uses a bullhook to pull down the baby's back. The elephant is held to the ground for thirty to forty-five seconds, given a break, and then subjected to more training.

To stand a baby elephant on its head, trainers attach a rope to the baby's trunk and pull the trunk between its front legs. Trainers poke the elephant in the tender spots on its hind feet so it will keep its legs raised and hook the sensitive spot behind its head so the baby won't lift upward.

Haddock learned his trade at the hands of head trainer Gary Jacobson, Theodore Svertesky, Gary Hill, and Buckles Woodcock, the trainer who worked with Billie, and beatings were common, Haddock wrote. "Buckles had warned me, 'If you see the whites of the elephant's eyes, they're eyeballing you and that's cause to correct them on the spot.' 'Eyeballing' meant that they were looking for an opportunity to attack."

Early on, Haddock had no problem punishing the elephants. In 1977 he was hauling hay to the stockcars when an elephant named Vance struck him with his trunk, sending Haddock flying and knocking him out. "I went after Vance with a hot shot in the stockyard," he wrote. "I burned out two hot shots and fried him for about ten minutes. He was screaming and regurgitating water."

A year later Haddock was assigned to "square away" the tough elephants, beating them to keep them in line. When an elephant named Major knocked him into a barn wall, Haddock struck back. He came up behind the elephant, thumped him for five minutes with a bullhook, and then pulled out a hot shot. "I took a break, then beat him more," he recounted. "I laid him down and hooked him repeatedly in his ear canal. The second beating lasted ten minutes. Major was screaming bloody murder."

The bullhook has one purpose, "and that is to inflict pain and punishment," Haddock wrote. "I should know, I used to make them. I built them to where you can't break them, no matter how hard you hit the elephant."

He saw elephants being beaten who had no idea why they were being punished. "They will start randomly lifting one leg, then another and another, lifting their trunk, hoping some trick will satisfy the trainer and make the beating stop." During USDA inspections the bull men would hide the hot shots and conceal rope burns and other injuries on the elephants by rubbing mud on their skin, Haddock wrote. He said it was his understanding that Ringling had an arrangement allowing USDA to conduct just two announced and one unannounced inspections a year at the Ringling center.

Later, Haddock worked with Jacobson on a six-year-old elephant named Tina at the JA Nugget casino in Reno, Nevada. They had six weeks to train her and they accomplished their goal "with brute force." They worked Tina twice a day, ninety minutes at a time, and beat her every day. "She was a smart elephant and caught on quick," Haddock wrote. "She had quite a few hook marks on her and we used quite a bit of electricity." In addition to the usual repertoire of tricks, he and Jacobson taught her to bottle walk on small pedestals, synchronizing her front and opposing back leg while walking forward and backward. Tina could also walk a balance beam, pull slot machines with her trunk, roll into a headstand and perform hind leg and front leg stands. She opened for a number of famous entertainers, including Red Skelton, Dick Clark, Bo Diddley, and Susan Anton.

Toward the end of his career, when someone asked Haddock what he did for a living and he told them he trained elephants for Ringling, people would ask: Is it true you have to beat elephants to make them perform those tricks?

"I stopped telling people what I did for a living," he wrote. "I was ashamed."

The animal welfare community welcomed Haddock's affidavit. For the first time, someone from the inside was exposing the atrocious training methods being used on baby elephants. "When someone like Sam Haddock says there's a problem with what's going on here, it's from the perspective of someone who lived through it and participated in it," Leahy said. "It totally contradicts what the circus has been telling the public for years."

But Haddock never got to experience the ripples caused by his confession. Diagnosed with liver cancer, he died a few weeks before PETA went public with his affidavit. Ringling Bros. denied everything he alleged. Confronted with Haddock's statement, Jacobson claimed it wasn't in Ringling's interest to mistreat elephants. "Those things are worth a tremendous amount of money." He added that he couldn't believe his former colleague had signed the statement. "He was always a stand-up guy," Jacobson said. "What does it say about humanity?

"The last thing they're afraid of is me, these little elephants," Jacobson said.

—————✦———————

Finally, in February 2009, nine years after the lawsuit against Feld Entertainment was first filed, the trial got under way. Over a six-week period, Tom Rider and twenty-nine other witnesses took the stand.

The animal welfare groups wanted Judge Sullivan to stop Ringling Bros. from harming its elephants during performances and punishing them for behaving imperfectly. "For nine minutes of performing, these elephants live a life of misery," lead attorney Katherine Meyer said.

At the trial, witnesses testified to a number of practices that Feld Entertainment would have preferred to keep hidden. For example, nearly all of Ringling's adult elephants suffered infected and abscessed feet that were full of ulcers. In addition, the elephants were made to perform forty-eight weeks a year and they traveled under grueling conditions, averaging twenty-six hours straight on the road, sometimes seventy hours, even a hundred hours, without a break.

Haddock's disclosures dovetailed with those of other whistle-blowing handlers. In a deposition taken prior to the trial, James Stechcon stated that at Ringling's Center for Elephant Conservation, older elephants were let outside from 7:00 A.M. to 3:00 P.M. and tied up the rest of the time, anchored to the concrete floors so ruinous to their feet. Other elephants were let out only an hour and a half a day.

"Those guys really don't get to walk around, ever," Stechcon said of baby elephants in his sworn testimony. "Almost their entire life, like, more than four-fifths of their life, is spent standing or laying down. And the only times they ever get to do any walking is either between the train and the building on the animal walks, when we first get to a town and when we leave, or when they're going from their pen area to the show and back. That's all the walking they ever do."

Stechcon echoed Haddock's tale of how baby elephants were separated from their mothers while they were still nursing and locked down in chains for weeks and months at a time. Trainers thrashed the calves to get them to memorize new tricks. Stechcon said the sounds of the thumpings would disturb all of the grown elephants within earshot. "They really freak out, pull on their chains and get all freaked out and everything."

Stechcon recalled how handlers singled out an elephant named Nicole for abuse when she flubbed up during a performance. Nicole would urinate excessively before climbing onto a tub. In Denver one night, the ABC show *Nightline* was taping a performance and the grooms were on their best behavior. But a few nights later, a trainer named Randy struck Nicole three or four times. Two weeks after that Pat Harned walloped her so hard he broke his bullhook.

Stechcon likened the sound of the beatings to a baseball bat hitting a body bag: *whack, whack, whack.* "There's no mistaking it," he said, "not to mention the fact the elephant is making lots of noise because of the pain." He said he'd seen Harned laugh and joke and smile "quite a bit" during the beatings.

Ringling's Center for Elephant Conservation offered no place for elephants to swim, something they adore doing. The purpose of keeping the elephants there was to train them for the circus and breed them. Elephants who weren't suited for circus work were loaned out for breeding to other circuses.

Beatings were frequent, witnesses testified. Ringling's records frequently mentioned scars on the elephants' left sides, the same side their handlers stood on. In a sworn affidavit given to USDA, former groom Sonnie Ridley testified that he saw puncture wounds caused by bullhooks probably three to four times a month on the circus's Blue Unit and hook boils on the elephants an average of twice a week. Some of the favorite spots for punishing the elephants were on their sides and under their trunks, on the underside of their legs, inside their ears and on top of their flanks. Places where injuries couldn't be seen.

Trial testimony revealed that Buckles Woodcock used a hot shot on at least one Ringling elephant after the circus hired him to fill in for the head elephant trainer, who'd been killed in an accident. On the witness stand, Kenneth Feld said Woodcock was spoken to about the incident, but he continued to work for the circus for more than a year and a half.

Judge Sullivan expressed concern about the living conditions described on the stand, and he indicated that the way the elephants reacted to the bullhooks suggested they feared they were going to be hit and hurt. Defense lawyer John Simpson argued that while there was a mild feeling from a prod, there was no sensation of pain—an elephant's hide is thick enough to avoid harm. To counter Meyer's claim that bullhook marks sometimes developed into infected boils, Simpson showed videotape of elephants in the wild with bleeding fly bites juxtaposed next to elephants with bleeding hook marks. The injuries look similar, he said: in reality a boil was nothing more than a pimple.

As for transporting the elephants, Simpson claimed that, despite being chained in train cars and left to stand in their own urine and feces for hours at a stretch, the elephants actually enjoyed riding across the country. The long trips satisfied their nomadic urge to roam. "They know that when they get on that railcar that they're going to a new place," Simpson told the courtroom. "It stimulates them. The whole concept stimulates them." He likened the chains fastened to the elephants' legs to seat belts humans wear when they get in a car.

Attorneys for Ringling said no one had evidence to prove that chaining elephants in place caused them to engage in stressful behavior. Asked about that on the stand, the Elephant Sanctuary's Carol Buckley, a witness for the animal welfare groups, disagreed. "Oh, I think we surely do," she said. "By observation, we can tell." Buckley's own elephant, Tarra, wasn't chained when Buckley first met her. But after Tarra was trained by Smokey Jones, Buckley took his advice and began keeping her elephant on chains. Within three weeks Tarra started weaving about repetitively.

Buckley talked about the anxiety she'd witnessed in the Hawthorn elephants since their arrival at the Sanctuary three years earlier. In particular, she talked about Billie.

"She's a very fearful individual," Buckley said. "Over the past year she's made a lot of progress and so now it isn't a daily routine of her swaying. She has spent many afternoons out in the habitat dusting and grazing, but there are times, still, that she will fall into that [repetitive movement], and it's usually when she wants to go into the barn and the others don't. . . . She doesn't want to be outside when it's dark."

One of the trial's most dramatic moments occurred when

Feld was called to the witness stand. Sworn to tell the truth, he admitted seeing Ringling employees strike elephants with bull-hooks, including under the chin. The term he used to describe the hits was "bopping," and he said he didn't see any reason to reprimand an employee for doing it. Trainers needed to use bull-hooks to keep elephants under control, Feld said. Without them the circus would not be able to have elephants, and Ringling was determined to have elephants.

"It is an absolute escape, it is good, wholesome family enter-tainment and [audiences] know that they get to see something they can't see anyplace else," Feld said of the circus. "The public speaks out and they vote whenever they come to our show and they buy a ticket."

The trial lasted six weeks. Much rode on the outcome. If Sul-livan found Ringling Bros. in violation of the Endangered Spe-cies Act, the circus would have to stop handling elephants the way they did or else obtain an exemption from the Interior De-partment, which oversees the law.

But in spite of the evidence of abuse, the plaintiffs faced an uphill challenge. They needed to demonstrate that the key plaintiff, Rider, had suffered emotional injury as a result of the elephants' mistreatment. Rider testified that seeing Ringling employees abuse the elephants he'd worked with for two years caused him suffering, and the suffering continued because, hav-ing quit his job with the circus, he could no longer visit or work with the elephants again. But Rider's testimony turned out to be highly flawed. Sullivan listed the reasons why in his fifty-seven-page ruling in Ringling's favor.

The judge noted that, shown a video of the elephants in ques-tion, Rider was unable to identify them by name, calling into question how emotionally disturbed he was by their treatment. Rider never complained to anyone about the mishandling of the elephants until the lawsuit was filed, the judge said—an indication that Rider either failed to witness any mistreatment or wasn't affected to the point of suffering emotional injury. Even if Rider had been injured emotionally, the court said, banning Ringling from using bullhooks and chains would not ensure that he would ever see the elephants and suffer emotionally again.

The judge also was troubled by the fact that Rider himself had used a bullhook after he left Ringling and joined a circus in Europe. The judge didn't like the fact that, as the case dragged on for years, the animal groups paid Rider, or that, as a side note, Rider neglected to pay taxes on the money. He wound up reaching a settlement with the IRS.

The plaintiffs argued that Ringling should have to apply for a "takings" permit from the federal government every time it abused its elephants—and because the circus did not do so, animal welfare organizations were deprived of information about the circus they would have received under the Endangered Species Act's public notice and comments requirements. But Judge Sullivan said the U.S. Fish & Wildlife Service had not required Ringling to apply for a permit. The animal groups would have been entitled to the notices and comments only if Fish & Wildlife had done so, and then their claim would need to be filed against the agency, not the circus.

The U.S. Court of Appeals upheld Sullivan's dismissal.

Animal welfare groups blamed Feld's victory on a technicality and scrambled to find something salvageable from the outcome. If nothing else, the case had given the groups the wherewithal to expose Ringling's practices. Now the public could conclude for itself how badly the elephants were treated and how weak the laws designed to protect them actually were. In future cases, a plaintiff claiming to have suffered an emotional injury from seeing circus animals abused could keep a case alive long enough for animal advocates, using the discovery process, to learn everything they could about the circus's practices. But the people most likely capable of proving emotional injury would be trainers or handlers who had worked with the animals in question, and rare was the worker willing to blow the whistle on his employer.

"The fact is that Feld Entertainment admitted that they strike elephants with sharp bullhooks, under oath," said Carter Dillard, director of litigation for the Animal Legal Defense Fund. "The evidence put forward in the case overwhelmingly showed that to get those elephants to perform, they abuse them."

Feld Entertainment countersued Rider, the attorneys, and the animal welfare groups, claiming they had violated racketeering laws by relying on a chief witness who had been paid. Feld asked for more than $19 million in legal expenses.

In December 2012, the ASPCA agreed to settle the suit for $9.3 million. Four months after that, Judge Sullivan ordered the other plaintiffs to pay Feld's legal fees, which were said to total more than $20 million. The trial had unearthed scathing facts about elephant training. But in the eyes of the public, the lasting impression was that animal activists had failed to mount a case that circus elephants deserved to go free.

In the years since, USDA has clamped down a bit more on behalf of circus elephants. In 2010 the Animal Care unit announced that it had formed a team of veterinary medical officers that would inspect traveling elephant exhibitors at regular intervals. Inspections would be timely, problems could be identified earlier and Animal Care would be able to respond more quickly to complaints.

The government fined Cole Bros. Circus $15,000 after PETA complained that two elephants, Tina and Jewel, had been deprived of veterinary care and were hundreds of pounds underweight. The government confiscated the elephants and turned them over to the Los Angeles Zoo.

And in 2011, USDA fined Ringling Bros. $270,000 for numerous violations of the Animal Welfare Act over a three-year period, including forcing a sick elephant to perform in the ring and failing to safely handle an elephant who escaped. The company was also charged with delivering meat to tigers in the same wheelbarrows that were used to carry away their feces.

The fine against Ringling set a record penalty under the Animal Welfare Act. As a result of the settlement, Ringling must now train all employees who handle animals and hire someone to ensure the company complies with the Animal Welfare Act. But Ringling admitted no wrongdoing or violation of USDA policy.

Interestingly, the person Ringling hired to fill its new compliance officer position was none other than Kenneth H. Vail—the same Kenneth Vail who'd looked the other way as USDA's chief legal counsel on animal welfare cases, and the same Kenneth Vail who admitted to *Mother Jones* magazine, in a blistering article about Ringling's practices: "If I were an elephant, I wouldn't want to be with Feld Entertainment. It's a tough life."

A NEW WAVE OF ELEPHANTS

World War II brought a jarring halt to the animal importing business. America needed to employ every ship it had to claim victory in the Pacific. The only way the military and materials could reach the war zone was by boat. America was now at war with Germany, so no German steamships were going to be docking on American shores. Zoos and circuses in the United States could no longer place orders for exotic wildlife. They needed to make do with the animals they had.

The end of the war in 1945 ended the animal-import drought. American dealers again began procuring animals, thousands of them, and shipping them to zoos, circuses, and showmen clamoring for fresh inventory. Elephants were the scarcest: Importers paid $2,000 for an elephant overseas, then turned around and sold them for anywhere from $3,800 to $5,000 in the States.

One circus alone, Ben Davenport's Dailey Bros., bought sixteen elephants, increasing the size of its herd to twenty-five. When importers M. Kahn and Harry Rimberg of New York ran an ad offering elephants for sale, forty-five circuses, zoos, and carnivals flooded them with requests for 125.

New Yorker Henry Trefflich claimed to be the first importer to fly animals, including elephants, to the States. A steamship company had commissioned an airplane to deliver a propeller, and when he found out the plane would be flying back empty, Trefflich arranged for the pilot to fly a load of exotic animals on the return trip.

Chartering the plane cost $15,000, nearly twice what it would have cost to transport the animals by boat. But air travel cut food costs significantly: the flight from Singapore to New York took just six days and nights, much shorter than the six weeks it would take by ship. And it reduced the risks of an animal dying en route. (More than once Trefflich had lost $10,000 worth of animals in a single storm at sea. When that happened, he would drink away his misery, swigging three or four slugs of Canadian whisky and chasing it with beer.)

Trefflich had an assistant, Genevieve Cuprys, who acquired a modicum of fame as "Jungle Jenny," procurer of elephants and other wildlife. After two or three plane shipments, Jenny confidently set out to bring home another shipment from Siam. She was especially excited by this shipment because she had traveled to Siam by herself and outbid three other American dealers, as well as a recognized Indian exporter, for a half dozen female baby elephants caught by native trappers. She walked the young animals eighteen miles to the railhead, where a train took them to Bangkok. Waiting for her in Bangkok was a DC-4 from Seaboard & Western Airlines chartered by Trefflich.

In addition to the elephants, Jenny procured two adult leopards and a pair of leopard cubs; two golden cats, 116 Javanese monkeys, four gibbons, and a twenty-three-foot-long python—13,000 pounds of unpredictability. The elephants weighed roughly 1,500 pounds apiece, and Jenny spent six hours building a ramp and enticing them to walk up it into the cylindrical cargo area. Once the elephants were inside, Jenny and her assistants used ropes fashioned from vines to hobble each animal's front legs, then chain one hind leg of each to a ringbolt embedded in the floor of the plane. The elephants were surrounded by canvas covered with heavy grass, on which they could lie down.

The elephants had no interest in resting. The plane had scarcely taken off when two of them managed to unfasten their chains. From her seat in the middle of the cargo compartment, Jenny glanced up to find the elephants looming over her, capable of squashing her each time the plane lurched. The pilot landed the plane long enough to secure the elephants again. But no sooner had the plane left Bangkok again than more elephants got loose. For six days and six nights as the aircraft touched down first in New Delhi then Karachi, Abadan, Damascus, Rome, Geneva, Shannon, and Reykjavik, anywhere from one to three of the elephants roamed the cabin.

Jenny couldn't keep asking the pilot to make an emergency landing every time an elephant began wandering. Instead, she kept a close eye on the untethered elephants for hours at a time, waiting until they grew tired enough that she could reach over and grab hold of the chains around their legs. In the meantime, the elephants tugged at everything in sight. They tore insulation from the walls of the plane and sheeting from the ceiling. One elephant figured out how to maneuver the rheostat with its trunk, constantly dimming the lights. Another discovered how to pry open the door to the pilothouse. Before anyone could stop him he snaked his trunk inside, ripped the gas stick from the pilot's hand and snapped it in half.

The pilot finally fought back: when the elephants became too mischievous he lifted the plane another couple of thousand feet, where the shortage of oxygen tired them out. Jenny later wrote that that flight was her worst experience ever. "For the first time in my entire life I really knew stark unforgettable fear."

By the 1950s, U.S. dealers were importing more animals than they had for nearly two generations. As a marketing gimmick, Wanamaker's department store in New York offered an elephant for sale. Alongside its puppies and kittens, orangutans and chimpanzees, was a fourteen-month-old pachyderm named Trunkles, just in from Thailand. She weighed 750 pounds, stood fifty-two inches high and was kept in a glass-enclosed cage, the equivalent of a humongous aquarium.

The public had no idea how difficult it was to procure an elephant like Trunkles. "Customers can almost call up and buy an elephant as you'd get a can of soup from the grocery store," Trefflich lamented.

EIGHTEEN

BAD DAYS, GOOD DAYS

It didn't take long to discover that Billie had two very different personalities. At times she seemed placid, emotionally stable. But on other days a caregiver could walk in the barn and immediately sense that something about her wasn't right. She'd be standing a little defiantly, a bit squared off.

Billie wasn't the only elephant to experience dramatic mood changes, but her pain seemed to go deeper. It really boiled down to trust—Billie had none. She'd been labeled a dangerous elephant almost her entire life, when what she really was was a distrusting soul. When anxiety engulfed her she retreated back into herself. It was as if she'd closed her heart so long ago she was too frightened to dare open it again.

One morning three years after Billie's arrival at the Sanctuary, Blais was four-wheeling across a meadow when he spied Frieda and Liz across the gate. The elephants came over and began talking with Blais: trumpeting, doing a little dance with their heads, and touching one another quickly. Suddenly Billie approached the fence, squeezed between Liz and Frieda, and rested her head against the slats. Clearly she wanted attention from Blais. He stood on the four-wheeler so he could be eye level with the elephants and for a good ten minutes they talked animatedly.

"Billie was in a super-soft place," he recalled.

Then, all of a sudden, Billie's guard flared back up as if to say: *Wait a minute. This is not supposed to happen. This goes against my rules.* Blais accepted her mood shift and backed away. Billie needed her space.

Blais had learned the hard way how mercurial an emotionally wounded elephant could be. In 2006, months after the Hawthorn elephants arrived, the Sanctuary experienced the worst thing imaginable with Winkie, the fickle elephant who'd been abused in the past. Looking back, Blais may have grown a bit complacent with Winkie because she behaved so well around him. She had a habit of making little *shwew, shwew, shwew* noises—a sign that she was in a good mood—and she seemed to have overcome the anger that stemmed from her past.

No one will ever know what was racing through Winkie's mind when Blais and another caregiver, Joanna Burke, pulled up in a four-wheeler to water the elephants. Winkie happened to have a swollen eye, and Burke, thirty-six, who'd worked as a primary caregiver for eight years, climbed off on the far side of the four-wheeler to try to get a look at Winkie's eye. Burke was standing twenty feet from the elephant, but for a twelve-foot-long elephant with an eight-foot-long trunk, twenty feet is no distance at all. In two quick steps, Winkie was within reach of Burke. The elephant unfurled her trunk, knocked Burke down, and began kicking and stomping her. Blais tried to intervene but Winkie ignored him and turned back to Burke.

Anyone who has ever watched an elephant rampage take place gains a new respect for her capacity to inflict injury. Winkie attacked Burke for forty-five agonizing seconds. She then turned on Blais, stopping only after Blais yelled out in desperation:

"Winkie, Winkie, *Winkie!*" The elephant froze in place. Her meltdown over, she now stood perfectly still. Blais, badly bruised, his ankle fractured, hobbled over to Burke, but it was too late.

Burke's death shocked everyone, even, seemingly, Winkie herself. For weeks afterward the elephant shut herself off from the world, including her best friend, Sissy. Blais and Buckley wondered if Winkie suffered from post-traumatic stress disorder from the years of abuse in her previous life. The only person she allowed in was Blais. Two days after the attack, he limped over to a fence where Winkie stood, reached his hand through the slats, and patted her on her rump. She turned to him, exhaled heavily and cooed back with her *shwew, shwew, shwew* sounds.

For so many years in their past, the elephants at the Sanctuary were forbidden to express their feelings. Their handlers would punish them for showing the slightest hint of displeasure. The elephants became powder kegs, their anger and frustration bubbling to the point that an elephant that seemed compliant one second might throw someone on the ground the next. The Sanctuary staff tried to alter this dynamic by encouraging the elephants to communicate in small ways, to convey, if they felt it, that *Hey, I'm good, but don't push me too far*. Blais hadn't seen any warning signs from Winkie that fateful day. But that didn't mean she hadn't given them.

Billie hadn't injured anyone at the Sanctuary, yet she could be just as unpredictable. Sanctuary staff worried about how Billie would react when, a couple of years later, her cherished friend Liz grew lethargic and stopped eating. A battery of tests confirmed the veterinarian's suspicions: Liz was suffering from an active case of tuberculosis. For the sake of the other elephants, the Sanctuary needed to separate her from the rest of the herd.

The Sanctuary is comprised of three habitats: Asian, African, and Quarantine, with subhabitats within each so the elephants can be segregated based on personality clashes or medical needs.

The staff moved Liz to the Sanctuary's original barn, dubbed the Q Barn for quarantine. Until they could get the symptoms of her disease under control, that's where she would remain. And because Billie and Frieda were such close friends of Liz, the Sanctuary moved them to the Q Barn too. Keeping the elephants together heightened the chances that Frieda and Billie might contract tuberculosis also. But separating them would be too traumatic: the three girls had grown that close. Their new arrangement offered far less room to wander—just two acres now, for the time being—but the elephants would have one another. To Billie, Frieda, and Liz, that's all that mattered.

Caregivers waited until after breakfast one morning to open the gate leading to the Q Barn. To protect Frieda's aching feet from the gravel driveway, the staff rolled out a rubber mat—a red carpet of sorts—and beckoned to the three girls, holding buckets of treats as an extra incentive. The invitation worked. The elephants tried so hard to beat one another through the gate that they caused gridlock. Frieda got through first, followed by Liz. Billie brought up the rear.

For the next several weeks the caregivers focused their attention on Liz. They needed to concoct the right mix of pharmaceuticals to treat her tuberculosis with a minimum of side effects. The process was both time-consuming and maddening because in the beginning the medication actually made Liz feel worse. Some days she absorbed the drugs well, but other days she struggled. When she wasn't feeling herself she lost her appetite, often for days at a time: she'd stop eating grain and produce and she'd hesitate to step into the restraint chute for her treatments.

Liz's daily treatments were hard on everyone. Before administering them, caregivers Richard Treat, Barbara Anderson, and Ashleigh Smith had to don hot and sweaty Tyvek suits and cumbersome respirators. Billie and Frieda picked up on higher stress levels, too. On days when Liz acted fluish and achy, Billie would refuse to go through the chute—in turn preventing Liz from entering the chute for her treatment. It was obvious that Billie was trying to do all she could to help Liz.

The three elephants were so fond of one another they took turns playing the role of protector. While Frieda napped Liz stood over her, keeping watch. At times Liz would even sit on her friend. Liz and Billie sometimes stood together over Frieda as she lay on a sand pile, resting her damaged feet.

Billie's emotions could be intense: one morning Frieda was napping on the sand pile when a bird nose-dived near her. Startled, she leapt up and Billie dashed over frantically, trumpeting and swinging her head around in search of the interloper. The three elephants let loose with a cacophony of rumbles, honks, and squeaks.

There was no way to tell whether Billie had ever experienced this degree of friendship before she was taken from the wild, or if the devotion she felt toward Frieda and Liz was entirely new. But it was good to see her develop such a tight bond.

The Sanctuary's caregivers were so wrapped up in Liz they didn't notice Billie's own transformation. Moving to the Q Barn with her newfound friends meant she was now separated permanently from assertive Minnie, and that enabled Billie to shed some of her angst. She made the most of her new arrangement. Instead of retreating to the top of the hill, she began to amble off on her own discovery tours.

Out in the field an elephant walks slowly, stopping every couple of feet or so to investigate the grass, the bushes—everything around her. Ears flapping, her tail swishing away flies, she sweeps her massive trunk back and forth, sniffing and foraging. Another couple of steps and she might halt again, this time tossing a snoutful of dust onto her back to block the sun.

Billie's caregivers began to see her wandering a few feet beyond Frieda and Liz. She ventured out earlier and stayed out longer, sniffing out the wild mint, blackberries, and passion fruit that dotted the landscape. She might pick up a branch with her trunk, lift it above her head, gaze through the leaves for a few minutes, and then consume it, delighting in her surroundings.

She began to sing out more—chirping spontaneously, the elephant equivalent of whistling a happy tune. Before, Billie felt uneasy once darkness fell; she'd charge inside the barn, anxious to pass through the big rubber flaps that separated outdoors from in. The barn's four walls offered safety and comfort, and once the sun set she was ready for their embrace. Now, late at night when the other elephants had settled in, caregivers could hear Billie scavenging outside, drinking in the silence that came with the darkness, cheeping with pleasure. Inside the barn, she amused herself by kicking a squishy ball around her stall or by grabbing hold of a toy that dangled on a wire.

Snow falls rarely in Tennessee, and Asian elephants designed for much warmer climates could be forgiven for wanting nothing to do with the white stuff. But that winter, after one snowfall, Liz ventured out, crunching loudly with each footfall. The snow enchanted her: she began frolicking, kicking up the snow and chirping. Frieda had to investigate the hubbub and Billie galloped over too, full of curiosity. The threesome spent hours exploring the snow-covered grounds, knowing they could return to the warm barn whenever they liked. Back inside, Billie rubbed up against the walls, the guardrails in her stall, even the other elephants to dry herself off.

In the spring of 2010 Middle Tennessee experienced hammering rains and its worst flooding in modern history. The Sanctuary's creeks spilled over, trees collapsed, and some of the dirt paths washed out. The elephants handled the deluge remarkably well. Minnie was captivated by a large round plastic culvert unearthed by the floods; she dropped sticks inside the culvert, knocked it down a small bank and stuck her entire head inside.

Elsewhere, Lottie and Ronnie scraped together bouquets of up-rooted plants and heaped them on their backs. Even Sissy, who'd nearly drowned nineteen years earlier during the Texas zoo flood, took the occasion to cavort with Winkie. Billie weathered the bad weather, too. Once stressed easily by the sounds of heavy equipment, she now seemed unperturbed when construction vehicles rumbled past to repair the damage.

Even a simple event, like the sight of a caregiver driving up to the barn on a four-wheeler to deliver a meal, could send Billie and Frieda into spasms of excitement, Frieda trumpeting and bellowing and scampering in circles, her ears and long tail projecting outward, and Billie roaring, squeaking and pirouetting. Their voices overlapped, forming a chorus. They sounded unmistakably happy.

To an outsider, the elephants' escapades might seem mundane, of no importance. But to these retired circus elephants, the freedom to move about, to roll around in a wallow of red mud, to coat their bodies in dust, to splash about in a pond and simply walk about unchained, sampling nature's delectables—not just once, but every day—must have seemed miraculous. The staff never grew tired of witnessing their adventures. Too many circus elephants would never taste this kind of freedom.

Billie still wrestled with her insecurities, so it was especially gratifying to see her silly side. One morning she waited outside the barn for Liz to emerge from her tuberculosis treatment, and then followed her friend out to the yard. Billie liked nothing better than to have both Liz and Frieda by her side. Billie checked in with Frieda and then, whimsically, she maneuvered backwards down the hill to where Liz was munching on a pile of hay. Back and forth Billie went, trying to encourage one or the other elephant to join the others.

She took utter delight in a large blue ball she discovered in the Q Barn, and staffers frequently found her kicking it around as if

she were a one-elephant soccer team. With surprising adroitness, Billie dribbled the ball between her enormous feet and maneuvered it under her belly. She dived for the ball so passionately
that her face would land in the mud and she would swish her ropy
tail back and forth with exhilaration. One afternoon a caregiver
heard a loud thump from the Q Barn and peered around the corner to see Billie's ball flying through the air. She frequently bat-
ted the ball so high it got stuck in a nearby tree.

Her happy fits didn't last long—maybe five minutes—but when
they erupted they were full-bore. For those few suspended moments, Billie felt safe and comfortable enough to shed her anx-
ieties.

Her growing sense of ease extended to her caregivers. In the
circus her handlers had touched her whenever, wherever, and
however they wanted to to get her in line. Long after her rescue,
Billie continued to avoid contact of almost any sort with humans.
But even if she had wanted to get to know her caregivers, it was
difficult. In her first three years in Tennessee, a number of new
faces rotated in and out of the barn. Now, under quarantine,
Billie interacted with just three direct caregivers, and the better
she got to know them the calmer she became. For the first
time in years she began to let the humans in her life caress
her trunk or touch the side of her massive gray body without
flinching. She could bathe herself in the pond, and did so often,
but now she let the staff wash her down with a hose as well. She
stood still, eyes shut, basking as the water cascaded off her wrinkly skin. The company of her caregivers seemed to enhance the
experience.

In spite of her fear and distrust, her fretfulness, she was learning to enjoy life, to savor the ordinary pleasures of the day. That
spring one of the caregivers decided to celebrate her own birth-
day with piñatas for the elephants—paper bags filled with berries
and other aromatic fruits. Some of the elephants took their time

with their gifts, shaking the piñatas and letting the contents strew about. Billie gulped her piñata down without a moment's hesitation, bag and all.

The Sanctuary's Web site chronicled the elephants' escapades, and Billie developed a fan club of sorts. Supporters knew her as the elephant who still wore a chain around her leg—a potent reminder of her previous life. The chain was more of a bracelet now; most of the four-foot attachment that trailed behind Billie had fallen off in the woods one day, worn down by her excursions. Billie was literally starting to shed her past.

Blais wasn't kidding himself; Billie had a long way to go. Her pain was so profound it seemed to exist in layers. She needed to work through each of them on her own terms and on her own timetable. Because of his other duties, Blais could spend only a fraction of his time around the fragile elephant. He hadn't realized how dramatically she'd blossomed until one afternoon when, as a result of the flood, the staff discovered a new toy for the Q girls: a three-foot-long plastic oblong-shaped capsule that had previously been buried under debris. Frieda and Liz hung back but Billie, inquisitive, stepped forward instantly to examine the bright orange toy. She grazed it with her trunk and rolled it back and forth. Next she mashed the ball, first with her foot, then with her shoulder. She maneuvered the pill-shaped item under her belly and lowered her immense body until she had pushed the ball flatly to the ground. She'd tested the object every way she knew how and now deemed it safe enough to smack and chase.

Free from any cares, Billie played all afternoon with her new toy, so enamored that at one point she abandoned the ball and galloped a lap around her companions, trumpeting victoriously. Blais watched her almost with disbelief. The elephant he'd once ranked at the worst possible level of apprehension now seemed capable of utter delight. Billie might look as though she were in a bad mood, the way she planted herself resolutely, with that distant gaze in her eye. But then she would let out her distinctive squeak, the tweet of a mouse magnified by a thousand. The squeak seemed to say that, for a moment, anyway, Billie was okay. More than okay. She was content.

CHAINS, HOOKS, AND HOT SHOTS

Circuses still rely on dominance training. In addition to bullhooks, trainers use ropes, chains, and, in modern days, electric prods, and hot shots to force an elephant into performing stunts she would otherwise never perform on her own. The key to dominance training is to strip an elephant of every ounce of autonomy by depriving her of even the smallest of choices—forcing her to perform a variety of tricks and inflicting pain on her when she fails to measure up.

Trainers see this as necessary: Circus elephants are uncaged and freer than most animals to walk about, and as a result they have to be taught to respect their handler. Most elephant men still insist that the only way to instill the right attitude is through fear: fear that disobeying a handler might bring about discomfort or, worse, pain. Rewarding an elephant with food for following a command and withholding the food if the command is ignored simply doesn't work, trainers believe. The old-timers maintain that once an elephant understands she will be disciplined only if she chooses to disobey, she will work for praise.

In the early days of the circus, trainers spoke candidly of how, to get an elephant to perform, they literally had to beat it into their heads. It was common to see an elephant's ears torn to tatters and her hide slashed bloody before she finally learned to understand what was expected of her.

Some elephants could and did form strong attachments to their trainers. Circus annals have noted many times how an elephant rescued a trainer from being attacked by another elephant or lashed out in fury at what appeared to be a malevolent move on the part of a third party. In 1940, an elephant at the Fort Worth Zoo, Queen Tut, stepped in after another elephant knocked down and tried to crush the zoo director. Queen Tut ran off the menacing elephant, Sugar, and kept watch over the director until help arrived.

The blind loyalty shown by some elephants was remarkable. In 1942, Ringling Bros. and Barnum & Bailey's menagerie tent caught fire in Cleveland, burning to death four elephants and leaving many others with scorched ears and bodies. Seared skin hung from the elephants in sheets. Yet in spite of their injuries the elephants stayed put, refusing to budge until the bull man, Walter McClain, arrived. Once he shouted his orders, the elephants dutifully reached down and pulled out the stakes that tied their front legs to the ground, then grasped the tail of the elephant in front of them and stumbled out of the chaos. The veterinarian who was on hand witnessed frantic shouting, blinding smoke, stench of burned flesh—and nothing but silence from the elephants. "Not one elephant trumpeted. I think they just trusted that us men would get them out of their pickle," the vet recalled years later. "It was one of the most touching experiences I've ever had around a circus—or anywhere."

Early trainers believed that elephants knew which handlers were true elephant men: they could smell the scent of elephants in their clothes, their hair and their shoes. The more conscientious trainers brushed their elephants twice a day, scrubbed them once a week and oiled their leathery skin twice a year. Circumstances didn't always allow it, however. Trainer Smokey Jones once said he'd like to wash his elephants, but Ringling told him it would be a waste of water. "Ain't one elephant around here's been washed in twenty years," Jones complained. "If there was a river or a lake near the lot I'd take them in myself."

Back in the day, keepers periodically used a blowtorch to burn off what little hair an elephant had. Right before a performance, they'd sweep the elephants' hides with brooms. To warm them in cold weather, keepers often dosed their elephants with brandy. Ringling Bros. and Barnum & Bailey fed its herd cracked corn, molasses, wheat bran, alfalfa meal, crimped oats, wheat bran, seed oil, calcium carbonate, iron and other minerals, and iodized salt. The baby elephants also got a dose of sorghum, charcoal powder, resin, soda and extra salt. When nobody was looking circus workers smuggled them doughnuts, coffee (including the cup), cotton candy, Coca-Cola, hot dogs, Popsicles, toasted cheese sandwiches, and Tums. Between gigs the elephants foraged the grounds for bits of dirt, gravel, coal, and cigarette butts. Before an elephant entered the ring her trainer often made her stand on her hind legs repeatedly to trigger her bowels.

To this day, show animals are often traded like pieces of machinery and forced to acclimate to new trainers or presenters, many of whom are ordered to make the animals perform acts they simply cannot master. And grooms still bring to the job an intense desire to right some wrong in their own lives—"because life has warped them with some low roundhouse blow," as trainer Bill Ballantine wrote in his 1958 memoir *Wild Tigers & Tame Fleas*.

NINETEEN

—⊷◈⊶—

UNCHAINED AT LAST

Years passed. John and Herta Cuneo continued to live a life of splendor. In 2009 they joined with the Cuneo Foundation to donate John Cuneo's childhood home, the hundred-acre Cuneo Museum and gardens in Libertyville, Illinois, valued at $50 million, to Loyola University Chicago. The school announced plans to construct a new building on its Lake Shore campus and call it Cuneo Hall.

USDA inspectors stepped up their scrutiny of Cuneo's circus tigers, citing his Hawthorn Corporation numerous times for failing to provide the animals with adequate space and exercise. Activists protested Cuneo's hiring of trainer Lance Ramos, also known as Lancelot Kollman. Ramos had such an extensive rap sheet for abusing exotic animals that the federal government revoked his exhibitor's license. Now he was working for Cuneo.

Meanwhile, the Elephant Sanctuary continued to grow. Supporters showered the Sanctuary with donations to help care for the elephants. Membership grew to 100,000 and contributions continued to exceed $4 million a year. The Sanctuary itself remained closed to visitors, but it opened a welcome center in downtown Hohenwald, where visitors could watch the elephants via a network of solar-powered cameras stationed throughout the habitat, attend talks by caregivers, watch videos of the elephants, and learn more about their past and present lives.

There'd been several setbacks. In the summer of 2009, eight employees tested positive for tuberculosis—caused by the pressure-washing of the barn where Liz was being treated for the disease. Elephants can excrete TB bacteria through their trunks and feces, and the pressure-washing created a mist that transmitted the bacteria throughout the barn supervised by Buckley and into an administrative building next door, the Tennessee Department of Health and the federal Centers for Disease Control and Prevention determined. Luckily none of the employees became ill. Staffers chose to take the medication regimen to prevent them from coming down with active TB. On the advice of the National Institute for Occupational Safety and Health, employees began wearing more protection around the elephants and using lower-pressure hoses to clean the barns.

The relationship between Buckley and Blais deteriorated. A year later, Blais announced that he was leaving the Sanctuary, which meant the daily supervision of all the Sanctuary's elephants would fall to Buckley. Blais agreed to stay on after the Sanctuary's board of directors removed Buckley from her position as CEO. The board and consultants from the Center for Nonprofit Management spent months working to define a role for Buckley that emphasized her strengths but, unable to agree on an arrangement, the board let her go in March 2010. Buckley sued, seeking $500,000 in damages and the right to visit Tarra. The board filed a counterclaim, supported by letters from current and former staff, that Buckley had mistreated staff, engaged in volatile outbursts, and failed to carry out infection controls suggested by regulators before the tuberculosis breakout. Buckley went on to start a new nonprofit organization, Elephant Aid International.

Her replacement was Rob Atkinson, former head of wildlife for the United Kingdom's Royal Society for the Prevention of Cruelty to Animals. Atkinson had led efforts in England to expand awareness about the suffering caused from keeping elephants in captivity, and had developed strategy for four wildlife centers. A year after Atkinson's arrival, Blais left the Sanctuary and began negotiating the release of a elephant in Chile who had spent sixty years with the circus. He married former caregiver Kat Haselau. Atkinson lasted another year before he, too, left in 2012.

The circus and zoo communities still looked with disdain at the Elephant Sanctuary. The AZA began referring to the sanctuaries in Tennessee and California as "elephant ranches" and said they were tantamount to large, unaccredited zoos. Circus veteran John Milton Herriott protested the Elephant Sanctuary's closed-door policy—"We don't know what's going on there." And he insisted that former circus elephants could not possibly enjoy life in an open field—that trying to get animals with so many divergent personalities to live as a herd would cause nothing but headaches.

By 2013, the Sanctuary had taken in twenty-four elephants and lost eleven, including three from Hawthorn. Queenie died in 2008, as did Delhi, the last of Billie's comrades from her Hawthorn Five days. Delhi passed away in her sleep. Lottie, the emotional leader of the Hawthorn herd, died suddenly in 2010. Caregivers discovered her one morning lying beneath a large cedar tree. Zula, one of the African elephants, and Asian elephant Bunny died in 2009, as did Ned, a painfully ill elephant who'd been confiscated the previous November from Lance Ramos. Ned was one of the few elephants born in captivity who survived to adulthood. He succumbed much too soon, at the age of twenty-one.

Billie, though, was making progress.

It seemed like a simple enough repair. The Q Barn's weighing scale had grown rusty from sitting just inside the entrance and it no longer worked. Facilities employee Daniel Bledsoe figured out a way to cover the scale from the elements and sent off for new parts. He installed the parts when they arrived and screwed in place the metal plate that covered the wiring. The scale was back in working order.

At least until the next morning. One of the caregivers arrived to find the scale torn apart again, the wiring busted and hanging down. Someone had unscrewed the bolts holding down the metal plate and was grasping it proudly in her trunk.

Billie.

Bledsoe sent off for another set of new parts, installed them, and once again got the scales working. The following morning Liz was undergoing her tuberculosis treatment when she shook some shavings off her back. Along with them tumbled a knob from the scale's display panel, which hit the ground with a loud clank. A few feet away stood the culprit holding the panel with her trunk: Billie again.

Bledsoe learned his lesson. This time he rewired a new display panel eight feet from the barn in a nearby shed and buried the conduit underground. Billie was watching. The next day her caregivers found dirt flung in every direction and the conduit lying on top of the ground.

It took four attempts to keep elephant from outsmarting repairman. While caregivers distracted Billie, Daniel reburied the conduit, disguised the dug-up soil and, for good measure, created piles of dirt and debris to lure Billie away from the scene.

The episode was vintage Billie. She was smart enough to dismantle the scales, not once but several times, so skillfully that Sanctuary staff were forced to outfox her. Employees learned they had to figure out how to keep doors shut. How to store the haycart. How to protect the wheelbarrow. Billie had a habit of demolishing those, too.

It would be easy to write off these incidents as vandalism, but an elephant wouldn't look at it that way. Billie had tackled the scales the same way a young child might disassemble a TV set, and seemed quite proud of her handiwork. She'd just waited to exercise her intelligence until no one was around.

Seven years had passed since her arrival at the Sanctuary. At fifty-one, she was physically in great shape. Unlike Frieda, Billie's feet were holding up well. Her cast-iron stomach was capable of processing anything she devoured. But, emotionally, for every two steps forward Billie made, she took one back. She might reach out her trunk to investigate the hands that beckoned to her, but only for a second. Then she'd withdraw it again.

Her caregivers began trying to coax Billie to leave the barn and follow them to a different corner of her habitat each morning so she wouldn't interfere with Liz's tuberculosis treatments. This was difficult on several fronts. First, Billie was reluctant to leave Liz and suspicious of anyone who suggested she do so. Offered a treat as a lure, she would stretch out her feet as wide as she could, try to grasp the treat and, if she succeeded, withdraw back into the barn. Or she might pick up a rock with her trunk and rake it along the fence line, back and forth, back and forth, as if she were stalling for time. If she did make it out of the barn, she often got stuck at the gate. It took a lot of encouragement to get her through the gate—sometimes forty-five minutes' worth of reassurances. Caregivers could see the fear and hesitation in her eyes. But over time, with much encouragement and patience on the part of the staff, Billie whittled her stalling to just ten minutes or so before she'd walk through.

The restraint chute was another challenge. Caregivers needed Billie to get used to the chute because it was the best possible place to carry out medical procedures. But the idea of being closed up in the same sort of crush she'd been locked in and beaten years earlier caused her extreme anxiety: the instant she stepped into the chute she'd back out of it again, a look of panic in her eyes. But she was learning. Eventually she grew brave enough to step inside the chute and stand still for several minutes before her caregivers opened the door again and let her back out.

Around Billie, caregivers needed to be aware of everything—because Billie noticed everything. She was ten times more aware of her surroundings than the human beings in her orbit would ever be.

And yet the unbridled joy she demonstrated on good days was undeniable. One summer afternoon the Sanctuary staff gave Billie a new toy: a giant rectangular cube with lopped-off corners, full of treats. Billie approached the cube, turned it over a couple of times, and *voilà*—the treats spilled out. All of them. That fast.

Her trumpets were the loudest of any elephant in the Q Barn. Frequently she backed up against the bars to let caregivers stroke her enormous rear end. When four-wheelers puttered into view, bearing food, she raced them along the fence line, trumpeting and twirling with glee. Entering the barn at night, she would roar so loudly she sounded like an airhorn.

The turnaround began in 2011, the year the Sanctuary brought in some consultants to offer target training. The Sanctuary needed to be able to administer medical procedures to the elephants—USDA required it—in a way that kept employees safe. The Sanctuary's other elephants had undergone target training with great success. Now it was the Hawthorn girls' turn, and no one needed the training more than Billie and Minnie.

The Sanctuary hired consultant Gail Laule to help them overcome the problem. Ever since she'd received her master's degree in behavioral science from California State University and gone to work at Marineland in California in 1979, Laule has been a pioneer in the animal welfare field. She helped develop training techniques that earned the trust of marine mammals and got them to cooperate with husbandry and medical procedures. In 1985, she and her partner, Tim Desmond, started a consulting business, Active Environments, and began working with captive animals of all kinds, including elephants. Laule and Desmond developed the concept of protected contact—of putting a barrier between humans and animals to keep both parties safe. Elephants were killing and injuring too many people in zoos and circuses and the only solution, as Laule saw it, was to implement a hands-off policy, a practice already in use throughout much of Europe.

Here's why: With protected contact, a trainer no longer needs to use tools to keep safe. She already is safe. Up to this point the Elephant Sanctuary had relied too much on passive control, and with passive control there was only so much caregivers could ask an elephant to do, Laule explained. With volatile elephants like Billie, they simply couldn't achieve the level of husbandry USDA required.

To help her, Laule brought in another Active Environments consultant, Margaret Whittaker, who'd first worked with elephants in the mid-1980s as a keeper at the Houston Zoo. Whittaker coordinated the first protected contact program involving a herd of breeding elephants in the country. She'd worked as a consultant for Active Environments since 1996.

Using protected contact, Laule and Whittaker found they could practice the exact same training techniques with an elephant that they used with a gorilla or a giraffe or a sea lion or anything else—and, moreover, they could ask elephants to do things they normally wouldn't choose to do. The trick lies in target training. Laule and Desmond wrap a paper towel around one end of a bamboo pole—it looks like a giant Q-tip—and use it to teach an elephant to touch his head to it, or his foot, or some other body part. Early on in the training, when an elephant doesn't know what the trainer wants her to do, the trainer blows a whistle every time the elephant makes even a small move in the right direction and gives her a treat. The treat is given the instant the whistle is blown.

Target training is crucial to teaching an elephant who is free to wander off to, instead, rest her foot on the side of a fence so a caregiver can file down her cuticles or stand still long enough for veterinarians to conduct trunk washes or draw blood. Elephants quickly begin to understand that good things happen if they choose to cooperate, and they begin to enjoy target training.

"They're smart animals," Laule said. "They like to learn. But they want to learn like the rest of us—no negative consequences for making a mistake. (With target training) they can say no if they want to. You provide them that kind of a context, they love to learn."

Billie responded quickly to target training. She learned to lean in toward the fence, to raise her feet so caregivers could trim her cuticles, to raise her trunk for tuberculosis testing and to have blood drawn from the veins in her ear. Sometimes she was even playful about it. If someone asked to work on her foot, she'd volunteer her ear. Clearly she trusted her caregivers, Laule reasoned, or she wouldn't have let them get that close.

Still, she remained volatile.

Blood draws are one of the riskier procedures to perform on elephants because they require a trainer to stand right up against the opposite side of the fence, within easy reach. The elephant must stand patiently and even endure a little pain from the prick of the needle. It's a two-person task: one trainer will stand on the opposite side of the fence from the elephant, near the elephant's head, to get her in position. The person doing the blood draw will stand on a ladder near the elephant's ear, desensitizing it by touching it first with a finger, then with a needle that has a cap on it, next with the needle itself, and finally inserting the needle to draw blood.

The lead trainer standing next to the elephant's ear blows the whistle each time the elephant does as she is asked, prompting the support caregiver at the elephant's head to give her a treat. If the animal decides to be aggressive, both employees have to be prepared to jump out of the way.

Most animals grow accustomed to target training: they relax and allow themselves to enjoy the bounty of treats. For blood draws, trainers haul out the fun food—fruits and vegetables, but also Cheerios, Froot Loops, marshmallows, and gummy bears—anything to bring an elephant to the table. Billie's favorite treat was jelly beans. She couldn't scarf them up fast enough.

In spite of that, Laule and Whittaker quickly discovered that they could never relax around Billie. She remained wary through-out the procedures. Elephants can enlist a whole array of aggressive behaviors and Billie showed them all: she would throw her trunk at her caregivers, charge at them, swing around quickly, and reach out and try to grab the person closest to her. Laule suspected what was going through Billie's mind. When an elephant offers an ear or foot or trunk, she has to be willing to give the caregiver on the other end some control. And for former circus elephants, control is a huge issue because they'd gone so many years without it. For an elephant like Billie, the act of relinquishing even a little bit of control is a big deal.

Over time Billie's aggression diminished by about two-thirds, but it still lingers, and Laule expects it always will. Sometimes she thinks Billie lashes out just to scare or surprise her caregiv-ers. But Laule also believes Billie is angry—angry at the people who mistreated her in her past, who forced her to sacrifice the life she should have had, who made her live on the edge. All those years, circus handlers struck Billie for no reason at all, and now she was striking back just as erratically.

For five years Billie remained defiant, unable to forget her past. Her chain was a daily reminder of who she was and where she had come from. She'd worn it for so long she no longer seemed bothered by the noise it made. But to her caregivers, not to mention the Sanctuary's supporters, the chain was an ugly symbol of Billie's past. They were more than ready to see it go.

So Laule and Whittaker went to work. First Laule convinced Billie to present her foot when she was asked. Her caregivers lavished her with so much praise when she responded to their requests that Billie began to offer up her foot before she was even asked. Next, the consultants had two caregivers who worked on Billie, Richard Treat and Jennifer Hampton, familiarize her with the sight of the bolt cutters and how it felt when they rested against her chain. Three days a week for nearly three weeks, they practiced this routine.

One sunny May afternoon, Billie seemed ready. Whittaker stood just on the other side of the fence from Billie's trunk, talking reassuringly to her and poised to feed her a whole bucket of snacks. From the other side of the fence, Treat asked Billie to raise her foot. She did so willingly and rested it on one of the slats in the fence. Treat approached her gingerly, bolt cutters in hand. He reached through the slats and carefully snipped at one of the links in the chain. The link gave a bit. It was weathered and weak.

Whittaker and Treat waited a few moments, trying to gauge Billie's mood. It was crucial not to push her too far. Twice more Treat approached, knelt and made cuts with the bolt cutters. Billie swatted the fence with her tail, hard. Whittaker and Treat spoke to her gently to calm her down.

Each time Billie backed away from the fence, the caregivers' reassurances brought her back. It was almost as if Billie realized what they were attempting to do. The expression on her face softened and she stopped swinging at the fence. She lifted her foot again, this time higher than before, pushed up against the bars of the fence and rotated her ankle first one way and then another.

Half a dozen times Treat applied the bolt cutters to the chain on Billie's leg. After the sixth cut the chain remained in place, just barely. Treat set the bolt cutters down and, kneeling at Billie's foot, he reached out to disconnect the links. The instant he touched the chain it clattered to the ground.

If Billie understood the significance of the moment, she gave no sign. She glanced down at the worn chain, picked it up with her trunk, then dropped it and walked away. The small crowd that had gathered swallowed back emotion at the milestone, but the elephant had better things to do. She headed out to the sand pile to wake Frieda from her nap.

NOTES

✦━━ ✦◈✦ ━━✦

PROLOGUE: FACING THE FUTURE

1   Interviews with Scott Blais, April 1, 2011, and December 8, 2012.

2   **The first elephant:** Bill Ballantine, *Wild Tigers & Tame Fleas* (New York: Rinehart & Company, 1958), 274.

3   **Then, around 1800:** E. S. Hallock, "The American Circus," *Century Illustrated Magazine*, August 1905, 568.

3   **She, too, was put on display:** Ballantine, *Wild Tigers & Tame Fleas,* 275.

3   **Little Bet followed:** Ibid.

3   **In 1880, the first elephant:** A. W. Rolker, "Babies of the Zoo," *McClure's Magazine*, October 1903, 608.

3   **Four years later:** David Lewis Hammarstrom, *Fall of the Big Top: The Vanishing American Circus* (Jefferson, NC: McFarland & Company, 2007), 17. Jumbo's career in America was short-lived: three years after his arrival Jumbo backed into the path of a locomotive in Saint Thomas, Canada, while the circus was unloading. The train struck and killed him, but not before he allegedly threw his best friend, a dwarf clown elephant named Tom Thumb, and his keeper out of the path of the train. Jumbo's taxidermied

hide was displayed at Tufts University's Barnum Hall in Boston until the building burned in 1975. tuftsjournal.tufts.edu.

3 **The phrase "seeing the elephant":** Vanessa Remmers, "Civil War comes alive at Dinwiddie Park," *Petersburg* (Va.) *Progress-Index,* April 7, 2013.

CHAPTER ONE: LOSING A FAMILY

6 **age of four:** Association of Zoos and Aquariums 2010 North American Regional Studbook—Asian elephant, 67. http://www.elephanttag.org/professional/2010AsianElephantStudbook.pdf

6 **By the time:** Jane Harriman, "Wild Animals Rule Cow Farm," *The Boston Globe*, October 18, 1964.

6 **Most of the elephants Southwick's imported:** John Krausz, *How to Buy an Elephant and 38 Other Things You Never Knew You Wanted To Know* (New York: Skyhorse, 2007), 1, and phone interview with Justine Brewer, October 8, 2012.

7 **Junior Clarke:** Buckles blog, http://bucklesw.blogspot.com, October 5, 2005.

8 **The rival circuses:** Michael Daly, *Topsy: The Startling Story of the Crooked-Tailed Elephant, P. T. Barnum, and the American Wizard, Thomas Edison* (New York: Atlantic Monthly Press, 2013), 160.

8 **Adam Forepaugh tried to trump:** Ibid.

8 **Barnum countered:** Ibid.

8 **In the early 1800s, hunters:** Lawrence Perry, "The Wild Beast Traffic," *Frank Leslie's Popular Monthly,* July 1903, 229.

8 **In Africa, native hunters:** Richard L. Garner, "Man Likeness in Jungle Beasts: Studying Animal Intelligence in Africa's Wilds," *American Periodicals Series,* 1919.

9 **Other hunters tracked down:** Janet M. Davis, *The Circus Age: Culture and Society Under the American Big Top* (Durham, NC: University of North Carolina Press, 2002), 196.

9 **"[Natives] don't cost much":** Ibid.

CHAPTER TWO: DRAWN TO THE BIG TOP

10   **Young Mr. Cuneo:** Margaret Scully, "Training Animals His Hobby, and He Finds Bears Exciting," *Chicago Daily Tribune*, March 21, 1950, 2.

10   **Bears:** Ibid.

11   Cuneo family background: John B. Byrne, *Cuneo Museum and Gardens* (Mount Pleasant, SC: Arcadia Publishing, 2009), 8–9.

11   **Sears, Roebuck:** Ibid., 85.

12   **Julia Shepherd:** Ibid., 77.

12   **Samuel Insull:** Ibid., 8–9. A British native, Insull served as private secretary to inventor Thomas Edison and later partnered with him to create Commonwealth Edison, the company that supplied power to Chicago and to surrounding towns that were just becoming electrified. Insull also later salvaged People's Gas, Coke and Light Company and chaired the Chicago Rapid Transit Authority, which operated the city's electric streetcars and elevated trains. And he acquired three local railroads: the Chicago, North Shore and Milwaukee; the Chicago, South Shore and South Bend; and the Chicago Aurora and Elgin Railroad. He was able to enjoy his pink palace for only a few years before his highfaluting ways crashed down. He had thousands of investors in his companies, and to make sure he retained control, he had developed an intricate series of holding companies. The Depression caught him up short. He had no choice but to sell the Libertyville property. A number of investors lost everything along with him, and when they rose up against Insull, the Franklin D. Roosevelt administration went after him. He ran away to Greece, but was later extradited. A trial eventually cleared him of the charges, but by then Insull wanted nothing more to do with America. He and his wife, Gladys, retired to Paris, where Insull died of a heart attack in a subway station several years later. See John B. Byrne, *Cuneo Museum and Gardens.*

12   **For years, Insull:** Ibid., 9.

12   **Locals called the house the Pink Mansion:** Ibid., 60. The

Cuneos reveled in their rural splendor. The outdoor swimming pool was limited to warm weather, so they added one indoors, too. Julia Cuneo's bedroom featured one of the first water-cooled air conditioners in existence, a souvenir from the House of the Future at the 1933 Century of Progress World's Fair in Chicago. (John Handley, "Museum-Quality: The Eras may change, but top-of-the-line homes share an uncommon history," *Chicago Tribune,* July 19, 2000, 16.) The couple kept a gilded Steinway piano in the dining room (Dean Geroulis, "Museum paints a portrait of how wealthy once lived: Print mogul's mansion, grounds overflow with beauty, sense of history," *Chicago Tribune*, October 23, 2002, 22.) Surrounding the piano were four floor lamps that originally hailed from Napoleon's palace in Corsica. In another corner of the room sat an eighteenth-century Madame Récamier cameo table, named for a woman in the French court who was exiled by Napoleon in 1805 and allowed to return only after Napoleon lost the fight at Waterloo a decade later.

The driveway to the house was equally impressive. It crossed a fieldstone and mortar bridge straddling a bucolic pond, winding its way through seventy-five acres of gently rolling gardens, lawns and woods—nothing like the flat prairie the land had started out as. Visitors who strolled the grounds at the rear of the house would come upon a sunken garden and a glistening outdoor pool.

A devout Catholic, John Senior converted Insull's sun porch into a private chapel framed with stained glass and murals designed by well-known artist John Mallin. Cardinal Samuel Stritch, the archbishop of Chicago and a close personal friend, consecrated the chapel, a move that necessitated approval from the pope. (Byrne, *Cuneo Museum and Gardens.)*

John Senior loved movies—he co-owned several movie theaters in Chicago—and he had a movie theater built in the basement. He and Julia threw lavish parties. They had two long dining room tables that, with added leaves, could accommodate sixty-four guests. John Junior later recalled his parents' annual New Year's Eve galas, when fifty of Chicago's most important leaders would be invited to dinner. Year after year the Cuneos served the same rich menu: caviar for starters, followed by white fish in a cream sauce, then pheasant and, for dessert, chocolate sundaes served in coconut shells. See Handley, *Chicago Tribune,* July 19, 2000.

13   **Family kept an apartment:** Ibid., 77.

13   **"Hampton among the cornfields":** Ibid., 7. Illinois governor and two-time presidential candidate Adlai Stevenson and shoe magnate Irving Florsheim joined John Cuneo Sr., in buying some of the four thousand acres Samuel Insull needed to unload. Newspaper mogul Joseph Medill Patterson used his mansion in the area as a writer's escape. See Byrne, *Cuneo Museum and Gardens.*

13   **To protect their:** Information given during tour of Cuneo Museum, October 28, 2011.

13   **A photograph of John Cuneo Jr.:** Byrne, *Cuneo Museum and Gardens,* 70.

13   **Ponies:** James Segreti, "Cuneo Entries Pile up Honors at Horse Show," *Chicago Daily Tribune,* November 7, 1945, 30.

13   **Two thousand acres:** Ibid., 9.

13   **Started the Hawthorn Mellody Farm:** Ibid., 91.

13   **Chicago's third-largest supplier of milk:** Ibid.

13   **"Home of Champions":** Ibid., 95.

14   **more than a quarter of a million children:** Ibid., 102.

14   **Dean Martin:** Ibid., 112.

14   **two guanacos:** Leigh Atkinson, "Gee Whiz, Kids! That Big Cow's Got a Trunk!" *Chicago Daily Tribune,* June 1, 1951, 9.

15   **Noah's Ark:** Byrne, *Cuneo Museum and Gardens,* 107

15   **Frontier Town:** Ibid., 109–111.

15   **car collided:** "John Cuneo Jr. Seriously Hurt in Auto Crash," *Chicago Daily Tribune,* November 30, 1950, B6.

16   **arrested for speeding:** "Cuneo Jr. Fined $30 and Costs in Speeding Case," *Chicago Daily Tribune,* March 27, 1952, 3.

16   **warrant for his arrest:** Ibid.

16   **Asa Candler Jr:** Ann Uhry Abrams, *Formula for Fortune: How Asa Candler Discovered Coca-Cola and Turned It into the Wealth His Children Enjoyed* (Bloomington, IN: iUniverse, 2012), 254.

16 **Delicious, Refreshing:** Ibid., 256.

16 **two-year-old baby elephant:** "Baby Elephant and Sun Bear Arrive for Zoo," *Chicago Daily Tribune,* March 29, 1951, 10.

16 **stewardess brushed her hide:** Ibid., back page.

17 **one of 264 elephants:** Tom Parkinson, "Billboard Calls Elephant Roll," *Billboard,* April 12, 1952, 1.

17 **Jessie loves to dance:** "Gee Whiz, Kids!" 1.

17 **Photos showed the elephant:** Buckles blog, May 28, 2012.

18 **Miss Eloise Berchtold:** Eleanor Page, "John F. Cuneo Jr. Takes Cincinnati Girl as Bride," *Chicago Daily Tribune*, February 29, 1956, 1.

18 **Eloise had worked at:** John Herriott, "Eloise Berchtold," *The Circus Report*, May 29, 1978, 18.

18 **Paramount Bears:** A link to the video appeared on Wade Burck's Circus No Spin Blog, August 30, 2010.

18 **"World's only uncaged":** An advertisement proclaiming this appeared in *Billboard* magazine, March 16, 1959.

19 **Cuneo suffered burns:** "J. F. Cuneo Jr. Burned While Starting Bike," *Chicago Daily Tribune*, October 17, 1956, B2.

19 **Paul Lemery, was mauled to death:** "Bear Kills Man in Libertyville," *Chicago Daily Tribune*, October 10, 1956, 1.

19 **tough time for circuses:** *Billboard*, March 16, 1959.

20 **"when the next P. T. Barnum":** Gabe Kaimowitz, Newspaper Enterprise Association, *The Chillicothe* (Missouri) *Constitution,* April 15, 1060.

20 **Wild Animal Fantasy:** *Billboard,* April 28, 1958.

20 **The act featured:** An ad describing Cuneo's Wild Animal Fantasy appeared on Wade Burck's Circus No Spin Zone blog, January 31, 2011.

21 **Cirque d'Hiver:** *Billboard*, March 16, 1960, 51.

21 **Cuneo's horse as the most:** Circus No Spin Zone blog, December 31, 2008.

21 **In 1960, Cuneo sold:** *Billboard*, December 26, 1960.

21 **Cuneo had divorced Berchtold:** Pat Jameson confirms this in her

response to a query posted on the Circus History Message Board Aug. 2, 2006. www.circushistory.org.

21 **One of his bears pedaled:** A page from a circus program advertising this appeared on the Circus No Spin Zone blog, February 25, 2011.

22 **Boo Boo was the best known:** Ibid., October 14, 2012.

22 **Cuneo and Klauser were married:** Loyola Stritch School of Medicine press release, November 3, 2011.

22 **A photo from that time:** Buckles blog, November 8, 2012.

22 **To round up the elephants:** Stephen French Whitman, "Elephant Catchers," *Current Literature,* May 1903, 568.

22 **The operation was arduous:** Ibid.

23 **Once the elephants:** Ibid. Two other articles: "Capturing Elephants: Chasing the Beasts Through Their Native Jungle," *Boston Daily Globe,* July 10, 1892, 27, and "Kraals: How Our Ancestors Captured Elephants," Sri Lanka *Sunday Observer,* October 5, 2008, also provided valuable insight.

23 **An account of a hunting expedition:** Sir James Emerson Tennent, *The Wild Elephant and the Method of Capturing and Taming it in Ceylon* (London: Longmans, Green, 1867), 118–54. Hunters relied on tamed elephants to help lure the wild ones. According to Tennent's account, a domesticated elephant would lure a newly caught elephant away from the herd and woo it by rubbing its ears, caressing its trunk, and showing signs of affection until it had won it over. Then a second elephant would approach and do the same thing. The tame elephants wore collars about their shoulders fastened to thick ropes. While the tame elephants entwined their trunks about the trunk of the wild animal, native capturers quickly fastened ropes to his hind legs. By now the untamed elephant was trapped, unable to move unless the elephants sandwiching him moved, too. The tame elephants didn't hesitate to pull their wild peers in line. More than once, Tennant wrote, he watched an elephant named Siribeddi push aside a wild elephant to keep it from seizing a rope before it could be wrapped around

his hind leg. In another instance, a decoy elephant waited patiently until a wild elephant lifted his hind foot, and then shoved her own leg beneath it, propping the wild elephant's leg up until a nooser could wrap the rope around it and pull it tight. If a wild elephant flung himself on the ground, trained elephants would ram the animal with their trunks and push him up again. Tame elephants would kneel down and pin a captive elephant down, if need be. Tennent was astonished that none of the captive elephants' trunks were injured by their writhing. One coiled and uncoiled his trunk back and forth in agitation, while another beat the ground slowly with the tip of his trunk in despair.

23   **Captors deliberately starved:** C. Knight, *The Elephant, Principally Viewed in Relation to Man* (London: Charles Knight & Co., 1844), 129.

23   **Once a captured elephant calmed down:** Tennent, 155.

24   **The elephant invariably:** Ibid., 156.

24   **Hobbled and surrounded:** Ibid.

CHAPTER THREE: LEARNING THE ROPES

25   **Born in 1935:** Dominique Jando, "William Woodcock Jr., elephant trainer," *Circopedia*. www.circopedia.org.

25   **His father:** Ibid.

25   **Her grandfather:** Ibid.

25   **Six foot two:** Letter written by Bill Woodcock Sr., November 7, 1955.

25   **got his nickname:** Ibid.

26   **Later, Woodcock helped his dad:** Ibid.

26   **"eats everything in sight":** Buckles blog, May 28, 2007.

26   **Anna May:** Jando, *Circopedia.*

26   **Bill Woodcock Sr. had a saying:** Ivan M. Henry, Legend City #2," The Circus Blog, April 18, 2013, www.thecircusblog.com.

26   **One of his strategies:** Buckles blog, June 3, 2012.

26   **He even married:** Ibid.

27   "Practiced all three rings": Ibid., July 25, 2013.

27   He spent several years: *The Circus Report*, January 10, 1972.

27   he got the call from Cuneo: Buckles blog, January 8, 2007.

27   Dorey Miller . . . asked: Ibid., November 19, 2007.

27   Teddy, the elephant: Ibid., December 27, 2012.

28   The first thing: Ibid.

28   "You gotta be kidding!": Buckles blog, July 29, 2005.

28   Billie and Peggy Ray: Ibid., September 18, 2012.

28   Cuneo had his lawyer: Ibid., March 8, 2012.

28   Trainer Hugo Schmitt: Circuses and Sideshows blog, circuses andsideshows.com/performers/hugoschmitt.html

28   Woodcock phoned Cuneo: Buckles blog, March 8, 2012.

28   MacDonald and his wife: A photo of the stunt appeared on Buckles blog, November 6, 2012.

29   Cuneo was undeterred: Buckles blog, March 8, 2012.

29   rule of thumb: Corinne Flocken, "Circus Vargas, a Show You See Up Close, Opens Its County Run," *Los Angeles Times*, February 3, 1990.

29   A dog trainer once: Ibid.

29   The driver was: Buckles blog, November 19, 2007.

29   Woodcock named the newest: Ibid.

30   secret formula: Ibid., March 30, 2012.

30   With Kelly: Ibid., November 19, 2007

30   "Come get your elephant": Ibid., December 28, 2012.

30   Never one to miss: Ibid.

30   first stop was in Texas: Ibid., May 1, 2005.

30   At thirty-six, Engesser: Mark Zaloudek, *Sarasota Herald Tribune*, August 1, 2008.

31   By 1972 Engesser: Stephen Miller, "Gee Gee Engesser: A 'Blonde Bombshell' of the circus was comfortable around predators," *The Wall Street Journal*, August 23, 2008, A7.

31   Thrust her trunk: Stephanie Hayes, "Circus animals had special hold on her," *St. Pete Times*, July 17, 2008.

31   Jones had a reputation: Bill Ballantine, *Wild Tigers & Tame Fleas* (New York: Rinehart & Company, 1958), 265.

31   His strategy was straightforward: Ibid.

31   Jones also carried: Ibid., 267.

31   Jones was looking to buy: Buckles blog, September 21, 2006.

32   Woodcock had planned: Ibid., September 18, 2006.

32   an elephant named Bimbo: *Amusement Business,* March 11, 1972.

32   Yet Woodcock, for one: Flocken, "Circus Vargas, a Show You See Up Close, Opens Its County Run," *Los Angeles Times,* February 3, 1990.

33   The day after Woodcock's entourage: Buckles blog, May 1, 2006.

33   Clifford Vargas came from: "A Profile: Clifford Vargas," *The Circus Report,* October 25, 1976, 5.

33   That night, Vargas threw a party: Buckles blog, October 25, 2007

34   Reviews were lackluster: *The Circus Report,* February 21, 1972, 1.

34   In the thick of winter: Ibid., January 17, 1977, 2.

34   The circus's spring-summer tour: Ibid., April 17, 1972, 2.

34   It was the first time: Ibid., February 7, 1972.

35   Hugo Schmitt: *Amusement Business,* August 26, 1972.

35   Bunny, a fourteen-week-old: Ibid., March 11, 1972.

35   advertised as the "fastest": Buckles blog, September 18, 2006.

35   mistakenly described: Ibid., January 4, 2008.

35   Cristiani elephants would carry out: Ibid., March 31, 2008.

35   glitzy headpieces: A copy of the photo was published on Buckles blog, September 18, 2006.

35   Barbara Woodcock entered: Ibid., June 19, 2012.

35   A photo from that time: Ibid., January 8, 2007.

36   In later years: Ibid., June 25, 2012.

36   Anna May: Andrew Meacham, "Ben Williams rode to his niche on the backs of elephants," *Tampa Bay Times,* October 6, 2009.

36   The elephant acts were sandwiched: *The Circus Report,* April 17, 1972, 2.

36   By the end of May: "Show Schedule," *The Circus Report,* April 10, 1972, 6.

36   The spring show drew raves: Bill Caldwell, "I Like It," *The Circus Report,* April 23, 1973, 4.

37   **By July, the newsletter:** Ibid., July 24, 1972, 5.

37   **Rival shows had encountered:** Ibid., August 28, 1972, 2.

37   **Buckles and Barbara Woodcock peeled off:** Buckles blog, May 1, 2006.

38   **Woodcock told a friend:** Phone interview with John Milton Herriott, July 24, 2013.

38   **In his *Mirabilia Descripta*:** *The Wild Elephant,* 157.

39   **In what was then called Ceylon:** Ibid., 165.

39   **The elephant's shame:** Ibid.

39   **In Malay, trainers:** Charles Mayer, *Trapping Wild Animals in Malay Jungles* (New York: Garden City Publishing Co., 1920), 77.

39   **Her trainer led her:** Ibid.

39   **For two weeks:** Ibid.

39   **Gradually the elephant:** Ibid., 78.

CHAPTER FOUR: ONE-LEGGED STANDS

41   **A native of Broumana:** www.hamidcircus.com.

41   **Cuneo had provided:** Cuneo interview, *The White Tops,* January/February 2011, 68–69.

41   **To sweeten his offer:** Ibid.

41   **The Hawthorn Five had begun:** Buckles blog, April 24, 2006.

42   **After she trampled:** Charles Wilkins, *The Circus at the Edge of the Earth: Travels with the Great Wallenda Circus* (Toronto: McClelland & Stewart, 1998), 169.

42   **one day he turned his back:** Ibid., 170.

42   **Now Gibbs was ready:** Ibid., 172.

42   **Gibbs spent the next two weeks:** Ibid., 170.

42   **He gave her:** Ibid., 172.

42   **For the first few months:** *The Circus Report,* May 28, 1973, 7.

43   **At forty, Bombay:** Buckles Blog, April 24, 2006.

43   **Culturally, the early 1970s:** The Year 1972, www.thepeoplehistory.com/1972.html.

44   **By 1972, 132 temples:** *The Circus Report,* April 24, 1972.

44   **four days in Wichita:** Ibid., Jan. 29, 1973.

44   **The season was barely under way:** Ibid., March 26, 1973.

44   **praised the show:** *The Circus Report,* May 28, 1973.

44   **Elephants walk with their weight:** Testimony of Dr. Philip Ensley, associate veterinarian at the Zoological Society of San Diego, in American Society for the Prevention of Cruelty to Animals, et al., vs. Feld Entertainment, February 24, 2009, 49.

45   **But in captivity:** Ibid., 51.

45   **A typical elephant:** Ibid.

45   **That November:** "Annual Shrine Show at Dallas/Fort Worth," *The Circus Report*, November 26, 1973.

45   **The next month:** *The Circus Report,* December 4, 1973.

45   **A photo from that year:** The photo appeared on www.thecircusblog.com on September 8, 2011.

46   **Daniels worked for Cuneo:** E-mail exchange with author, January 15, 2013.

46   **Lockard was one of five:** Ibid., April 16, 2013

46   **A few years before:** Ibid.

47   **Cuneo fed her extra grain:** Ibid

47   **Cuneo could handle Billie:** Phone interview with John Cuneo, October 24, 2011.

47   **"If I was an elephant":** E-mail exchange with author, April 16, 2013.

48   **In Africa, hunters:** "The Wild Animal Trade," *New York Tribune,* March 22, 1896, 27.

48   **Many elephants failed to survive:** Mayer, *Trapping Wild Animals,* 50.

48   **traders used slings:** Ibid., 92.

48   **Others placed:** Tennent, *The Wild Elephant,* 102.

48   **In the early 1700s:** Ibid., 103.

49   **On board, elephants were led down:** "Capturing Elephants," *Gleason's Pictorial Drawing Room Companion,* June 21 and 28, 1851.

49   **In 1894 the British:** "Toodles, The Baby, Survives," *The New York Times,* February 6, 1894.

49   **One circus's passage:** Charles Theodore Murray, "At Sea with the Circus," *McClure's Magazine,* May 1898, 76.

49   **A ship from Calcutta:** "Elephants Overboard: Leopard a Suicide," *The New York Times*, April 8, 1905.

50   **On one boat from Singapore:** *Trapping Wild Animals,* 95–96.

50   **In 1936 a pygmy elephant:** "Hippo Kills Elephant Aboard Ship in Storm," *Daily Boston Globe,* March 31, 1936, 1.

50   **Newspapers chronicled:** "Rum Jumbo Too Much for Lady Elephant," Ibid., January 9, 1948, 1.

50   **on a steamer from Europe:** "Some Babies from Over the Water," *Outlook*, March 7, 1876, 438.

CHAPTER FIVE: THE HAWTHORN FIVE

52   **In 1974, gasoline was scarce:** Letter to elephant enthusiast Chang Reynolds from historian Richard Flint, February 11, 1974, Circus World Museum archives.

52   **A listless economy:** Billy Barton, "76–77," *The Circus Report,* November 1, 1976.

52   **A circus needed three years:** Ibid.

53   **By late September:** Ibid.

53   **Circus Vargas:** "Today and Tomorrow," *The Circus Report*, October 25, 1976, 9.

53   **Hamid-Morton did well:** Frank Hoopes, Ibid., May 24, 1976.

53   **Bill Golden presented:** Ibid., June 14, 1976, 11.

53   **The Cuneos' white tigers:** Dan Geringer, "Now He's the Cat's Meow," *Sports Illustrated,* July 21, 1986.

53   **Three of them:** Ibid.

53   **Cuneo's star, Bagheera:** Ibid.

54   **Cuneo's baby elephants:** *The Circus Report,* June 14, 1976.

54   **He trucked his animals:** Ibid., December 8, 1975, 5.

54   **Germaine's latest production:** "Ready for Police Date," *The Circus Report,* August 16, 1976, 3.

55 **One trainer fed his fox:** Pat Derby, *The Lady and Her Tiger* (New York: Dutton, 1976), 171.

55 **Derby knew of elephants:** Arlene Mueller, "Animal Stunts: Circus Delights and a Sober Note of Concern," *The Christian Science Monitor,* September 14, 1988.

55 **She'd divorced her husband:** Christine Mai-Duc, "Pat Derby Dies at 70, Rescuer of Exotic and Performing Animals," *Los Angeles Times*, February 20, 2013.

55 **Page-Cavanaugh's fall show:** "The Program," *The Circus Report,* September 17, 1976, 7.

56 **Adam Forepaugh's 1899 show:** William L. Slout, *Olympians of the Sawdust Circle: A Biographical Dictionary of the Nineteenth Century American Circus* (Rockville, MD: Wildside Press, 1998), 301.

56 **The John Robinson Circus:** On August 4, 2009, Buckles blog reproduced a 1905 story about the circus.

56 **The crowd favorite:** Official program, John Robinson's 10 Big Shows, 1900 season, reprinted in *Hobby Bandwagon*, March 1949, 10–11.

56 **Tillie was 120:** Andrew Chu, "John Robinson's Circus of Terrace Park, Ohio," Circus4Youth.org, May 10, 2009.

56 **That changed in the early 1900s:** Frank Tripp, "Once Famed Elephants Just Marchers Now," *Ellensburg* (Wash.) *Daily Record,* May 18, 1950, 42. Tripp wrote that Jeanne Power, Bill's widow and George's mother, once described elephants as inquisitive animals with mischievous trunks that would "snoop, pull down lights, open water faucets and undo each other's chains, as children might." In one incident, one of the Powers' elephants, Roxie, chewed up a quart jar of jam, glass and all. Another elephant, Jennie, devoured a bushel of coals and, in a separate incident, swallowed an entire barrel of road oil. She was sick for weeks and lost several hundred pounds, but she lived.

57 **Powers' Dancing Elephants had spent:** Ibid.

57 **In elaborately choreographed skits:** Ibid.

57   **A perennial trick:** Ballantine, *Wild Tigers & Tame Fleas,* 298.

57   **Hollywood studio trainer:** Frank Whitbeck, "Elephants," *Toledo Blade,* April 23, 1950, reprinted in *The Circus Report,* November 6, 1978, 12.

57   **In the late 1800s:** George Lockhart, "About Elephants," reprinted in *The Circus Report,* January 30, 1989, 28.

58   **The popular hind-leg maneuver:** Buckles blog, June 6, 2012.

58   **"We have an art":** Ballantine, *Wild Tigers & Tame Fleas,* 279.

58   **Legendary trainer Gunther Gebel-Williams:** Curry Kirkpatrick, "The Greatest Showman on Earth," *Sports Illustrated,* September 26, 1977.

58   **One non-circus elephant even learned:** "Queenie the Water-Skiing Elephant Dies at 59," www.gothamist.com, June 5, 2011.

59   **Trainer Gene Garner festooned:** Buckles blog, November 11, 2010.

CHAPTER SIX: LIFE ON THE ROAD

60   **Circuses were thriving:** C&B Show, *Circus Report,* April 25, 1977, 8.

60   **Packs was a veteran:** Ryan Easley, "Tom Packs Elephants," September 28, 2010, www.showmeelephants.com.

60   **The State Department learned:** Ibid.

60   **The captain messaged:** Ibid.

61   **Finally, the U.S. Navy:** Ibid.

61   **The elephants were malnourished:** Ibid.

61   **Mac MacDonald took one look:** Buckles blog, June 24, 2012.

61   **Vintage photos:** Ibid.

61   **The act suffered**: www.showmeelephants.com.

62   **Packs sold them:** Ibid.

62   **Some if not all:** Photos, Wade Burck's Circus No Spin Zone blog, October 3, 2011.

62   **Dorey Miller:** Cherie Valentine, "The End of an Era," *Back Yard,* September 15, 1999, 6.

62 **In 1977, a twenty-five-year-old elephant:** *The Circus Report,* February 11, 1974.

63 **But John Cuneo Jr. seemed more captivated:** Phone interview with author October 20, 2011.

63 **"Billie was not a nice elephant":** Ibid.

63 **An elephant's personality:** Ibid.

63 **"She did everything for me":** Ibid.

63 **Burck was a hotshot:** *Sports Illustrated,* July 21, 1986.

64 **He left home:** Ibid.

64 **Five years later:** Ibid.

64 **Burck tried to emulate his idol:** Ibid.

64 **He appreciated the fact:** Circus No Spin Zone blog, July 20, 2010.

65 **"In the old days":** Eric Levin, "In the Eye of the Tiger He is Trainer, Equal and Potentially Lunch," *People,* July 1, 1985.

65 **One of their regular stops:** Circus No Spin Zone blog, May 31, 2011.

65 **But he remained very involved:** Ibid., January 31, 2011.

65 **Cuneo wrote the playlist:** Ibid.

66 **Cuneo insisted that an animal:** Ibid.

66 **A series of photos:** Buckles blog, July 29, 2008.

66 **Sometime in 1978:** The video appeared on Burck's Circus No Spin Zone blog, March 30, 2012.

68 **Years later, a trainer for Ringling:** Gary Jacobson testimony, American Society for the Prevention of Cruelty to Animals v. Feld Entertainment, U.S. District Court for the District of Columbia, October 24, 2009.

68 **More remarkable is the scene:** A copy of the video was posted on Wade Burck's Circus No Spin Zone blog, March 30, 2012.

70 **He didn't object:** *People,* July 8, 1985.

70 **Years after the video:** Circus No Spin Zone blog, May 24, 2012.

71 **Burck wrote that the scene:** Ibid., March 30, 2012.

71 **In some of their actual performances:** Ibid., April 28, 2008.

71 **John Milton Herriott scolded:** Ibid., October 3, 2009.

71   **"Took a great amount of precision":** Ibid., August 26, 2010.

72   **"Joyce was on a roll":** Ibid., December 7, 2011.

72   **Joyce struck a groom one day:** Ibid.

72   **In the winter of 1978:** Michael Sneed, "Shrine Circus Elephant Kills Keeper; Probe Abuse," *Chicago Tribune*, March 13, 1978, 1.

72   **She plucked Farr:** Ibid.

73   **Herta Cuneo defended:** Ibid.

73   **Cuneo insisted:** Ibid.

73   **Hawthorn elephant handler:** Ibid.

73   **One of the horse groomers:** UPI, March 14, 1978.

73   **Cuneo gave a detailed account:** Phone interview, October 28, 2011.

74   **Two months after Joyce:** "National Woman Killed by Elephant," Associated Press, *Tuscaloosa News,* May 7, 1978, 3A.

75   **In the 1830s, with great flourish:** "Step Right Up: Bob Brooke Presents the History of the Circus in America," *History Magazine,* www.history-magazine.com.

75   **The climax of his act:** *The New York Mirror,* July 7, 1838.

75   **Trainers would clip the claws:** Harvey Sutherland, "Training Wild Animals," *Current Literature,* June 1902, 709, and "Attachment B: Major issues with animals used in circuses and rodeos," memo to Santa Clara County, Calif., Board of Supervisors from CEO Pete McHugh, February 12, 2008.

76   **Horses endured whippings:** "Former Ringling Bros. Employee Speaks Out Against Abuse," PETA, www.peta.org.

76   **Trainers have long:** George Lewis with Byron Fish, *I Loved Rogues: The Life of an Elephant Tramp* (Seattle, WA: Superior Publishing, 1978), 149.

76   **To learn new tricks:** Ibid.

76   **Cheerful Gardner:** Cheerful Gardner, "Big Berthas of the Big Top," *Back Yard,* September 30, 1998, 1.

76   **He preferred to start:** Ibid., 5.

76   **Gardner and his crew:** Ibid.

77   **Teaching an elephant to lie down:** *I Loved Rogues,* 30.

CHAPTER SEVEN: ACTING OUT

78   **he was badly injured:** *People,* July 8, 1985.

79   **He was a mess:** Ibid.

79   **Burck immediately returned:** Ibid.

79   **At a performance:** George C. Bingaman, "Hamid-Morton Circus," *The Circus Report,* June 14, 1982, 25.

79   **Billie knocked her down:** John Milton Herriott interview.

80   **Photos taken the following year:** Circus No Spin Zone blog, July 29, 2008.

80   **In 1988, he went after:** PETA files, citing USDA and Canadian law enforcement records.

80   **"If you don't stay":** *The Palm Beach Post,* April 3, 1978.

80   **In years to come:** USDA files, courtesy of PETA.

81   **The Hawthorn Five were part:** Fred D. Pfening III, "1989: The Circus Year in Review," *Bandwagon,* January-February 1990, 15.

81   **the circus played just two cities:** Ibid.

81   **"We'll never see the likes":** "Interview with Cuneo," *The White Tops,* January-February 2011, 69.

81   **Ringling Bros. appealed:** "Contract Dispute Detains Ringling Animals in Japan," UPI, September 7, 1989.

82   **Years later, a man:** Buckles blog, December 21, 2008.

83   **Cuneo had replaced:** *Back Yard,* December 31, 1998.

83   **In a videotaped interview:** KTVU/San Francisco, June 25, 2007.

83   **Billie attacked Wells:** www.elephant.se.

83   **The official write-up:** Gordon Taylor, "Elephant Show," *The Circus Report,* September 3, 1990, 16–17.

84   **A spectator witnessed:** A commenter identified only as "Mary" described the scene in the comments section of the Circus No Spin Zone blog, April 2, 2008.

84   **Wells's father-in-law:** John Milton Herriott interview.

85   **"Bombay and her four":** Marita Lowman, "Circus Opens with Monkey Business, and Elephants Too," *Wilkes-Barre Times Leader,* March 23, 1993, 1D.

85 **Three months later:** Comments section, Buckles blog, December 13, 2005.

85 **Wisconsin has a rich:** "The Great Circus Parade," *Milwaukee Journal,* July 3, 1993.

86 **The Hawthorn Five:** Bill Hall, "Circus Scene: Stars of the Moscow Circus Head to Hawaii," *Amusement Business,* August 23, 1993.

86 **Hawaii was where Billie:** John Milton Herriott interview.

86 **Wells chose to resign:** Ibid.

86 **Cuneo boasted:** Cuneo interview, *The White Tops,* January-February 2011.

87 **It's unclear whether Wade Burck:** comments section, Circus No Spin Zone blog, April 3, 2008.

87 **Trainers often chained:** "Elephants at School: Teaching Rough and Many Never Learn Much," *Boston Daily Globe,* July 21, 1895, 24.

87 **The first time:** Ibid.

87 **To teach that trick:** Sutherland, *Current Literature.*

88 **To train an elephant to hop on two legs:** *Back Yard,* 5.

88 **The "tightrope" he taught:** Ibid.

88 **A more difficult trick:** Ibid.

88 **To teach an elephant to whirl:** Sutherland, *Current Literature.*

88 **To perform on a seesaw:** Ibid.

88 **Only the most daring of trainers:** Ballantine, *Wild Tigers & Tame Fleas,* 284.

89 **Too much pressure:** Ibid., 284.

89 **In 1954, cereal boxes:** Buckles blog, February 13, 2012

89 **A male elephant once sideswiped:** Lewis, *I Loved Rogues,* 159.

CHAPTER EIGHT: A SANCTUARY TAKES SHAPE

90 **During a performance:** Performing Animal Welfare Society (PAWS) and PETA files, April 21, 1993.

90 **The next day:** PETA files, April 22, 1993.

90 **Three months later:** PAWS and PETA files, July 23, 1993.

90   **Cuneo had ready explanations:** Vicki Croke, "Don't Blame the Elephant," *Boston Globe,* September 3, 1994, 69.

90   **On August 23, 1994:** PETA files.

91   **John Lehnhardt:** Croke, *Boston Globe.*

91   **Carol Buckley and Scott Blais couldn't understand:** Scott Blais interview, December 8, 2012.

91   **Buckley discovered elephants:** Craig Walker, "Tarra, the Roller-Skating Elephant," www.ojaihistory.com.

93   **The elephant with the:** Carol Buckley, *Tarra & Bella: The Elephant and Dog Who Became Best Friends* (New York: Putnam, 2009), 4.

93   **She was captivated:** "Carol Buckley," *Animal News Center,* Animal Liberation Front, July 2003.

93   **"Being away from her":** "Tarra & Bella," *Dallas Morning News* blog post, September 5, 2009.

93   **When Tarra was six:** David Larsen, "Baby Tarra on Roller Skates," *Los Angeles Times,* February 13, 1980.

93   **At one point Buckley:** Ibid.

94   **In 1984, after a performance:** William Mullen, "Where the Elephants Roam," *Chicago Tribune,* May 29, 2005.

94   **As a baby:** Tarra's bio on the Elephant Sanctuary Web site, www .elephants.com.

94   **To make a living:** Carol Buckley's bio on the Elephant Sanctuary Web site.

94   **Buckley wound up taking:** Tarra's bio on the Elephant Sanctuary Web site.

95   **A native of Maine:** Scott Blais interview, December 8–9, 2012.

95   **The following summer:** Ibid.

95   **Blais saw other elephants:** Ibid., April 8, 2011.

95   **Like almost all elephant exhibitors:** Ibid., December 7–9, 2012.

96   **Blais did so:** Ibid.

96   **This time Blais:** Ibid.

97   **The beatings appeared to work:** Ibid.

97   **The male elephants posed:** Ibid.

97   **Blais was just seventeen:** Ibid.

98   **He helped train Mugwamp:** Ibid.

98   **Then Buckley arrived:** Ibid.

98   **Rascha was a good example:** Ibid.

99   **Buckley's initial idea:** Ibid.

99   **Buckley flew back:** Ibid.

100   **Steele was an old-school:** Ibid.

100   **Buckley and Blais began contacting:** Ibid.

100   **Blais and Buckley:** Ibid.

101   **Tarra's pregnancy:** Ibid.

101   **Buckley and Blais:** Ibid.

101   **Something else gave them pause:** Ibid.

101   **They noticed that:** Ibid.

102   **After Tarra lost her calf:** Ibid.

102   **They originally planned:** Ibid.

102   **A month after:** Ibid.

102   **Local banker Sandra Estes:** Interview with Sandra Estes, August 23, 2012.

103   **George Arstingstall, the first American:** "Elephants Ruled by Fear," *New York Mail and Express,* April 28, 1885, 7.

103   **"Don't imagine that you can":** Horace Townsend, "Animals and their Trainers," *Frank Leslie's Popular Monthly,* December 1888, 728. Elephant trainer Jim Coughlin described his approach this way: "You finally get it convinced in its mind that you will beat it to DEATH. But it must be convinced. It calls for respect. You work 'em, chain 'em, feed 'em. Business is business." "Amusement Business First Elephant Census," *Amusement Business,* May 31, 1969, 30.

CHAPTER NINE: TROUBLE FOR CUNEO

105   **Tyke's demise triggered:** Dennis O'Brien, "Exhibitor Denies: Cuneo Hopes to Win Back His License," *Chicago Tribune,* McHenry County Edition, February 20, 1997, 1.

105 **USDA fined the Hawthorn Corporation:** Ira Dreyfuss, "Elephants seized from trainer whose Tyke stomped Kakaako," Associated Press, March 19, 2004.

105 **In a memo:** USDA document dated January 20, 1995, courtesy of PETA.

106 **A fourth Cuneo elephant:** "Circus and Ride Elephant Incidents," PAWS, July 24, 1983.

106 **In 1994, in Salt Lake City:** Ibid., April 4, 1994.

107 **Two years later:** Ibid., June 14, 1996.

107 **In 1983, while she was:** Ibid., May 25, 1983.

107 **Frieda crushed the chest:** Associated Press, "Woman trampled by elephant she tried to ride," July 6, 1985.

107 **In 1993, Frieda:** "Circus and Ride Elephant Incidents," PAWS, March 16, 1993.

107 **Frieda exchanged blows:** Ibid., July 10, 1995.

108 **Frieda and Debbie:** Blanca Quintanilla, "Berserk Elephants Are Repeat Offenders," New York *Daily News,* July 12, 1995.

108 **A year and a half:** Ibid., June 18, 1996.

108 **The Hawthorn barn:** Scott Blais interview, April 8, 2011.

108 **Their pen was roughly:** Ibid.

108 **When anyone needed:** Ibid.

109 **Outside was a small:** Ibid.

109 **Few people noticed:** PETA, citing USDA documents, December 17, 1994.

109 **Or that USDA:** Dennis O'Brien and Andrew Buchanan, "Animal Renter Cries Foul Over Suspension," *Chicago Tribune,* February 11, 1997.

109 **Joyce, Billie's longtime:** Deborah Belgum and David Terrell, "Elephant Deaths Draw Spotlight's Glare," *Los Angeles Times,* August 10, 1996.

109 **Three days after:** Ibid.

109 **Autopsies found:** Ibid.

109 **The federal government charged:** Tresa Baldas, "Settlement over elephants' TB deaths costs Cuneo," *Chicago Tribune,* March 27, 1998, 8A.

110   **Just two years earlier:** Global Action Network, citing the cut-line of a March 2, 1994, photo in *The Toronto Sun,* depicting "30-year-old Asian elephant named Joyce" giving a ride to a small child at the Garden Bros. performance at the SkyDome.

110   **New Mexico officials:** USDA documents, August 15, 1996, courtesy of PETA.

110   **Florida officials:** Ibid., October 22, 1996, courtesy of PETA.

110   **Hawthorn had leased elephants:** PETA, citing USDA documents identifying facilities that had housed Hawthorn elephants, January 4, 1997.

111   **four Hawthorn employees:** PETA, citing USDA documents, August 28, 1996.

111   **"PETA has infiltrated":** *Chicago Tribune,* August 9, 1997.

111   **"People at circuses":** Ibid., February 20, 1997.

111   **Two years later:** USDA documents, November 20–21, 1997, courtesy of PETA.

111   **When the inspector:** Ibid., May 13–17, 1998, courtesy of PETA.

112   **Lota was diagnosed:** Ibid., July 7, 1997, courtesy of PETA.

112   **Still, Lota continued:** Ibid., February 6, 1997, courtesy of PETA.

113   **A fluid-filled abscess:** Ibid., October 15, 2001, courtesy of PETA.

113   **Walker Bros. was performing:** PETA, citing *Chicago Sun-Times,* April 13, 2001.

113   **"The trainer began":** Ibid.

113   **The complaint subsequently:** Ibid.

113   **In Harlan County:** PETA, citing USDA documents, October 1, 2001.

113   **USDA cited Hawthorn:** Ibid., October 2, 2001.

113   **Liz had been taken:** Elephant Sanctuary's biography of Liz.

114   **Walker Bros. kept:** USDA document, October 2, 2001, courtesy of PETA.

114   **Delhi, especially, was suffering:** Ibid., October 5, 2001, courtesy of PETA.

115   **Outside an arena:** PETA files, October 27, 2001.

115 **And two months after that:** Ibid.

115 **By January 2002:** USDA document, January 2, 2002, courtesy of PETA.

115 **Now fifty-six, her front legs:** Ibid., May 4, 2002, courtesy of PETA.

115 **Her front feet:** PETA files, April 26, 2002.

116 **"I don't believe":** Jeff Long and Jon Yates, "Citing Abuse, U.S. Seeks to Shut Circus-Animal Farm." *Chicago Tribune,* May 14, 2003, 1.

116 **In the past, Oosterhuis:** Among other things, Oosterhuis defended the 1988 beating of Dunda about the head at the San Diego Zoo as "an appropriate and non-harmful place in which to administer required discipline." See Jane Fritsch, "Zookeepers Aim Angry Barbs at Animal Park, Superiors in Dunda Case," *Los Angeles Times,* July 30, 1988.

116 **He prescribed a laundry list:** USDA document, September 11, 2003, courtesy of PETA.

116 **Inspectors found Cuneo's African:** Ibid., May 24, 2002, courtesy of PETA.

116 **Handlers were keeping:** Ibid., September 1, 2003, courtesy of PETA.

116 **One of them:** Ibid.

117 **A six-year-old tiger:** Ibid.

117 **In Norfolk, Virginia:** PETA files citing stories in the *Virginian-Pilot,* September 4–5, 2002.

117 **In March 2003:** PETA files, citing a story in *The Edmonton Sun.*

117 **Billie and Frieda now shared:** USDA document, July 11, 2001, courtesy of PETA.

117 **Elephants are large:** Testimony of Philip Ensley, 81.

118 **Since 1990 alone:** PETA files.

118 **Circuses had a way of beating the rap:** Lewis, *I Loved Rogues,* 114.

119 **If the elephant never did surrender:** "Elephants at School," *Boston Daily Globe,* July 21, 1895, 24.

119 **Conklin's men chained Chief:** Ibid.

119   Conklin instantly regretted: Ibid.

119   "He couldn't stand any more clubbing": Ibid.

119   He kept his elephants: Lewis, *I Loved Rogues,* 63.

119   The circus changed her name: Ibid.

120   In 1903, Thomas Edison: Daly, *Topsy.*

120   At twenty-eight, Topsy had killed a man: Ibid., 302.

120   Edison had already electrocuted: Tony Long, "Jan. 4, 1903: Edison Fries an Elephant to Prove his Point," *Wired,* January 4, 2008, www.wired.com.

120   The zoo erected a gallows: Daly, *Topsy,* 316.

120   Topsy refused to climb: Ibid., 317.

120   Later that year: Ibid.

120   In 1911, the Yankee Robinson Circus: "Big Elephant is Drowned," *Cumberland* (Wisconsin) *Journal,* June 30, 1911, reprinted in *The Circus Report,* January 10, 1972, 6.

121   Circus employees made light: Ibid.

CHAPTER TEN: SPACE AND SILENCE

122   Elephants are migratory: "Elephants," factsanddetails.com.

123   Buckley took care: Scott Blais interview, December 8–9, 2012.

123   Behind the scenes: Ibid.

123   Buckley and Blais were living: Ibid.

123   Their phone carrier: Ibid.

124   Almost immediately: Ibid.

124   Now someone else: Ibid.

124   He sat in his car: Ibid.

124   Relief also came: Ibid.

126   At an Elephant Managers: Ibid.

126   Born in Sri Lanka: Elephant Sanctuary bios, www.elephants .com.

126   Blais and Buckley took turns: Scott Blais interview.

126   Captured in 1973: Elephant Sanctuary bios, www.elephants.com.

126   The circus wanted nothing more: Ibid.

127   **Caring for and feeding:** www.elephants.com.

128   **The sanctuary's second phase:** Ibid.

128   **Shirley had traveled:** Ibid.

128   **National Geographic filmed:** Ibid.

129   **Elephants have remarkable memories:** Joyce Poole, *Coming of Age with Elephants* (New York: Hyperion, 1996), 131–33, 143–44, 155–57. Poole writes that an elephant's cerebrum temporal lobes, the parts of the brain that store memory, are much larger than those of a human.

129   **Blais slid open the door:** Scott Blais interview.

129   **Bunny, forty-seven, was the fifth:** www.elephants.com.

129   **Sissy came in 2000:** Ibid.

130   **Shipped to America:** Ibid.

130   **In October 2001:** Ibid.

130   **Thirty-three and plagued:** Ibid.

130   **Zula and Tange:** Ibid.

130   **Flora:** Ibid.

131   **Elephant-handling is hazardous:** Tony Perry, "Elephant Behavior Studied in Hands-Off Training," *Los Angeles Times,* July 12, 2004. In 1991, then–National Zoo manager John Lehnhardt calculated that, with an average of one fatality a year occurring among 600 handlers over the previous fifteen years, elephant-handling was three times more likely to prove deadly than coal mining, then considered the riskiest job in the country. See Eric Scigliano, *Love, War, and Circuses: The Age-Old Relationship Between Elephants and Humans* (New York: Houghton Mifflin Company, 2002, 279–280).

131   **The risks inherent in the job:** Ballantine, *Wild Tigers & Tame Fleas,* 270.

131   **Pat Derby:** Derby, *The Lady and Her Tiger,* 72.

131   **And once a beating started:** Ballantine, *Wild Tigers & Tame Fleas,* 266.

131   **The severity of the beating:** Scott Blais interview, December 8, 2012.

131   **The trainer would approach:** Ibid.

132 The elephant might start: Ibid.

132 Once the elephant was on the ground: Ibid.

132 Trainers aimed for spots: Ibid.

132 seasoned trainers approached: Ballantine, *Wild Tigers & Tame Fleas,* 266.

132 They used to allege: Ibid.

132 In most places: Ibid., 295.

133 One alternative to a beating: Ibid., 266.

133 In one instance: Lewis, *I Loved Rogues,* 110.

133 At one point she tried to escape: Ibid.

133 Tears ran down her face: Ibid.

133 "But we saw and heard": Ibid.

CHAPTER ELEVEN: THE CRACKDOWN BEGINS

134 Finally, on April 9: USDA records, courtesy of PETA.

135 USDA identified: Ibid.

135 Debby Leahy: Jeff Long and Jon Yates, "Citing Abuse, U.S. Seeks to Shut Down Circus-Animal Farm," *Chicago Tribune,* May 14, 2003.

135 The Elephant Sanctuary's Carol Buckley: Ibid.

135 He shrugged off the charges: Ibid.

135 "Where are the marks": Ibid.

135 "If these animals": Ibid.

136 Instead, Cuneo spent: "Top of the Market" blog, *Sarasota Magazine,* February 1, 2002. sarasotamagazine.com.

136 Federal inspectors: USDA records, courtesy of PETA.

136 Two months after: USDA records, June 4, 2003, courtesy of PETA.

136 Hawthorn had failed: Ibid., July 28, 2003, courtesy of PETA.

136 Elephant superintendent Gary: Ibid.

137 Nothing had been done: Ibid.

137 Federal regulations required: Ibid.

137 They spent long days: Ibid.

137 The federal Occupational Safety and Health: Yates, "Animal

Trainer Cited in TB case: Employees May Have Contracted It From Elephants," *Chicago Tribune,* September 26, 2003.

137 **In late November:** USDA records, Nov. 21, 2003, courtesy of PETA.

137 **The following day:** Ibid., Nov. 22, 2003, courtesy of PETA.

138 **Four more months:** Marc Kaufman, "USDA seizes circus elephant," *The Washington Post,* March 18, 2004, A3.

138 **The settlement was unprecedented:** Ibid.

138 **But USDA spokesman:** Ibid.

138 **Carol Buckley said:** Ibid.

138 **Richard Farinato:** Richard Farinato, "USDA seizes the moment, orders Hawthorn to give up 16 elephants," Humane Society of the United States.

139 **One of them, Ena:** Lewis, *I Loved Rogues,* 110.

139 **In 1928, the Sells-Floto Circus:** "Grave of Thirsty Mary the Elephant," *Roadside America,* www.roadsideamerica.com.

139 **If the animal is really serious:** Lewis, *I Loved Rogues,* 146.

139 **In her book *Elephants on the Edge*:** G.A. Bradshaw, *Elephants on the Edge* (New Haven, CT: Yale University Press, 2009), 14.

140 **By some accounts:** Ballantine, *Wild Tigers & Tame Fleas,* 286.

140 **One elephant, Dumbo:** Diane L. Beers, *For the Prevention of Cruelty: The History and Legacy of Animal Rights Activism in the United States* (Athens, OH: Ohio University Press, 2006), 105.

140 **After Black Diamond:** Robyn Ross, "Corsicana's 'Killer Elephant'," *Texas Observer,* October 1, 2012, www.Texasobserver.org.

140 **In Corsicana, Texas:** Ibid.

140 **Prickett and Black Diamond:** Ibid.

140 **Black Diamond responded:** Ibid.

141 **The owner of the Barnes Circus:** Ibid.

141 **Black Diamond was smart enough:** Ibid.

141 **Black Diamond's death:** Lewis, *I Loved Rogues,* 50.

141 **The manager of Barnes:** Ibid.

141 **In truth, he was:** Ibid., 134.

141 **And powerful:** Ibid., 8.

141 **The chains alone:** Ibid., 42.

142   **Handlers pummeled pins:** Ibid., 120.

142   **The chains around his legs:** Ibid.

142   **By 1952:** Ibid., 6.

CHAPTER TWELVE: MIRED IN BUREAUCRACY

143   **And in exchange:** "Trainer Gets Deadline to Give Away Elephants," *Chicago Tribune,* March 19, 2004, 3.

143   **"Cuneo has made":** Marc Kaufman, "USDA seizes circus elephants," *The Washington Post,* March 18, 2004, A3.

144   **The settlement authorized:** Ibid.

144   **"We think they need":** Ibid.

144   **The general counsel:** Letter from Bernadette Juarez to Hawthorn attorney Derek Shaffer, May 21, 2004.

145   **Cuneo proposed:** Ibid.

145   **By late May:** Jeff Long, "PETA sues to block transfer of four elephants from farm," *Chicago Tribune,* June 17, 2005, 1.

145   **The head of the facility:** Ibid.

145   **Five years earlier:** Undercover video of elephant trainer Tim Frisco: A copy of the video is available on YouTube. Circus owner Barbara Byrd said the video was spliced together and dubbed over, and defended the use of bullhooks as common and humane.

146   **To avoid going to court:** *Chicago Tribune,* June 17, 2005.

146   **From 1995 to 2001:** Ibid.

146   **USDA vetoed Carson & Barnes:** Letter from USDA legal counsel Bernadette Juarez to Benjamin Boley, attorney for Hawthorn, April 30, 2004, courtesy of PETA.

147   **That left Sue:** Ibid.

147   **Run by the:** Popcorn Park Zoo Web site, www.ahscares.org.

147   **But at the last minute:** Marc Kaufman, "Illinois Elephants' Fate Remain Uncertain; Battle Over 'Hawthorn Herd' Pits Circus World Against Animal Rights Backers," *The Washington Post,* A6.

147   **On November 22:** USDA records, courtesy of PETA.

148 **when Cuneo tried to make her:** Misty's biography, Elephant Sanctuary Web site, www.elephants.com.

148 **"You look at Misty":** Jeff Gard, "Local Elephants in need of home," *Northwest Herald,* November 29, 2004.

148 **Tess, one of the:** USDA report, January 20, 2005, courtesy of PETA.

149 **"These four are considered":** Ibid., February 5, 2004, courtesy of PETA.

149 **And because of what had happened:** Wade Burck's Circus No Spin Zone blog, January 11, 2009.

149 **But three years after Hawthorn:** Ibid.

150 **He wound up in a:** USDA inspection report, February 7, 2005, and Circus Protest, http://circusprotest.com.

150 **The following January:** USDA records, January 5, 2005, courtesy of PETA.

151 **Lota seemed fascinated:** Elephant Sanctuary's *Trunklines* newsletter, Spring 2005, 5.

151 **She died at 3:00 A.M.:** www.elephants.com.

152 **The elephants weren't:** USDA report, January 20, 2005, courtesy of PETA.

152 **One of the sticking points:** Letter to USDA legal counsel Bernadette Juarez and Hawthorn attorney Derek Shaffer from Elephant Sanctuary attorney Michael Stagg, February 15, 2005, courtesy of PETA.

153 **The Sanctuary had raised:** Ibid., March 3, 2005, courtesy of PETA.

153 **In the meantime:** Jeff Long, "Talks in works to move elephants," *Chicago Tribune,* February 18, 2005.

153 **Three months passed:** Marc Kaufman, "Illinois Elephants' Fate Remains Uncertain," *Chicago Tribune,* May 30, 2005.

154 **The head of the foundation:** Ibid.

154 **USDA initially rejected:** Letter from USDA general counsel Bernadette Juarez to attorney for Cuneo, April 30, 2004.

154 **PETA, which had spent years:** *Chicago Tribune,* June 15, 2005.

154   **That left the Elephant Sanctuary:** Jeff Long, "Deal to Transfer Elephants OK'd: 9 of 11 Animals to go to Tennessee Sanctuary," *Chicago Tribune,* November 30, 2005.

154   **Cuneo signed:** "In Memory of Lota," www.elephants.com.

155   **By 1900:** Lawrence Perry, "The Wild Beast Traffic," *Frank Leslie's Popular Monthly,* July 1903, 229.

155   **Born in New York:** Jeffrey Wayne Maulhardt, *Jungleland (Images of America)* (Mount Pleasant, SC: Arcadia Publishing, 2011), 7.

155   **Goebel boasted:** Ibid., 8.

155   **He purchased twenty-six:** Ibid., 12.

155   **He rented out dozens:** Ibid.

156   **In 1940 a fire ignited:** Associated Press, "'Sally and Queenie,' Movie Elephants, Perish in Blaze," *The Milwaukee Journal,* July 10, 1940, 4.

156   **Attempting to escape:** Ibid.

156   **Queenie had appeared:** Frank Whitbeck, "On the Esquire Screen," *The Southeast Missourian,* December 21, 1962, 7.

CHAPTER THIRTEEN: SETBACKS IN ILLINOIS

157   **At one point:** Scott Blais interviews, April 8, 2011, and December 8, 2012.

158   **Six of the elephants:** Ibid.

158   **Debbie, thirty-five:** www.elephants.com.

158   **Ronnie:** Ibid.

158   **Debbie and Ronnie:** Scott Blais.

158   **Imported from the wild:** www.elephants.com.

158   **At the other end:** Ibid.

158   **Lottie, forty-three:** Ibid.

158   **Before she was sold:** Ibid.

158   **At forty-nine, her trunk:** Elephant Sanctuary, Scott Blais.

158   **With nothing else to do:** Scott Blais.

158   **Billie, Sue, and Frieda:** Ibid.

159   The keepers didn't ask: Susan Mikota interview, August 2012.

159   Nic loved water: Wade Burck's Circus No Spin Zone blog, May 15, 2011.

159   Burck described her: Ibid.

159   To keep her: Ibid.

160   Each winter, Sue: Ibid.

160   Billie was "the bitch": Scott Blais interview.

160   Hawthorn's veterinarian: Ibid.

161   Over the next several days: Ibid.

161   From a distance: Ibid.

162   Volunteers stepped forward: Elephant Sanctuary's *Trunklines,* Spring 2006.

163   Eleven days after: Ibid.

163   Later, writing about: Debbie Leahy, "An Elephant Named Sue," PETA files blog, May 10, 2007.

164   One of importer Frank Buck's: Frank Buck, *Bring 'Em Back Alive,* (New York: Garden City Publishing, 1930), 161.

164   A few weeks later: Ibid., 164.

164   The trader then insisted: Ibid., 165.

165   Buck and his assistant: Ibid., 166.

165   The elephant had no idea: Ibid.

165   He cut off a piece of bamboo: Ibid., 169.

165   A couple of hours later: Ibid., 170.

165   While one picture: Ibid., 172.

CHAPTER FOURTEEN: CARAVAN TO FREEDOM

167   the morning of: Scott Blais interviews, April 1, 2011, and December 9, 2012.

167   Three times over the last: Elephant Sanctuary's Ele-diaries, January 31, 2006, and February 2, 2006.

167   The elephants seemed: Ibid.

168   his employees had delayed: Ibid., February 6, 2006.

168   He headed to the barn: Scott Blais interview.

The saga of the Hawthorn: Keith Oppenheim, "Paula Zahn Now," CNN-TV, February 17, 2006.

168 **A Hawthorn employee tried:** Ibid.

168 **"She hates me":** Scott Blais interview.

169 **Once Burck moved:** Ibid.

169 **This time, Blais *asked*:** Ibid.

169 **Blais had dealt:** Ibid.

170 **He called for Billie:** Ibid.

170 **The elephant made her way:** Ibid.

171 **Suddenly, without hesitating:** Ibid.

171 **The inside of the trailer:** Ibid.

171 **Then he worked his way:** Ibid.

172 **Billie watched him intently:** Ibid.

172 **a couple of apples:** CNN.

173 **A few miles north:** Ibid.

173 **Shortly before seven:** Scott Blais interview.

174 **The elephant paused:** Ibid.

174 **Carefully she moved backward:** The video, "Liz, Frieda and Billie Arrive," is available on YouTube.

174 **"Very good":** Ibid.

174 **The elephant edged back:** Ibid.

175 **But if the injured party:** Lewis, *I Loved Rogues,* 4.

175 **Circuses typically had one groom:** Ibid., 20.

175 **When they weren't walloping elephants:** Ibid., 34.

175 **Circus owners were known to carry:** Ibid.

175 **Red Eldridge:** Joan Vannorsdall Schroeder, "The Day They Hanged an Elephant in East Tennessee," *Blue Ridge Country,* May 1, 1997.

175 **The star was Big Mary:** Sparks Circus ad, which ran in the *Johnson City* (Tenn.) *Staff* newspaper on September 14, 1916. Reprinted in Vince Staten's blog, April 17, 2010, vincestaten.blogspot. com.

175 **Mary's reputation for violence:** Schroeder, *Blue Ridge Country.*

176 **The showstopper came:** Article reprinted in Vince Staten's blog, April 17, 2010.

176   **After the performance:** Schroeder, *Blue Ridge Country*.
176   **According to the best-known version:** Ibid.
176   **The circus managed:** Ibid.
176   **At the following day's performance:** Ibid.
176   **A crowd of more than 2,500:** Ibid.
176   **Authorities latched the boom:** Ibid.
177   **Sparks kept Mary dangling:** Ibid.

CHAPTER FIFTEEN: THE START OF A NEW LIFE

178   **In front of her:** "Liz, Frieda, and Billie Arrive," video on YouTube.
178   **Five of the:** CNN, February 17, 2006.
179   **It was eight thirty:** Scott Blais interview.
179   **Most of the elephants:** Interview with Sanctuary employee Angela Sherrill, August 23, 2012.
180   **Billie seemed immobilized:** Ibid.
181   **Since arriving, Lottie:** Ele-diaries, March 6, 2006.
181   **Because she was Lottie's:** Ibid.
181   **The elephants' day began:** Elephant Sanctuary FAQs, www .elephants.com
182   **The remaining two meals:** Ibid.
182   **That first couple of weeks:** Ele-diaries, March 1, 2006.
183   **Billie shied away:** Angela Sherrill interview.
183   **For the next three months:** Ibid.
184   **Even when she began:** Ibid.
184   **Elephants chirp:** "What Sounds Do Elephants Make?" www .elemotion.org.
184   **they also rely on:** Ibid.
184   **use the tips:** Mark Shwartz, "Elephants Pick up Good Vibrations— Through Their Feet," Stanford University News Service, March 5, 2001. By adjusting the volume and strength of the vibrations—by opening their mouths wide or closing them, by flapping their ears or keeping them still, holding their heads up high or down low— elephants can emit a whole vocabulary of sounds. The slack lower

half of an elephant's mouth contains a pharyngeal pouch, an apparatus believed to enable the low-frequency noises. The sounds are one to two octaves below what humans are capable of hearing and they travel much farther than high-frequency noises, no matter the terrain. The rumbling noises also enable elephants to communicate through the ground. Researcher Caitlin O'Connell-Rodwell first observed this in 1992, when she saw some elephants in Namibia freeze in place, then lean forward and lift one foot. It occurred to her that raising one of their feet required the elephants to stand more firmly on their other three legs, enabling the three legs to pick up subsonic rumblings from other elephants. Scientists eventually learned that elephants' underground noises travel as far as ten miles. Nervous or frightened elephants that are stomping around can send signals as far as twenty miles.

184   **Some days, if Billie:** Interviews with sanctuary employees Angela Sherrill and Kelly Costanzo, August 23, 2012.

185   **In mid spring:** Ele-diaries: April 4, 2006.

185   **On good days:** Angela Sherrill interview.

185   **Months passed before:** Ibid.

186   **Caregivers soaked:** Ele-diaries, March 20, 2006.

186   **Bananas were her favorite:** Scott Blais interview.

187   **One afternoon a couple:** Ele-diaries, March 26, 2006.

187   **Two of them:** Scott Blais interview.

188   **One day about a month:** Ibid.

188   **Every once in a while:** Ibid.

189   **Encouraged by her growing tolerance:** Ibid.

189   **She avoided him:** Ibid.

190   **The first American-bred:** As told by the breeder, Fred C. Alispaw, "Authentic Story of the First-Recorded American Bred Baby Elephant," *The White Tops,* October 1931, 6.

190   **His mother tried:** Ibid.

190   **Twice a day:** Ibid., 7.

190   **While the band played:** Ibid.

190   **Baby Hutch generated:** Ibid.

190   **on a trip to California:** Ibid.

CHAPTER SIXTEEN: THE CONUNDRUM OF ZOOS

191   **To provide a means:** Sarah Kershaw, "A 9,000-Pound Fish Out of Water, Alone in Alaska," *The New York Times,* January 9, 2005.

191   **Orphaned when her:** Ibid.

191   **The zoo recognized:** Ibid.

192   **Zoos had come a long way:** The most irresponsible thing done to an elephant occurred in 1962, when the Oklahoma City Zoo allowed researchers from the University of Oklahoma to inject a fourteen-year-old African male elephant with LSD to see whether the drug could induce musth. Five minutes later the elephant collapsed, lost control of his bowels, and went into a seizure. An hour and a half later he died. See Rob Collins, "LSD Experiment at Zoo in 1962 Killed Elephant," *Oklahoma Gazette,* October 4, 2007.

192   **Elephants need to be able:** Lisa Kane, Debra Forthman, and David Hancocks, "Best Practices by the Coalition for Captive Elephant Well-Being," Coalition for Captive Elephant Well-Being, 2005, www.elephantcare.org.

192   **"They end up living":** Michael Stetz, "San Diego Zoo Safari Park bashed for elephant breeding," *San Diego Union-Tribune,* January 27, 2011.

193   **That year, trainers:** Arlene Mueller, "Animal Stunts: Circus Delights and a Sober Note of Concerns," *Christian Science Monitor,* September 14, 1988.

193   **When Dunda acted:** Jane Fritsch, "Aftermath of Dunda beating: Elephant Care and Staff has Changed at S.D. Park," *Los Angeles Times,* July 17, 1989.

193   **One keeper described:** Ibid.

193   **Leading the sessions:** Ibid.

193   **He co-wrote a manual:** Alan Roocroft and Donald Atwell Zoll, *Managing Elephants: An Introduction to their Training and Management* (Athens, GA: Fever Tree Press, 1994).

193   **He said the serrated:** Jane Fritsch, "Zookeepers Aim Angry

Barbs at Animal Park, Superiors in Dunda Case," *Los Angeles Times,* July 30, 1989.

193 **But elephant keeper Lisa Landres**: Jill Howard Church, "The Elephants' Graveyard: Life in Captivity," from *A Primer on Animal Rights, Leading Experts Write about Animal Cruelty and Exploitation* (New York: Lantern Books, 2002), 134. Landres told Church: "When you're in the elephant 'biz,' it's like you're in a secret club. We all know each other's dirty little secrets." She went on to write her master's thesis about the abnormal behavior of captive elephants. She became a field investigator for the Humane Society of the United States, then worked for Friends of Animals before leaving the profession in utter frustration in 1992.

193 **USDA fined and reprimanded**: Tony Perry, "Zoo Hopes a Little TLC Goes Long Way with Elephants," *Los Angeles Times,* July 12, 2004.

193 **The Association of Zoos and Aquariums**: Jane Fritsch, "National Group Forms Elephant Task Force: Zoo Society Avoids Censure Over Dunda,*" Los Angeles Times,* October 12, 1988.

194 **Soon afterward**: Annie's bio, www.pawsweb.org. A video of Annie's training session at the Milwaukee Zoo is on YouTube.

194 **It took more than a decade**: www.aza.org.

194 **Since 1990**: PETA files.

195 **With the help**: Michael J. Berens, "Elephants are dying out in America's Zoos," *The Seattle Times,* December 1, 2012, 1.

195 **Don Moore**: "The Elephant (Not) in the Room," *Liberty City Press,* September 12, 2012.

195 **One of them was Southwick's**: Ashley Studley, "Southwick's on Animal Rights List of Worst Zoos for Elephants," *Metrowest* (Mass.) *Daily News,* January 19, 2011,

195 **In a letter to the editor**: Les Schobert, "L.A. Zoo needs to give its elephants a break," *Los Angeles Times,* September 27, 2005.

196 **Schobert acquired a number of calves**: Matthew D. LaPlante, "Dead Utah Elephant Suffered Tragic Life—and She Wasn't Alone," *The Salt Lake Tribune,* September 16, 2008.

196   **Zoos really hadn't changed:** Michael D. Lemonick, "Who Belongs in the Zoo?" *Time,* June 19, 2006, 51.

196   **In 2006, USDA's:** Kelly Garbato, "Elephants Have an Achilles' Heel, and It's Their Feet," *The Wall Street Journal,* November 6, 2006.

196   **One of them was an Asian:** D'Vera Cohn and Karlyn Barker, "Toni the Elephant Euthanized," *The Washington Post,* January 25, 2006.

196   **At the Oregon Zoo:** G. A. Bradshaw, *Elephants on the Edge: What Animals Teach us about Humanity* (New Haven, CT: Yale University Press, 2010), 105.

196   **the AZA drew up:** *The Wall Street Journal,* November 6, 2006.

196   **The Oregon Zoo:** www.oregonzoo.org.

197   **The Phoenix, Arizona, zoo's:** Hilda Tresz and Heather Wright, "Let them be Elephants! How Phoenix Zoo Integrated Three 'Problem' Elephants," *International Zoo News,* vol. 53, 3 (2006), 154–60.

197   **The AZA's new standards:** www.aza.org.

197   **The Oakland Zoo:** www.oaklandzoo.org.

197   **The Oklahoma Zoo's:** Carie Coppernoll, "Oklahoma City elephant exhibit debuts as largest in the country," *Oklahoman,* March 17, 2011.

198   **the Denver Zoo:** Ray Mark Rinaldi, "Making Elephants—and Humans—Feel at Home at the Denver Zoo through state-of-the-art architecture, engineering," *The Denver Post,* June 3, 2012.

198   **Woodland Park's exhibit:** www.freewpzelephants.com.

198   **The Honolulu Zoo's:** "City Dedicates new elephant exhibit," Honolulu city government press release, December 12, 2011.

198   **But a former zoo curator:** Peter Stroud, "An Ill-fitting New Home for the National Zoo's Elephants," *The Washington Post,* August 22, 2010, C5.

198   **But the zoo's walking trail:** Ibid.

199   **After twenty-two years:** James C. McKinley Jr., "What to Do

With Traumatized Elephant Stirs Up Dallas," *The New York Times,* August 15, 2008.

199 **Weary of handling her:** Ibid.

199 **It kept Jenny:** Ibid.

199 **The zoo opened**: David Flick, "New Elephants Coming Two by Two to Dallas Zoo," *The Dallas Morning News,* March 6, 2010.

199 **At the Los Angeles Zoo:** "Closing Arguments in Elephant Trial Held," City News Service, June 26, 2012. A lawsuit filed in 2007 by the late actor Robert Culp alleged that keepers used bullhooks and hot shots to control Billy. In 2012, Zoo Director John Lewis testified that those weapons would never be used again as long as he was in charge.

199 **In the meantime, the city council:** The Associated Press, "Billy the L.A. Zoo elephant welcomes new company," November 11, 2010.

199 **In a 2012 decision:** Carla Hall, "L.A. Zoo is not a 'happy' place for elephants," *Los Angeles Times,* July 24, 2012.

200 **By 2013, 288 elephants:** Michael J. Berens, "Elephants are dying out in America's zoos," *The Seattle Times,* December 1, 2012, 1.

200 **in a 1975 letter:** Circus World Museum archives, Baraboo, Wisconsin.

200 **The Woodland Park Zoo:** Berens, "Elephants are dying out in America's Zoos."

200 **When elephant sperm:** Ibid.

201 **Normally timid:** Ibid.

201 **The USDA fined the zoo:** Ibid.

201 **Artificial insemination:** Ibid.

201 **By contrast:** Jeffrey Kluger, "Free Dumbo! Zoos are Bad for Elephants," *Time,* December 11, 2008.

201 **Chai finally succeeded:** *The Seattle Times,* December 1, 2012.

201 **In a groundbreaking series:** Ibid.

201 **The herpes virus has surfaced:** Ibid.

202 **Even after she gave birth:** Ibid.

202 **The Times discovered:** Michael J. Berens, "Portland's Baby

Elephant Belongs to Traveling Show," *The Seattle Times,* December 3, 2012.

202 **In exchange for using:** Ibid.

202 **videotape secretly shot:** David Whiting, "Were zoo elephants abused?" *Orange County Register,* May 31, 2011; www.ad-interna tional.org/animals_in_entertainment/go.php?id=2119.

202 **The Johnsons said:** "Have Trunk Will Travel Responds to Alleged Abuse of Tai the Elephant," waterforelephantsfilm.com.

202 **The outcry over Lily:** Alexa Vaughn, "Baby Elephant at Oregon Zoo Won't Go to Traveling Show," *The Seattle Times,* February 8, 2013.

203 **Seventy-three accredited zoos:** Jon Shainman, "Elephants coming to the Treasure Coast," WPTV-TV (West Palm Beach), February 20, 2013.

203 **Officials have said:** Eric Pfahler, "Elephant Center shifts north to Fellsmere from St. Lucie County," TCPalm.com, September 7, 2011.

203 **The AZA has given its members:** Shaun Tandon, "US zoos step up elephant safety rules," Agence France-Presse, August 24, 2011.

203 **But many zoos that claim:** Interview with Gail Laule, Active Environments, July 28, 2013.

203 **In the fall of 2007:** "Operation Maggie Migration update," PAWS Web site, November 2007.

204 **One of America's most famous elephants:** Andrew Friederici Ross, *Let the Lions Roar* (Brookfield, IL: Chicago Zoological Society, 1997), 62.

204 **Lewis implored the zoo:** Ibid., 76.

204 **Lewis defended Ziggy's cell:** Lewis, *I Loved Rogues,* 92.

204 **But in 1969:** Michael Sneed, "Story bring response; appeals filed for Ziggy," *Chicago Sun-Times,* March 13, 1969, S3.

204 **The zoo began raising money:** Ross, *Let the Lions Roar,* 144.

205 **Several times the elephant:** Lewis, *I Loved Rogues,* 93–94.

205 **For the next four years:** Ibid., 95–96.

CHAPTER SEVENTEEN: SPOTLIGHT ON ABUSE

206   **Organizers collected whistle-blower accounts:** Eyewitness accounts of elephant abuse were cited in the ASPCA's complaint against Ringling Bros. and Barnum & Bailey, March 10, 2009, 18. An incident involving handlers pinching baby elephants with pliers was caught on video at the Cow Palace in San Francisco in 1990, according to the Wildlife Advocacy Project.

206   **In 1989 the Acme Boot Company:** *The Circus Report,* April 24, 1989.

206   **In 2001, *Time* magazine:** Richard Corliss, "That Old Feeling IV: A Tale of Two Circuses," *Time,* April 20, 2001.

207   **A number of countries:** Animal Defenders International, www .ad-international.org/animals_in_entertainment/go.php?id-281.

207   **To critics who questioned:** Thomas K. Arnold, "Circus Elephant Trainer Talks Kindly, But Still Carries a Stick," *Los Angeles Times,* July 8, 1988. Trainer Axel Gauthier told the newspaper: "Elephants can get spoiled very easily if you always let them have their way . . . .You show affection when they do things good, by talking nicely and giving them something they like, maybe an apple or a carrot. When they do something bad, you talk harshly to them, or, if they really misbehave, you rap them on the behind with a stick." Five years after that interview, Gauthier was killed by an elephant he was working with at the Ringling Elephant Farm in Williston, Florida.

207   **Circuses claimed that by:** Corinne Flocken, "Circus Vargas, a Show You See Up Close, Opens its County Run," *Los Angeles Times,* February 3, 1990. Trainer Buckles Woodcock told the paper: "If [elephants are] going to be saved, it's going to be in this country. Look at all the poaching that's going on. In the wild, Joe's ivory would be a death warrant."

207   **Seeing elephants up close:** Jim Myers, "Debate rages on over circus elephants," *The Tennessean,* January 25, 2013. Steve Payne, spokesman for Feld Entertainment, said Ringling Bros.' breeding

program would help ensure that "future generations are able to see these animals, that they don't vanish from the earth." As of January 2013, twenty-five elephants had been born at Ringling Bros.' facility.

207 **Circuses further argued that elephants:** "Circus Draws Animal Cruelty Protest," *Las Vegas Review-Journal,* June 18, 2010. Joey Frisco, an elephant handler with Ringling Bros., said "If [the elephants] go on their heads, they're digging in the ground for water, or if they're on their hind legs, they're searching for food up high. It's natural behavior."

208 **A spokeswoman for Ringling, Catherine Ort-Mabry:** Liz Garone, "Circus Trainer Accused of Abusing Elephant," *The Washington Post*, December 19, 2001, A3.

208 **Yet under the glaring lights:** Circus No Spin Zone blog, March 30, 2012.

208 **Earlier in his career:** Curry Kirkpatrick, "The Greatest Showman on Earth," *Sports Illustrated,* September 26, 1977. Gunther Gebel-Williams told the reporter: "I try training only by voice. Spread the elephants out. Make three rings and everything. Maybe go here, go there, sit down, go a little further, always talking to elephants. Unbelievably hard because elephants so smart. They know when I am far away, they can fool around and not get smacked. So I come back and smack. Then I give elephants the carrots."

208 **Now Ringling Bros. began to depict:** Richard Severo, "Gunther Gebel-Williams, Circus Animal Trainer, Dies at 66," *The New York Times,* July 20, 2001. The article quoted Gebel-Williams as saying he never tried to break the spirits of animals and did not use brutality. "I'd say 'come here' to any one of the elephants and it would walk right over to me."

208 **No one defended:** Kenneth N. Gilpin, "The Circus Is Just One of His Acts," *The New York Times,* May 24, 1993.

208 **Irvin Feld:** Ibid.

209 **Eight years after:** Jeff Stein, "The Greatest Vendetta on Earth," Salon.com, August 30, 2001, and "Send in the Clowns: How

Ringling Bros. minions tormented a freelance writer for eight years," August 31, 2001.

209   **Feld was said:** Ibid.

209   **To oversee his vindication:** Ibid. According to Stein's article, Feld's vengeful scheme was divulged when his former sidekick, Charles F. Smith, had a falling-out with Feld and sued him. Attached to the lawsuit was the affidavit from George. Reading it, Pottker learned to her astonishment that Kenneth Feld had paid Clair and his assistant, Robert Eringer, $2.3 million to spy on Pottker. Pottker sued Feld for infiltrating her life and wound up settling the case out of court. The disclosures led PAWS to sue Feld, too. George's affidavit intimated that Feld created a special unit whose job was to try to ruin anyone who jeopardized his company's reputation for wholesome family fun. The unit was headed by Richard Froemming, an executive vice president for Feld. Among of his chief targets were PETA and other groups who were alleging that Ringling Bros. was taking poor care of its elephants.

209   **cronies even brainstormed:** Ibid.

209   **Feld created a:** Ibid.

210   **A full-age ad:** Leonora LaPeter, "Ringling jabs at animal rights groups," *St. Petersburg Times,* January 8, 2002.

210   **Of all the enterprises:** Kenneth Feld testimony, American Society for the Prevention of Cruelty to Animals v. Feld Entertainment, U.S. District Court for the District of Columbia, March 4, 2009.

210   **In 1998, USDA charged:** Deborah Nelson, "The Cruelest Show on Earth," *Mother Jones,* November-December 2011.

210   **Kenny was one of Ringling's:** Ibid.

210   **When he became:** Ibid.

210   **But Ringling's Gebel-Williams:** Ibid.

211   **The year before:** "Sick Circus Elephant Dies in Hot Truck," *Animal News Org.,* September 1997.

211   **a few months after Kenny's death:** *Mother Jones*, November-December 2011.

211   **Later that year:** Ibid.

211 **Lawyers for Derby:** Ibid.

211 **Stechcon was particularly upset:** Deposition of James Stechcon, Performing Animal Welfare Society v. Ringling Bros., Exhibit C, December 27, 1998, 27.

211 **Pat Harned:** *Mother Jones,* November-December 2011.

211 **Appearing with Benjamin:** Ibid.

212 **Feld's corporate counsel:** Ibid.

212 **A year later:** Ringling Bros. and Barnum & Bailey press release, July 26, 1999.

212 **Feld authorities concluded:** *Mother Jones,* November-December 2011.

212 **At least one USDA inspector:** Claudia Rowe, "Banning the Big Top," *The New York Times,* June 16, 2002.

212 **The hands-off arrangement:** Ibid.

212 **On a tour of the company's:** *Mother Jones,* November-December 2011.

213 **The head of the center:** Gary Jacobson testimony, ASPCA v. Feld Entertainment, Oct. 24, 2009.

213 **But instead of taking action:** *Mother Jones,* November-December 2011.

213 **Feld Entertainment objected:** Ibid.

213 **Moreover, the law gives:** Emily A. Beverage, "Abuse Under the Big Top: Seeking Legal Protection for Circus Elephants after ASPCA v. Ringling Brothers," *Vanderbilt Journal of Entertainment and Technology Law,* vol. 13, 1 (Fall 2010):155, 158.

214 **An earlier effort by Derby's PAWS:** Ibid., 167.

214 **Rider submitted a seven-page:** *Mother Jones,* November-December 2011. The problems had been noticed for years. In 1992, a veterinarian in Albany, NY, Holly Cheever, said she had seen Ringling Bros. elephants chained in dirty railroad cars, "many with old scars, some with fresh puncture wounds and many exhibiting behavior which indicates mental stress." In a July 9, 1992, story in the *Boston Globe,* she said that some of the elephants were so arthritic and lame they crept down the unloading ramps "in obvious pain."

214 **On Rider's behalf:** Ibid.

214 **Meyer suggested Derby:** Ibid.

214 **Several months after the lawsuit was filed:** Ibid.

214 **Among the wealth:** Ibid.

214 **She sued its parent company:** Ibid.

215 **Feld's attorneys quickly offered:** Ibid.

215 **She used the settlement:** Ibid.

215 **A month after Derby:** Ibid.

215 **The judge in the case:** Ibid.

215 **The appeals court disagreed:** Ibid.

215 **USDA fined the Clyde Beatty–Cole Bros.:** Christina Headrick, "Circus brings tradition, controversy," *St. Petersburg Times,* October 29, 2000.

216 **But the government:** Ibid.

216 **The following year:** Greg Winter, "Circus Trainer is Acquitted of Abusing a Rare Elephant," *The New York Times,* December 22, 2001.

216 **Ringling officials had to euthanize:** *Mother Jones,* November-December 2011.

216 **On the day he broke his legs:** Gary Jacobson testimony, ASPCA v. Feld, October 24, 2009.

216 **A couple of weeks:** *Mother Jones,* November-December 2011.

216 **USDA inspectors recommended:** Ibid.

216 **USDA's own inspector general:** Ibid.

217 **Animal Care's DeHaven:** Ibid.

217 **Jodey Eliseo:** PETA press release, July 5, 2006.

217 **Haddock had worked:** Affidavit of Samuel DeWitt Haddock Jr., signed and notarized August 28, 2009.

221 **"When someone like":** David Montgomery, "PETA, Ringling Bros. at Odds over Treatment of Baby Circus Elephants," *The Washington Post,* December 16, 2009, C1.

221 **Diagnosed with liver cancer:** Ibid.

221 **Confronted with Haddock's statement:** Ibid.

221 **"The last thing they're afraid of":** Ibid.

221 **"For nine minutes of performing":** Nedra Pickler, "Circus

Elephants' Rights Subject of Heated Legal Battle," Associated Press, March 18, 2009.

221   **For example, nearly all:** David Crary, "Groups Try to Stop Circus from Chaining Elephants," Associated Press, May 21, 2008. Ringling said elephants are chained in place at night to keep them from eating one another's food, and on trains to prevent them from shifting their weight suddenly and derailing the train car.

222   **at Ringling's Center:** Stechcon affidavit.

222   **"Those guys really don't":** Ibid.

222   **Stechcon echoed Haddock's tale:** Ibid.

222   **Stechcon recall how handlers:** Stechcon affidavit.

222   **Nicole would urinate:** Ibid.

222   **But a few nights later:** Ibid.

222   **Two weeks after that:** Ibid.

222   **Stechcon likened the sound:** Ibid.

223   **Ringling's records frequently:** *Mother Jones,* November-December, 2011.

223   **In a sworn affidavit:** Ibid.

223   **former groom Sonnie Ridley:** Ibid.

223   **Some of the favorite spots:** Ibid.

223   **On the witness stand:** Kenneth Feld testimony.

223   **Judge Sullivan expressed concern:** Associated Press, March 18, 2009.

223   **Defense lawyer John Simpson:** Ibid.

223   **To counter Meyer's claim:** Ibid.

224   **The injuries look similar:** Ibid.

224   **The long trips satisfied:** Associated Press, March, 18, 2009.

224   **Asked about that:** Carol Buckley testimony, American Society for the Prevention of Cruelty to Animals v. Feld Entertainment, U.S. District Court for the District of Columbia, February 23, 2009.

224   **Buckley talked about:** Ibid.

224   **"She's a very fearful individual":** Ibid.

224   **"Over the past year":** Ibid.

225   **Sworn to tell the truth:** Kenneth Feld testimony.

225   **The term he used:** Ibid.

225   **"It is an absolute escape":** Ibid.

225   **Rider testified that:** Tom Rider testimony, American Society for the Prevention of Cruelty to Animals v. Feld Entertainment, U.S. District Court for the District of Columbia, February 12, 2009.

225   **The judged noted that:** Del Quentin Wilber, "Judge rules in favor of circus in lawsuit over treatment of Asian elephants," *The Washington Post,* December 31, 2009.

225   **Rider never complained:** Ibid.

226   **Even if Rider:** Ibid.

226   **The plaintiffs argued:** Beverage, *Vanderbilt Journal of Entertainment and Technology Law,* 155.

227   **"The fact is":** Jim Myers, "Debate rages on over circus elephants," *The Tennessean,* January 25, 2013.

227   **Feld Entertainment countersued:** "Ringling Bros. Awarded $9.3 Million in Elephant Case," Associated Press, December 29, 2012.

227   **the ASPCA agreed:** Ibid.

227   **Four months after:** Ibid.

227   **In 2010 the Animal Care unit:** USDA press release, September 1, 2010.

000   **The government fined:** Jason Babcock, "Circus Settles on Animal Cruelty Charges for $15,000," *Southern* (Maryland) *Newspapers* Online, May 9, 2012.

227   **And in 2011:** Leigh Remizowski, "USDA Fines Ringling Bros. Circus over Treatment of Animals," CNN, November 20, 2011.

228   **The fine against Ringling:** Ibid. An inspection report alleged that Ringling forced a thirty-five-year-old Asian elephant named Banko to perform even though she had been diagnosed with a form of colic and appeared to be suffering abdominal pains. Circus officials said separating Banko from the other elephants would have distressed her more. "Ringling Circus Agrees to $270K

USDA Fine Involving Alleged Violations of Animal Welfare Rules," Associated Press, November 28, 2011; www.huffingtonpost .com.

228 **the person Ringling hired:** Lloyd Grove, "USDA Complaint is PETA's Latest Salvo in War Against Ringling Bros.," *The Daily Beast* Web site, October 18, 2012. According to the group Public Integrity, Feld Entertainment spent $335,000 lobbying Congress and the federal government in 2012, up from $120,000 in 2007.

228 **World War II brought:** Jim McHugh, "Animal Kingdom Comeback: Imports Ease, Dealers Race," *Billboard*, June 15, 1946.

228 **American dealers again began procuring:** Ibid.

228 **Elephants were the scarcest:** Ibid.

229 **One circus alone:** "Animal Picture is Bright!" *Billboard,* March 27, 1948.

229 **New Yorker Henry Trefflich:** Henry Trefflich as told to Baynard Kendrick, *They Never Talk Back* (New York: Appleton-Century-Crofts, 1954). Trefflich wrote that many elephants in Siam were owned by four men, usually from different families, and each man owned a leg. Even with four owners, a well-trained elephant could earn enough money to support them all. Buying one was difficult, though, because all four owners had to consent to the sale. If any of them refused, the deal was off.

229 **More than once:** Frederick Woltman, "Henry Trefflich," *The American Mercury,* June 1954.

229 **Trefflich had an assistant:** Trefflich, *They Never Talk Back,* 134.

230 **The plane had scarcely taken off:** Ibid., 135.

230 **They tore insulation:** Ibid.

230 **The pilot finally fought back:** Ibid.

231 **As a marketing gimmick:** "Wild Animals Take a Bow with Tame at Pet Shop Debut," *The New York Times,* March 9, 1954.

231 **"Customers can almost call up":** Trefflich, *They Never Talk Back,* 221.

CHAPTER EIGHTEEN: BAD DAYS, GOOD DAYS

232 **three years after:** Scott Blais interview, February 21, 2011.

233 **Then, all of a sudden:** Ibid.

233 **Burke was standing:** Ibid.

233 **In two quick steps:** Ibid.

233 **Winkie attacked Burke:** Ibid.

233 **The elephant froze:** Ibid.

234 **For weeks afterward:** Ibid.

235 **The staff moved Liz:** www.elephants.com.

235 **To protect Frieda's aching feet:** www.elephants.com, August 24, 2008.

235 **The process was both:** Ibid., April 30, 2010, and June 21, 2010.

235 **Before administering them:** The Elephant Sanctuary's *Trunklines* newsletter, Spring 2011, 5.

236 **While Frieda napped:** www.elephants.com, January 25, 2010.

236 **Frieda was napping:** www.elephants.com, March 14, 2011.

236 **Moving to the Q Barn:** www.elephants.com, March 30, 2010.

237 **Now, late at night:** www.elephants.com, March 30, 2010, and Angela Sherrill interview.

237 **But that winter:** www.elephants.com, February 1, 2010.

237 **The elephants handled:** www.elephants.com, May 17, 2010.

238 **Even a simple event:** www.elephants.com, March 28, 2011.

238 **One morning she waited:** www.elephants.com, February 21, 2011.

239 **With surprising adroitness:** www.elephants.com, March 22, 2010.

239 **In her first three years:** Scott Blais interview.

239 **She could bathe herself:** www.elephants.com, April 5, 2010.

239 **That spring one of the caregivers:** Ibid., May 17, 2010.

240 **Frieda and Liz hung back:** www.elephants.com, May 24, 2010.

240 **Free from any cares:** Ibid.

240 **Blais watched her:** Scott Blais interview.

241 **Most elephant men:** Lewis, *I Loved Rogues,* 29.

241   **In the early days:** Ballantine, *Wild Tigers & Tame Fleas,* 296.

242   **In 1940, an elephant:** Lewis, *I Loved Rogues,* 71.

242   **In 1942, Ringling Bros.:** Ballantine, *Wild Tigers & Tame Fleas,* 298.

242   **The veterinarian who was on hand:** Ibid.

242   **Early trainers believed:** Balllantine, *Wild Tigers & Tame Fleas,* 267.

242   **The more conscientious trainers:** Ibid., 296.

242   **"Ain't one elephant around here":** Ibid., 319.

242   **To warm them in cold weather:** Ibid., 297.

243   **Ringling Bros. and Barnum & Bailey:** Ibid., 301.

243   **Between gigs the elephants:** Ibid.

243   **Show animals are often traded:** Wade Burck's Circus No Spin Zone blog, February 5, 2012.

243   **And grooms still bring:** Ballantine, *Wild Tigers & Tame Fleas,* 270.

CHAPTER NINETEEN: UNCHAINED AT LAST

244   **In 2009, they joined with the Cuneo Foundation:** Lorene Yue, "Loyola's $50M gift from Cuneo Family Sets School Record," *Chicago Business,* December 7, 2009.

244   **USDA inspectors stepped up:** PETA fact sheet on the Hawthorn Corporation, www.mediapeta.com.

244   **Membership grew:** Angela Spivey, Elephant Sanctuary spokeswoman.

244   **contributions continued to exceed:** Elephant Sanctuary Web site.

245   **In the summer of 2009:** Mike Stobbe, "Elephant Spread TB to Workers at Tenn. Sanctuary," Associated Press, February 16, 2011.

245   **Staffers chose to:** Janice Zeitlin, chief operating officer and vice president of the Elephant Sanctuary, August 24, 2013.

245   **began wearing:** Ibid.

245   **A year later:** Ibid.

245   **Blais agreed to stay on:** Ibid.

245   **The board and consultants:** Ibid.

245   **Buckley sued:** Malcolm Gay, "Sanctuary in Custody Fight over Elephant," *The New York Times,* October 27, 2010.

245   **The board filed a counterclaim:** Ibid.

246   **Atkinson had led efforts:** "The Elephant Sanctuary in TN getting new CEO," *The Tennessean,* September 7, 2010.

246   **The AZA began referring:** www.aza.org.

246   **Circus veteran John Milton Herriott:** John Milton Herriott interview, July 24, 2013.

247   **Facilities employee Daniel Bledsoe:** www.elephants.com, March 17, 2012.

247   **Bledsoe sent off for:** Ibid.

247   **This time he rewired:** Ibid.

248   **Offered a treat as a lure:** www.elephants.com, April 20, 2012.

248   **Caregivers could see:** Kelly Costanzo interview, August 23, 2012.

249   **One summer afternoon:** www.elephants.com, July 18, 2011.

249   **Frequently she backed up:** *Trunklines,* Spring 2013, 4.

249   **Ever since she'd received:** www.activeenvironments.org.

250   **Laule and Desmond developed:** Ibid.

250   **To help her, Laule brought in:** Interview with Gail Laule, June 28, 2013.

250   **Whittaker coordinated:** Active Environments Web site.

250   **Using protected contact:** Gail Laule interview.

251   **"They're smart animals":** Ibid.

251   **Billie responded quickly:** Ibid.

252   **Elephants can enlist:** Ibid.

252   **Over time Billie's aggression:** Ibid.

253   **First Laule convinced Billie:** Ibid.

253   **Whittaker stood:** Elephant Sanctuary's *Trunklines* newsletter, Summer 2011, 8.

253   **Whittaker and Treat:** Ibid.

254   **Half a dozen times:** Ibid.

BIBLIOGRAPHY

◆—◆〓◆—◆

BOOKS

Abrams, Ann Uhry. *Formula for Fortune: How Asa Candler Discovered Coca-Cola and Turned It into the Wealth His Children Enjoyed.* Bloomington, IN: IUniverse, 2012.

Ballantine, Bill. *Wild Tigers & Tame Fleas.* New York: Rinehart & Company, 1958.

Beers, Diane L. *For the Prevention of Cruelty: The History and Legacy of Animal Rights Activism in the United States.* Athens, OH: Ohio University Press, 2006.

Bradshaw, G. A. *Elephants on the Edge: What Animals Teach Us about Humanity.* New Haven, CT: Yale University Press, 2009.

Buck, Frank with Edward Anthony. *Bring 'Em Back Alive.* New York: Garden City Publishing Co., 1930.

Byrne, John B. *Cuneo Museum and Gardens.* Mount Pleasant, NC: Arcadia Publishing, 2009.

Daly, Michael. *Topsy: The Startling Story of the Crooked-Tailed Elephant, P.T. Barnum, and the American Wizard, Thomas Edison.* New York: Atlantic Monthly Press, 2013.

Davis, Janet M. *The Circus Age: Culture and Society Under the American Big Top.* Chapel Hill, NC: The University of North Carolina Press, 2002.

Derby, Pat. *The Lady and Her Tiger.* New York: Dutton, 1976.

Knight, C. *The Elephant, Principally Viewed in Relation to Man*. London: Charles Knight & Co., 1844.

Krausz, John. *How to Buy an Elephant and 38 Other Things You Never Knew You Wanted To Know*. New York: Skyhorse, 2007.

Lewis, George with Byron Fish. *I Loved Rogues: The Life of an Elephant Tramp*. Superior, NE: Superior Publishing, 1978.

Maulhardt, Jeffrey Wayne. *Jungleland (Images of America)*, Mount Pleasant, SC: Arcadia Publishing, 2011.

Mayer, Charles. *Trapping Wild Animals in Malay Jungles*. New York: Garden City Publishing Co., 1920.

Scigliano, Eric. *Love, War, and Circuses: The Age-Old Relationship Between Elephants and Humans*. New York: Houghton Mifflin Company, 2002.

Stallwood, Kim W. *A Primer on Animal Rights*. New York: Lantern Books, 2002.

Tennent, Sir James Emerson. *The Wild Elephant and the Method of Capturing and Taming it in Ceylon*. London: Longmans, Green, 1867.

Trefflich, Harry, as told to Baynard Kendrick. *They Never Talk Back*. New York: Appleton-Century-Crofts, 1954.

Wilkins, Charles. *The Circus at the Edge of the Earth: Travels with the Great Wallenda Circus*. Toronto: McClelland & Stewart, 1998.

SELECTED ARTICLES AND ESSAYS

Emily A. Beverage. "Abuse Under the Big Top: Seeking Legal Protection for Circus Elephants after ASPCA v. Ringling Brothers." *Vanderbilt Journal of Entertainment and Technology Law,* vol. 13, 1 (Fall 2010): 155, 158.

Michael J. Berens. "Elephants Are Dying Out in America's Zoos." *The Seattle Times,* December 1–2, 2012.

Deborah Nelson. "The Cruelest Show on Earth." *Mother Jones,* November-December 2011.

Jeff Stein. "The Greatest Vendetta on Earth." Salon.com, August 30, 2001, and "Send in the Clowns: How Ringling Bros. Minions Tormented a Freelance Writer for Eight Years," August 31, 2001.

INDEX